MIKE
SCOTT
ADVENTURES
OF A WATERBOY

MIKE
SCOTT
ADVENTURES
OF A WATERBOY

MIKE SCOTT
ADVENTURES OF A WATERBOY

A Jawbone Book
First Edition 2012
Published in the UK and the USA by Jawbone Press
2a Union Court,
20–22 Union Road,
London SW4 6JP,
England
www.jawbonepress.com

This edition published by permission of The Lilliput Press, Dublin, Ireland
www.lilliputpress.ie

ISBN 978-1-908279-24-8

EDITOR Thomas Jerome Seabrook
DESIGN Paul Cooper Design

Printed by Everbest Printing Co Ltd, China

2 3 4 5 6 20 19 18 17 16

Contents

THIS PAGE, CLOCKWISE FROM TOP LEFT: Mike, London, 1972; Mike's mother, Anne Scott, c. 1969; a Patti Smith pose, 1978; issue six of the *Jungleland* fanzine, November/December 1977.
OPPOSITE PAGE, CLOCKWISE FROM TOP LEFT: An advertisement for 'Heaven Gets Closer Everyday' by Another Pretty Face, 1980; Another Pretty Face, 1979; John Caldwell and Mike, London, 1979.

HEAVEN GETS
CLOSER
EVERYDAY

ANOTHER PRETTY
FACE
SINGLE: JAZZ 1

THE RED AND THE BLACK

HOPE AND ANCHOR THURSDAY JULY 15th   9pm £1.50   highbury and islington Tube

group with gigs. Keith-061-445 3639.

EXPERIENCED BASSIST required to join guitarist, drummer, keyboards. Bunnymen. Doors influences. Phone Sam 226 5817 daytime for audition.

FOR LEFT alternative anti-sexist danceable band. Manchester. Carol 061-660 5301. Mike 061-434 5707.

HARDCORE KILLING Joke/P.i.L. guitarist wants to join/form group. 01-627 1475.

M/F GUITARIST (Velvets, Sinatra, Bunnymen). Melancholy/Sunny sound. East London. Alan 981 4601. Yep!

THE WATERBOYS REQUIRE LEAD/ RHYTHM GUITAR PLAYER, 18-24. Ability, own style and appreciation of Patti Smith essential. No pop fans or Jacks of all Trades. Phone 01-221 2039.

TRUMPET FLUTE Sax Organ or piano for young Catford based band. Graham 778 1826/650 7583.

VOCALIST WANTED for energy Rock+Roll band, frontman essential. Into N.Y. Dolls, Clash, making record soon. Tel. Ted 01-428 8529.

VOCALS SUPERHUMAN? Wanted urgently. Banshees, Division Paraphenalia. Tel. Keith 735 0254/837 0740 evenings.

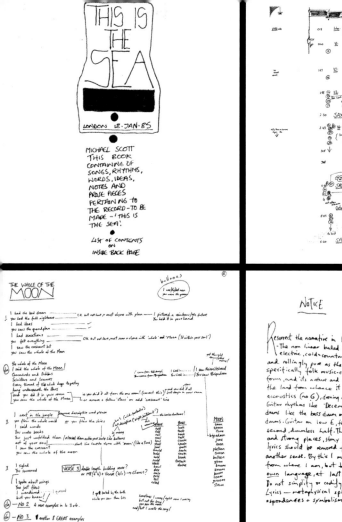

THIS IS THE SEA

LONDON 18 · JAN · 85

MICHAEL SCOTT
THIS BOOK
CONTAINING OF
SONGS, RHYTHMS,
WORDS, IDEAS,
NOTES AND
PROSE PIECES
PERTAINING TO
THE RECORD-TO BE
MADE – 'THIS IS
THE SEA'.

LIST OF CONTENTS
ON
INSIDE BACK PAGE

THE WHOLE OF THE MOON

balloons?
I was higher than the ground

I had the bad dream
you had the full nightmare ———— OK but not loud, a neat rhyme with plan — I pictured a rainbow/a/the picture
I had ideas   You held it in your hand
you saw the grandpa
I had sensations
you felt everything ———— OK but not loud, neat scene + rhyme with 'whole' and 'Moon' (& within your soul)
I saw the crescent but
you saw the whole of the Moon

the whole of the Moon!
I said the whole of the Moon!
Cannonballs and Debbies
Scimitars and Seasons
Every thread of the whole days together
having unsheathed the stars
and you did it in your room ———— so you did it all from the one room (connect this)   and you did it all
you saw the whole of the Moon!   "...or rename a fallin' 'stars' on add 'crescent' line   too simply in your room

I went in the jungle ———— Pagan descriptive and please
you flew the airplane ———— so you flew the skies
I said words
You wrote books
You just unfolded them / released them unlike your souls like balloons
out of your soul ———— short line twenties rhyme with 'moon' (like a Time)
I saw the crescent
you saw the whole of the moon.

I sighed
You screamed   VERSE 3 / double length building verse?
                                                        or Mid (6/7) + Verse (6/7) → Chorus?
I wondered
but you knew! / ———— I guessed!

— No 2   3 more examples in 3 v/s.

— No 3   8 another 8 GREAT examples.

NOTICE

Resurrect the narrative in Poetic/wild/Impressionistic form.
The non-linear ballad cometh. Create new acoustic
electric, cold country rock/folk music – jagged
specifically folk music-corresponds in its shape and
form, and its nature and character to the aspects of
the land from whence it springs. Bleak songs. 5 string
acoustics (no G), droning electrics, Pagan drums, bells,
Guitar rhythms like 'December' + 'A Pagan Place'. Pagan
drums like the bass drum on 'Be my Baby'. Bells with
drums. Guitar on low E, first half of line, high E on
second, drumless half. This is the sound of rocks, caves,
and strong places, stony places, fantastic places. The
lyrics should be removed from Word Reality – as in
another sense. By this I mean not to come into centre
from where I am, but to fearlessly voice and use my
own language, at last. My natural tongue require
Do not simplify or codify for ALL in these songs.
Lyrics — metaphysical spirit/soul analogies with corr-
espondences + symbolism. But NARRATIVE.

— fertile Songs

THIS PAGE, FROM TOP: **Steve Wickham and Anto Thistlethwaite, Werchter Rock Festival, July 1986; legendary drummer Jim Keltner, 1986; Steve and Anto at Mill Valley, California, December 1986.**
OPPOSITE PAGE, FROM TOP: **The Waterboys in Kenmare, Ireland, May 1987; Mike, Steve Wickham and Vinnie Kilduff aboard the Greenpeace ship *Siruis*, May 1987.**

THIS PAGE, CLOCKWISE FROM LEFT: Seamus Begley and Steve Cooney, 1989; Sharon Shannon on the Waterboys tour bus, 1989; The Waterboys at the Glastonbury Festival, 1989. OPPOSITE PAGE: Barry Beckett and The Waterboys, Spiddal, March 1990; Mike and Janette, Venice, March 1994.

ABOVE: **Universal Hall, Findhorn, Scotland.**
BELOW: **Mike in Findhorn, May 1994.**

CHAPTER 1

MUSIC IN THE HEAD

On a late afternoon in autumn 1968 an Edinburgh bus rumbles down cobbled streets. On its upstairs front seat, wearing a blue school uniform and dreaming through the window over the spires and rooftops, is a nine-year-old me. Music is running through my head, as always, a mighty stramash of pop melodies learned from the radio, only grander and louder and longer because in my head the music does whatever I want it to. And for accompaniment my feet are beating rhythm on the steel floor of the bus. The sound is bright and metallic and it has a depth, too, a reverberating blurred quality that delights my ear.

Then something unusual happens. I take this bus home every day and there's no stop on this stretch of the route, but we're slowing to a halt. I hear the muted sound of a door slamming, then heavy feet clambering noisily up the stairs – which, I note, are also metal, with the same pleasing reverberating sound.

Suddenly a huge man in a black blazer is towering over me, his face flushed and the skin of his cheeks quivering with anger. Glaring at me as if I've done him some terrible ill, he roars, 'Stop that bloody banging!' With a pang of horror I realise this is the bus driver and his head has been directly under the floor I've been drumming my feet on for the last fifteen minutes.

I splutter an apology and the driver turns and descends the stairs. I hear his cabin door slamming shut again and a few seconds later the bus starts moving. My heart's beating fast; being accosted by a furious stranger is shocking enough for a nine-year-old, and I was scared for a few moments there. But even more shocking is the realisation that the driver couldn't hear the accompanying music in my head, otherwise he'd have known it wasn't 'banging' at all, but a sophisticated rhythm to a magnificent soundtrack!

For it's a rude awakening to learn that the sound in my imagination is only in my imagination, and that its outward manifestations – foot-stomping, whistling or rhythmic beating with fingers on a schoolroom desktop – don't transmit the inner content. And though I don't yet know it, figuring out ways to let other people hear this music will become the occupation of my adult life.

I was six or seven when I first noticed the music in my head. It was there in the classroom, on the football pitch, at the dinner table, when I went to sleep and when I woke up. There was never a moment when it wasn't running in some form or other, whether melodies or rhythms, pop singles from start to finish or instrumental extravaganzas that spun perpetually for a day. And it's continued ever since. Sometimes I wonder if when I die I'll hear the whole however-many-years-long inner soundtrack of my life flashing by in one great mad cacophonous moment.

The fateful incident with the bus driver was only one of several that told me if I wanted to express this music in a way that other people could perceive it, I had to somehow process it and give it objective reality. Two solutions presented themselves: making music out loud with an instrument or recording myself on tape. I couldn't play an instrument so I tried the latter, getting together with my school friend Mike Graham and a reel-to-reel tape recorder. We did a version of The Beatles' 'Hey Jude', singing and clapping the 'nah nah' outro together into the microphone. Just like on the bus, the whole soundtrack was running in my head and as I mimicked McCartney's Beatle-ific 'Jude-ah, Jude-ah, Jude-ah!' ad libs. They sounded fantastic. But when we played the tape back and heard a child's tinny voice making silly exclamations, sounding as if he had a head cold, it was another shock. Tape recorders couldn't hear the music in my head either!

Another revelation came when I discovered that everyone saw different pictures in their imagination when they heard the psychedelic outro of 'Strawberry Fields Forever'. I assumed the images I 'saw' when I listened to any piece of music were somehow encoded in the record. Surely everybody knew the outro of 'Strawberry Fields' represented a procession of brightly clothed Beatles jigging in and out of traffic during rush hour in an Asian city, pursued by water buffaloes and snake charmers? But when I asked my friends, they imagined nothing at all or saw totally different images.

This was disappointing because it meant that what I perceived wasn't an absolute reality and humans weren't all connected in one big communal imagination. Yet it was exciting at the same time, for not only did it mean the images I saw were unique to me, and that everyone's else's were unique to *them*, but one day, when I came to make records myself, my own music could spark people's imaginations in ways I couldn't dream of.

Making records became my sole ambition during a sweet summer towards the end of the sixties when I started falling in love with pop singles; the same explosion of feelings that happened again a few years later when I became interested in girls. I'd get a crush on a top twenty hit – The Hollies' 'Listen To Me', for example, or The Turtles' 'Elenore' – and wouldn't be able to breathe till I heard it again. Its melodies would hang tantalisingly beyond the call of my memory in the same way a newly loved girl's face would later elude my mind's eye.

Pop records assailed my emotions, filling me with inexplicable longings. When I heard Jane Birkin's sexy 'Je T'Aime' at the age of ten I felt teetering towers of fire in my chest. And black music: Motown, The Elgins singing 'Heaven Must Have Sent You', The Four Tops ripping through 'Reach Out I'll Be There': their urgent voices seemed to make shapes in the air, dark-flashing and tangible, full of a flavour I later recognised as a cocktail of pain and desire, which awoke me as an adult ahead of my time.

So did the split-up of my parents. One of the last times I saw my father was on my tenth birthday when he came to the house and gave me an acoustic guitar and a Rolling Stones album. The guitar leaned against my bedroom wall, a sacred mystery, for a year, until one day the same school friend, Mike Graham, useful fellow, showed me some things he'd just learned called chords. I copied him and could soon play a rudimentary twelve-bar blues.

One of my mother's students, a twenty-year-old Dylan-mad piano player called Leonard, used to come round and make up songs on my guitar to entertain me. I realised I could make up songs too. Soon I had sheaves of papers covered with lyrical attempts influenced by writers like Hermann Hesse, who I found on my mother's bookshelves. And while my mum was teaching at night school I'd perform concerts in front of the living-room mirror to enthusiastic audiences that applauded wildly in the auditorium of my imagination. Just like the inner music, they did whatever I wanted.

My songwriting world was a private universe inhabited by one and its gods were Dylan, Lennon and George Harrison who lent their riffs to my creations and watched my progress from posters on the wall. Then another of my mother's students, a man called John Milroy, gave me an old upright piano, which I taught myself to play. Every day I'd get home from school, shut myself in my bedroom and bash away for hours. When I discovered the octave-hopping riff from Pink Floyd's 'Careful With That Axe, Eugene', I took to improvising twenty-minute opuses around it. Then I bought the songbook for The Who's *Tommy* and would play the entire double album from start to finish, the whole bleeding rock opera, which I hardly even understood.

I couldn't read music; I just followed the chord symbols and played everything my own way, using one finger for the bass and three fingers for chords and melodies. This created odd, lopsided rhythms, which years later resulted in the style of Waterboys songs like 'A Girl Called Johnny' and 'The Whole Of The Moon'. When several notes on the piano broke, their strings snapped through constant hammering, it never occurred to me to get them replaced. I just learned how to play using the black notes: consequently every song I wrote for several years in the late seventies was in D flat.

At sixteen I entered another world: the realm of the teenage band, a perilous domain from which my personal songwriting universe remained a secret. Subjecting my songs to the criticism of my bandmates, the rhythm-guitar-playing Caldwell brothers and lead guitarist Davy Flynn, seemed a bleak prospect so I kept them under my hat and we played covers instead, a jumble of Bowie and Stones tunes. Even when I started playing originals with subsequent bands a few years later, these didn't come from my private world but were sketchy co-writes with band members. Though by then I had a huge collection of songs, a few of which were even in danger of sounding not bad, the parallel worlds of my bands and my writing wouldn't fully merge till the advent of The Waterboys in the eighties.

Around the same time as I began playing in bands I started recording my songs on a little mono cassette machine. The sound was colourless and dry, not much of an advance on my early ascent up the north face of 'Hey Jude', but desire drove me forwards and it was only a question of time and opportunity before I found my way to a real recording studio.

In 1976, my mother and I went on holiday to London, as we did most summers, and I decided to record a few songs professionally while I was there. I had no plan to do anything with the results; I just wanted to hear myself with a decent sound and come away with a show-off tape to play my friends. In the small ads at the back of *Melody Maker* I found a place called Portobello Studios and phoned 'em up. 'How long do you need?' asked the guy on the end of the line. Well, I thought to myself, I'm going to do a six-minute version of Dylan's 'Like A Rolling Stone' and I'm going to play five instruments on it, that's half an hour, then two of my own piano-and-vocal songs at five minutes each – I'll need forty minutes. I innocently thought I would only use as long as it took me to physically play the songs. The man on the phone suggested it might take a little longer, so I booked the enormous timespan of three hours, asked him what tube station was closest, and started getting excited.

The big day came and I got off the train at Ladbroke Grove with my mother and trusty piano-playing Leonard, fortuitously in London on his own holiday. I expected the studio to be immediately obvious (perhaps with a big neon sign saying STUDIO) but there was just a busy West London street on a hot summer morning with nothing that looked like my idea of a recording studio. With a pang of dismay I realised I hadn't brought the address with me or even a copy of *Melody Maker* with the phone number. I was musically prepared, all right, with my notebook of songs and a hundred ideas primed for action, but as far as practical logistics went I'd blown it big time. We walked up and down the street wondering what to do, looking for someone who might know about recording studios, until I spotted a black guy with a yellow Mott The Hoople t-shirt. I asked if he knew where Portobello Studios was. 'Mmmm ... that's a difficult one,' he drawled as if I'd asked him a question in a quiz, hands on hips, eyes half-closed as he squinted in the sunshine. Then he said, 'Yeah, man. There's some kind of studio a few hundred yards up the road there,' and pointed.

His directions led up a leafy sun-dappled terrace and across Portobello Road, one of London's most famously bohemian streets, which to my delight was filled with canvas-covered market stalls manned by hard-faced, cockney-voiced geezers shouting out archaic descriptions of their wares while dreadlocked Rastafarians and important-looking hippie chieftains with long hair and flares promenaded like demigods along the sidewalks. Surely the great Portobello Studios must be close now! And sure enough a block farther on we came to the junction of Basing Street, on the corner of which stood a large church-type building with a broad wooden door wide open. We walked in. A girl sat at a reception desk. I asked her if this was the studio, and when she said yes I told her I had a booking.

'And what's your name please?' she asked with a slight edge that suggested she didn't really think I belonged here.

'Mike Scott,' I answered, trying not to let my cool slip. She consulted a sheet of paper on her desk then replied, 'No, I don't have your name here. Are you sure you're at the right place?'

'This is Portobello Studios, isn't it?' I said, at which a smile of understanding broke on her face. 'Ah,' she said gently, 'This is Island Records Studios. The one you want is round the corner on Lancaster Road.'

Island Records! The sleeves of all the albums I'd ever bought on the Island label flashed through my mind: King Crimson, Sparks, Traffic, Bob Marley, and I wondered how many of them had been recorded right here. An image arose in my mind of a huge, high-ceilinged hall bedecked with drums and Hammond organs, somewhere in the building, under my very feet perhaps, where some top band was making their record at this moment, and I wondered who they might be. 'Here you go,' said the girl, interrupting my reverie and handing me a sheet of paper with the correct address. I thanked her and the three of us stepped back out on the street.

Lancaster Road was the tree-lined terrace we'd walked up to get here so we retraced our steps, counting house numbers until we found the right one. But it was just a regular house with no studio sign or nameplate. I rang the bell and the door opened to reveal a bespectacled guy with an American accent (the first American I'd ever met) who confirmed this was indeed Portobello Studios, 'and you're Mike, right?' His name was Joe and he led us downstairs to the basement flat. The 'studio' comprised a small red-draped playing space – the front room of the flat – plus a mixing desk squeezed into a narrow hallway. With embarrassment I realised the vast difference between Island Studios and the one I'd booked. Instead of turning up at my allotted humble place, I'd walked into one of the most famous recording establishments in London, bold as brass, as if it were all there just waiting for me. And I'd do it again one day, as an Island artist and a Waterboy, in an as-yet undreamed-of future.

American Joe, it transpired, was the Portobello Studios engineer, and under his alien eye I embarked on my session. Quickly, shockingly, I discovered there was more to the recording process than I'd ever imagined. I expected the instruments to be miked up and already sounding like they did on all my favourite records: instant Beatlesound. But no, each had to be set up, individually miked and soundchecked from scratch. Joe was helpful enough, but he spoke a mysterious language I didn't understand, full of esoteric words like *cans* and *foldback*. And assessing the sound of the instruments, let alone directing Joe to modify them to my taste, was a task beyond my comprehension. The ad in *Melody Maker* had said the studio was equipped with a piano and I'd imagined a full-sized grand, but what awaited poor Leonard was a plastic-looking electric keyboard that sounded like a xylophone. At least the promised Fender Stratocaster guitar was present, but I'd never played one before and couldn't believe how thin and watery it sounded when I plugged it in.

Then came the job of giving a spirited performance, not a problem usually but suddenly difficult in the antiseptic studio atmosphere, using instruments that sounded like the band on *The Sooty Show*. And bloody hell, did my voice really sound like that? Even with reverb and turned up loud in the speakers, I sounded mushy and Scottish, nothing like the razor-sharp, all-knowing teenage rock'n'roll adventurer in my head.

With Leonard on piano and Joe guesting on rumbly bass guitar ('It'll save you time if I play it,' he said kindly) I led us through several dubious takes of 'Like A Rolling Stone' till we got a semi-acceptable version on tape. Next came the unspeakable process of overdubbing other instruments including, God help me, *drums*. When Joe played me back my efforts they sounded like a squirrel scurrying back and forth over a bunch of dustbin lids.

But eventually, stumbling like a dizzy explorer through a vast and inexplicable new country, I completed my version of 'Rolling Stone'. Then I recorded a pair of my own songs, long-forgotten one-take masterpieces, which I performed on the xylophone-like piano. By now I'd run several hours over time, an omen perhaps of the distant future when it would take me three years to record *Fisherman's Blues*, and with another session due to start after mine I had to wrap up fast. But before I left Portobello Studios one more bracing rock'n'roll revelation lay in wait. I was now to learn that behind every friendly creative person in the music industry there's a moneyman. For as helpful Joe packed away the microphones, a well-heeled young Englishman called Nigel materialised from nowhere to smilingly unburden me of a hundred quid, a sum far in excess of my budget. My financial calculations, which took no account of running over time, paying for tape or the mysterious workings of value added tax, had been as naïve as my time estimates. Luckily for me, my mum coughed up the balance.

Finally I emerged into the early evening sunlight with a reel-to-reel tape under my arm that I couldn't even play when I got home. A few weeks later I found someone to transfer it to cassette for me and sat back in my bedroom to take a listen. The results were dog rough and it would take me eight, maybe nine years to close the gap between the sound in my head and the sound on tape. But it was a start.

CHAPTER 2

THE REALM OF
THE TEENAGE
BAND

It's 1977. My band, White Heat, named after half a Velvet Underground song, is on stage in some kind of social club in rural Scotland. Well, I say 'on stage' but there's only a low triangular wooden platform, big enough to fit our drummer Crigg, while myself, guitarist Ronnie and bassist Jim are all on floor level. The locals sit at long tables or slouch against the bar at the far end of the room, and all seem to have long thin heads the shape of bricks and a look in their eyes like the flash of a razor blade.

We've been bashing through a selection of our own punky originals and rebellious rock anthems like 'My Generation' and 'Pretty Vacant' but the locals, surely wondering who the hell booked this lot, don't get it. We've even had a request to 'play a Jim Reeves number, son.' I'm singing my ass off. I've got that much together, though my guitar, as usual, isn't brilliantly in tune. Ronnie is widdling away and Jim's bass chunders along cheerily. Crigg is bashing cymbals and not taking events quite seriously, throwing in mock fills and madcap pressed rolls as if he's Keith Moon's naughty nephew. After every song a different brick-headed local approaches the stage, fixes us with his terrible eyes and tells us to turn down, until by now, near the end of the night, we're playing so quietly I can hear my guitar strings buzzing above the sound of the amp. We finish the number, a cover of the Stones' 'Sympathy For The Devil', which has gone down like a Sieg Heil at a Bar Mitzvah, when a youngish fellow comes up, leans over and speaks directly into my ear. In a wheezy voice he instructs me to 'play "God Save The Queen", pal.' 'You mean the Sex Pistols song?' I reply disbelievingly, though with a sudden rush of hope that

I've found a kindred spirit in this wilderness. 'No,' comes the dour response, 'the national anthem.'

My teenage years were spent in the bustling county town of Ayr, on the southwest coast of Scotland, the cradle of boot boys, hairdressers and hardworking folk with no airs or graces and a predisposition to anonymity. My mother had taken a job in a college there, and Ayr, as I quickly learned, wasn't the place to be spectacular or outrageous. The unofficial town motto, a harsh retort to any perceived vanity or self-glorification, was 'who do you think *you* are?'

I'd been a city boy, attuned to Edinburgh's rumble and uproar, profoundly at home amid its gothic towers and Enlightenment architecture without ever truly noticing any of it. Ayr was built on a lesser scale, though it wasn't without magic. Its charms were natural ones: a proximity to the western sea (so much more mysterious than Edinburgh's industrialised east coast), long hazy beaches and an abundance of green parks and woodlands under a backdrop of vast, ever-changing skies; a magnificent place for dreaming. And dreaming is what I did there, mostly, for seven years.

The nearest place to catch big rock concerts was Glasgow, an hour's train ride away. From the age of fourteen my friends and I regularly made the trek to the famous Apollo Theatre where we saw The Who, The Rolling Stones and Paul McCartney's Wings, among others. But for an idealistic, ambitious rock'n'roller in training there wasn't a whole lot of anything going on in Ayr.

My bandmates in White Heat were Jim Geddes, a scarf-toting Stones fan who played a Hofner fiddle bass with a set of ancient black strings of which he was fond of saying, 'they were in tune when I bought it'; Ronnie Wilson, our most accomplished musician, the chubby son of a music teacher who played a home-made guitar with an exotic tuning (which meant he couldn't play minor chords); and Crigg, a wiggy-haired mod drummer who'd been in the year below me at school where we'd been enemies. Crigg had been in a suedehead gang called The Mental Lords and spoke only three words to me all the years of our schooling: these, prompted by his disdain for my long hair and flares, were 'There's that poof!' But when Crigg realised the poof was a fellow Beatles fan and I discovered the suedehead was a handy drummer, we became friends. Now our band practised every Saturday afternoon in the sonic temple of my front room with curtains drawn and lights out.

When we were sufficiently rehearsed to venture out and actually do some shows, we found there was nowhere to play unless we bashed out top twenty hits at agricultural dances or polite 'soft-rock' in local hotel ballrooms, neither of which we wanted or were able to do. If we were to play what we considered a *real* gig, one in which we stepped out on the true road of rock'n'roll performing music we wrote or loved, we had to make it happen ourselves. There were three possible routes:

1. The humanitarian method: put on a charity gig and hustle venue, bouncers, ticket printing and coverage in the local paper for free.
2. The entrepreneurial method: club together with mates, hire a hotel function room (lots of those in seaside Ayr) and sell tickets to friends.
3. The deception method: lie to the booker at a venue that our music would work for his punters.

We tried all three. Our sole charity gig, a benefit for the local Cancer Research group, was at Alloway School on the outskirts of town, a spit and a hop from Rabbie Burns's Cottage, a lovingly preserved tourist landmark against the wall of which my under-age drinking pals and I used to gaily pee on our way home from discos. Alloway School Hall had a real four-foot-high stage, a thing of wonder that looked sublime bedecked with our two WEM P.A. columns and motley collection of amps and drums. And stepping onto it was a magnificent feeling. The wooden boards echoed under our heels and the generous vista of the broad hall stretched away below us. Yes, I was made for this!

The concert, on a cold night in January 1977, was well attended with a tangible sense of event. But halfway through some teenage thugs in David Bowie bum-freezer suits turned up and, unobstructed by our timid voluntary bouncers, smashed up the toilets causing damage amounting to more than the takings for the night. The Cancer Research office, instead of making a profit, had to shell out for repairs. Still, it was a killer show, youthfully heroic, legendary in the locality for about three weeks thereafter and tinged with a frisson of violence that, though scary at the time, lent the event a glamorous edge in hindsight.

The second method, the self-promoted function room gambit, yielded three gigs at local hotels. I found a college for the disabled that would print tickets cheaply, and we drew advertising posters by hand on huge sheets of coloured card, proudly sticking them up in Ayr's only hip record shop, Speed Records. Friends were then press-ganged into buying tickets, some proving uncannily resistant when there was no cause other than our career advancement, while the general public, passing our customised poster in the Speed Records window, paid no attention whatsoever.

These shows, two at the Blue Grotto on Ayr's seafront and one at the Golden Eagle in neighbouring Prestwick, were anti-climatic after the dramatic highs of Alloway School Hall. And with the complications of bar managers who told us to keep the music down and the lights up, embarrassed audiences that stayed magnetised to the bar, complaints about noise from hotel residents, and the financial gulf between the costs of putting on the gig and the takings, this method was almost more trouble than it was worth. We didn't even get to strut around on a decent stage. The Blue Grotto's was six inches high and narrow as a wardrobe, while the Golden Eagle had no stage at all. Each event was a massive contraction from the glorious shows constantly running on the film spool of my imagination.

The third method, by which we bogusly blagged gigs in places where the general public was gathered anyway, was where we really paid our dues and took tentative steps learning our trade as performers. But these were the toughest of all. Standing on a dance floor playing a smattering of punk covers at curtailed volume to an audience of brassed-off Scottish holiday-makers in a caravan park disco is challenging, especially when the owner insists on three separate forty-five minute sets. *Three sets?* We had to play everything we knew twice plus a couple of Chuck Berry medleys to manage that. So when one day I noticed an entry form for a Battle of the Bands contest winking at me from the counter of the town's musical instrument shop, the Keyboard Centre, I saw a new and hassle-free way to get myself and my mates on stage. The contest was in the ballroom of the Darlington Hotel, a straight-laced local nightspot. I submitted the form and got a phone call a few days later telling us we'd been drawn against a cabaret band called Revival and would play a two-band concert with them, the winner, after an audience vote, to go on to the next round. This was brilliant news; not only a free gig, but with our rock edge we would surely destroy these cabaret charlatans!

Come the date we arrived at the ballroom to discover there was no audience, or at least no audience made up of bona fide members of the public; there was only whoever the two bands had brought with them. We had a few mates and girlfriends with us, but Revival shipped in two rowdy busloads of rustics from the hinterlands of Ayrshire. Looking at the voting forms laid out on each table, the names Revival and White Heat each with a blank voting box next to them, then clocking our mates sitting dejectedly at a table in the far corner, their numbers countable on the fingers of one hand, I began to see the evening wasn't going to go as expected. Revival played first. They were twenty years older than us and their set featured all the middle-of-the-road groaner songs of the day: Neil Diamond's 'Red Red Wine', Peters & Lee's 'Hey Mister Music Man' and the high pinnacle of middle-of-the-road naffness, Daniel Boone's satanic 'Beautiful Sunday'. The busloads of fans lapped it all up, cheering and applauding like football supporters. Revival finished to rapturous response and even played an encore, something I'd only ever dreamed of.

Half an hour later, after moving our gear on stage in front of the bemused gaze of Revival's fans who stuck around for the fast-becoming-inevitable crowning of their favourites as the night's champions, we began our set. After the first number my self-proclaimed status as a teenage rock visionary was sorely punctured when I was approached by a middle-aged woman and handed a slip of paper that said: 'Play "Simple Simon Says" for the Grimmet Farm girls.'

And it got worse. Between songs women came up and complained, 'We cannae hear the words!' or 'Can you no' play somethin' we ken?' while the menfolk turned their backs and ignored us at the bar. The Grimmet Farm Girls, determined to enjoy themselves whether or not we played Simon Says, started doing jigs, linking arms and dancing cheerfully while we bashed out a doleful version of 'Waiting For The Man'. Staying in doomy rock mode while happy people are having a good time ignoring you is very hard to do, and we were sufficiently charmed by the girls' display to play a loopy Scottish march for them. Responding to the calls to 'Dae one we ken!' I even sang them an a cappella verse of 'Love Me Tender'. But the battle of the bands was lost, and after our last number, for which we reverted to type with a long and incomprehensible (to them), heroic and revolutionary (to us) version of Patti Smith's 'Land', we wheeled off our gear to no applause whatsoever. A few minutes later Revival were proclaimed winners by a Stalinesque margin of votes and our humiliation was complete.

We were fleeing the scene, dragging our amps through a corridor to the boot of my mother's waiting car, when one of Revival, a cheerful moustached fellow of about thirty-five, gregarious in his hour of victory, cornered me before I could escape and gave me some friendly advice: 'Get yourself a pedal-steel player, son. There's money in the cabaret business.'

During the year of its existence White Heat played a grand total of ten shows around Ayr, and despite playing music people didn't want to hear, and the weekend violence that was an inescapable part of local culture, we never got beaten up. To get publicity we hustled the writer of the *Ayrshire Post*'s pop column 'Discoround' until he sent a photographer to my house to take pictures of us in the living room where we rehearsed. One of these, with a tiny accompanying article, appeared in the paper the next Thursday. Inspired by this thrilling success we decided to send pictures of ourselves to the national music press. So we found a mate with a camera and embarked on the grand folly of all teenage bands: the photo session in a cemetery.

The cemetery was on a hill behind my old school, and we mugged and gurned around the gravestones, thinking we were pulling off some natty poses. Next Saturday at rehearsal we saw the results: exactly thirty-six holiday snapshot-sized photos, for our mate, being an amateur, had shot only one film and hadn't thought of enlarging them. The pictures were fascinating, though not in quite the way I'd anticipated. We looked like guys from four different bands: a mod, a chubby biker, a tanned bon viveur and a hairy rock starchild. Nor had we managed to project a unified attitude: if three people looked tough the fourth was simpering; if two were smiling, the others were grimacing. Or somebody had his eyes closed. Or somebody looked glazed. And our outfits and body language were all mixed up. The only one who had his look sorted was Crigg, with his Eddie & The Hot Rods hairdo and a series of half-decent mod poses. But guitarist Ronnie was cuddly and cheery, while bassist Jim looked like he'd come from a sports car rally and couldn't wait to go back. As for me, I was whippet-thin with flared jeans – even in the punk Year Zero of 1977 – tight velvet t-shirt, shoulder-length hair, and no sense of what to do with my body. Shall I put my hands on my hips, or here, halfway up my chest, or shall I make a funny face, or look wary, or suspicious? I hadn't yet quite landed.

The photos were deemed unusable and we divvied them up between us for souvenirs, each band member taking the ones that showed himself in the least-worst light. It was almost our final act as a band; at the end of summer Crigg split to form a mod trio, Ronnie gave up groups, Jim went to drama college and I moved back to Edinburgh, then ablaze with punk rock, where a new constellation of possibilities glimmered on the horizon. But before we went our separate ways there was one last local show to play.

We had a jostling friendship with a cabaret guitarist called Brian Noble who we used to accuse of selling out because he played the squeaky-clean Eagles-type rock popular at weddings and dances. Perhaps to teach us a lesson he got us a booking at a venue in a small town called Maybole, and ever eager for a gig we took the bait. We arrived early on a Saturday evening to find the place, the Three Steps Club, not much more than a shebeen clinging to a cliff overlooking a piece of waste ground at the arse-end of town. It turned out to be an Orange Lodge, whatever that was, and it looked grim and functional, some kind of private working men's club. 'Set up in the corner, boys,' said a man, pointing to a low triangular platform. Several club members were milling around and they looked hard, with dour, frozen features as if their faces had been chiselled from the cliff outside. We began to realise our cabaret guitarist friend had booked us here to take a rise out of us, but there was no way out.

Three hours later, as the last chord of 'Sympathy For The Devil' echoed uneasily through the smoke-filled air, I was instructed by the wheezy young local to play the national anthem. I was shaping up to say 'no way' when another native stepped up and addressed not me, but Ronnie, who hadn't sung a note all night, with the words, 'You're a good singer, son, sing the national anthem while Walter here accompanies you on the moothie.' And there on cue was Walter, a wee man I hadn't noticed before, pulling a little silver harmonica out of his jacket pocket.

Some beneficent angel must have been watching over us and prevented the Orange Lodgers from trying to make me sing the national anthem. Or perhaps the 'angel' was the native himself, recognising that a confrontation was brewing and tactfully moving to head it off. Whatever, Ronnie, wiser and less the firebrand than myself, duly sang 'God Save The Queen' (*mumbled* would be more accurate) while Walter backed him doggedly on the moothie and everyone in the place stood up. Except for our roadie Rab and me. The two of us remained seated throughout due to ideological objections, somehow managing to do so without a fight breaking out: another miracle. On the drive home I asked the others what an Orange Lodge was. Our Catholic bass player Jim told me.

CHAPTER 3

WHERE'S THAT SCOTTISH BOY?

At ten o'clock on a Sunday morning I sit alone in an elegant hotel dining room in west London. Antique mirrors in gilt frames hang on white walls, sunlight floods through a bay window and mellow soul music drifts lazily from the bar. I'm nineteen years old and four hours ago I stepped off the overnight train from Scotland. My breakfast, long finished, has been cleared away and I'm reading a book, The Last Battle *by C.S. Lewis. I've read it several times before, but I have it with me because it's good to have an old friend around on an adventure into the unknown.*

Suddenly a small, fragile voice calls my name. Twice. A white-cold wave of anticipation rushes through me. I rise from my seat and walk towards the voice, through an arched doorway, to the foot of the stairs. I look up and there, sitting on the top couple of steps in a white nightdress, is my New York rock'n'roll heroine Patti Smith. Her face is thin, her black hair a magnificent crow's nest, her arms spindly, all elbows and long fingers. I've admired her, listened to her recordings, read her words and thought about her for two years; have come to London solely because of her, tracking her to this hotel, but I've never met or seen her in the flesh before. So the vision before me, this sudden private glimpse behind the gloss of fame, is super-real, blowing the gates of my young perception wide open, confounding all expectations.

Questions clamour in my mind: Have I disturbed her? Is it always so easy to meet her or am I special and favoured above all fans? Why this degree of magic? How will I get my friends to believe me? Will I be worthy of this? And rumbling under them all: What does she think of me and who will I find myself to be in this new situation?

I climb the steps and take her outstretched hand. It's warm. She speaks to me in a kind of child-like half-asleep way, affectionate, with an older sister's concern, and I feel inadequate, curling at the edges, transparent. She's become a real living person, no longer my idea of Patti Smith-ness, and, paradoxically, under the penetration of her eyes, I've become a diminished shrunken idea of myself, an imposter, no longer real.

She says, 'I'm not getting up for ya 'cos I've gotta sleep, but I've booked you a room.' I thank her and she uncurls herself, stands to her full height, towering above me like a giantess on her higher step of the stairs, then disappears through a door to the hotel lobby.

I return to the basement lounge and pick up my half-read book. The sun is flooding through the window just as before, and the soul music plays softly. The world is still turning. I catch sight of my face in one of the mirrors. I'm becoming real again. I'm breathing.

I first read about Patti Smith and her band in the British music press in early 1976. Word had it they played 'intellectual garage rock', a phrase suggesting a mix of instinct, intelligence and primal energy, exactly what I wanted to hear in those becalmed days before punk re-lit the touch-paper and made rock'n'roll revolutionary again. I had a pen pal in Wales who imported bootleg records from America and when his latest list included a Patti album called *Teenage Perversity & Ships In The Night*, I ordered it, sight unseen and sound unheard.

With perfect timing it arrived in the mail the week I left school for the last time, at that golden shimmering moment when the world was wide open and everything was possible. It was a twelve-inch record in a plain white cover, shrink-wrapped, with reddish-brown photocopied insert bearing a picture of a crow-like, spark-eyed woman, and a set of unlikely song titles. These were unusual, charismatic, infinitely *other*: 'The Smooth Stone Beyond', 'Radio Ethiopia', 'Strained On Strange', 'Redondo Beach'. What weird new culture was I about to enter?

It turned out to be a live recording, tinny and thin but full of energy. First I loved Patti's scrawny voice, a threadbare raven full of defiance and spunk. Then her words were like the clamourings of an urchin visionary who, against all odds, has found the key to the universe. And thirdly her band; raw and fast, with rough guitars and hammering piano bouncing off tumultuous, explosive drums. There was no virtuoso show-off playing and the music was coloured with improvisation and a spirited sense of rebellion. It was the first punk record I ever heard, and the best.

A few days later I bought her official album *Horses*, which was brimful of the same scratchy, ecstatic energy. I started collecting everything of Patti's I could find and soon my attention alighted on her poetry books; slim, arty volumes available by mail order from esoteric-sounding bookshops in London and New York. That Patti was a proper published poet gave her an intellectual cachet that set her apart from other singers; imagining her poems, before I saw them, to be bulletins from a transcendent consciousness, I figured she must have access to worlds and phenomena normal people couldn't see. This impression was dented when I read the poems. They were by turns crude, druggy, obscure or dream-like, occasionally shot through with brilliance, and always deliciously pretentious. But pretentious or not, I took it all as holy writ because I was smitten. And anyway I was pretentious myself. Being a fan of the exotic Patti Smith Group – an initiate of their Mysteries, no less – put me several leagues closer to cool than any of my friends, and at seventeen that was just about the most important thing for a young man to attend to.

For the next two years I devoured Patti's work, played her songs with my band and raved about her in my home-made fan magazine, *Jungleland*, a photocopied medley of articles by me and mates illuminated by stolen photos chopped out of the music papers. As editor I adopted the ridiculous pen name of Velvet Lanier, after The Velvet Underground and Patti's boyfriend, Blue Öyster Cult keyboard player Allen Lanier.

In March 1978 Patti released her third album, *Easter*. It included the song she became best known for, 'Because The Night', but it was the title track that did weird things to my soul; a surreal lyric poem with a palpably sacred atmosphere, set to a processional rhythm with tolling, hazy bells and a vocal performance pitched between a child's wonder and a high priestess's invocation. At the song's gorgeous denouement the inspired addition of distant bagpipes pierced my heart like a rose thorn.

To coincide with *Easter*'s release Patti was due to play two concerts at the Rainbow Theatre in London, part of a European tour. I was in Scotland with no tickets, but I'd read that Patti always stayed at the Portobello Hotel when she was in London. I knew this joint, a discreet bohemian bolthole favoured by artists and musicians in a terrace of stucco-fronted houses close to the Portobello Road; I'd visited it once, trying to meet and interview ex-Velvet Underground member John Cale. So I took a chance. I phoned the hotel on the afternoon of Patti's first show and in my most confident voice asked to speak to her. To my amazement they put me through to her room without question. The phone rang twice, then a female American voice came on the line.

'Hello, this is Patti?' She said this with a kind of rising question mark at the end, subtly requesting the caller to identify himself.

'Hi, my name's Mike Scott. I sent some fanzines, called *Jungleland*, to your fan club address. Did you get them OK?'

' Yeah ...' This was clearly untrue as I could tell she had no idea what I was talking about, but it was said, kindly, to spare my tender fan's feelings. 'Where are you calling from?'

'Scotland.'

'Scotland? How far is that?'

'400 miles.' A decent distance in Britain, but nothing to an American.

'Wow ... what a long way! You gotta come to the show so you can tell the kids all about it up there.'

'You mean come to London?'

'Yeah, come to London and write about the show.'

This encouragement, casually given, acted on me like a wonder drug. My heroine had summoned me and I was going! And though Patti perhaps didn't quite count on me turning up at her hotel and laying myself on her mercy, I got the overnight train that night and presented myself at the Portobello Hotel at nine the next morning.

Some time after our dream-like encounter on the stairs, the hotel receptionist came to tell me my room was ready. It was on the top floor, a small Victorian chamber with deep red walls and wooden furniture that made me think of ship's cabins. An old fashioned painting of the Crimean war was hung above a dark mahogany dressing table, and a small window, with wooden blinds that split the streaming sunlight into golden stripes, overlooked gardens bustling with spring blossoms and clusters of cloud-high trees. I lay down on the bed in this gracious space, the first top-class hotel room I'd ever been in, and slept. I was woken by the phone ringing. It was Patti's guitar player, Lenny Kaye, who she'd delegated to look after me. I arranged to meet Lenny in his room and when I knocked on his door he was just out of the shower, drying his hair with a towel, a tall, thin, intellectual American. I liked him straight away. Lenny was a kind, soulful guy, easy to be with, and we spent an hour comparing notes on rock'n'roll, British punk bands and Patti bootlegs, of which Lenny showed me several he'd purchased on tour.

In the early evening Lenny took me to the theatre in a black chauffeur-driven car, another first. We drove past Hyde Park, through the West End and Kings Cross and into the greasy spoon hinterlands of North London, finally pulling up at Rainbow's stage door on a side street off the Seven Sisters Road. We walked down white corridors that smelt of disinfectant till we came to the dressing room, where the rest of the band, minus Patti but plus several people I didn't recognise whom I presumed were stage crew or friends, were hanging out on plush leather armchairs, strumming guitars and talking.

In an antechamber was a lordly spread of salads and sandwiches. Not understanding, at my tender age, about hotel room service, all

I'd had to eat that day were two biscuits I'd found in my room. I was so hungry I snuck in and helped myself to some morsels from the spread. The band's drummer Jay Dee Daugherty – blond, charismatic, younger than Patti and Lenny – walked in after me. 'Hi,' he said in a friendly but firm American accent, 'my name's Jay. I don't think we've met.' Ten years later, to the day, I would work with this man on The Waterboys' *Fisherman's Blues* album, and carry coal and turf to his rented cottage in the west of Ireland, myself the veteran and he the new boy. But for now he was a princeling in his own domain and I was a callow interloper, filching provisions.

I embarrassedly introduced myself, then from the dressing room I heard hands clapping for silence followed by Lenny's voice requesting 'everyone except members of the Patti Smith Group' to leave. I made my escape, slipped down to the side of the stage and got myself into a good position to watch the show.

To see my favourite band for the first time from such a super-close vantage point was a privileged, heady experience. A few feet before my eyes the players and music came to life and I felt their energy like a man standing in front of a fire feels the heat of the flames. I saw the musicians' interactions, noticed signals and glances pass between them, moments unseen by the audience, and I gained a sense of the balance of power and personality within the group; Patti, super-intense, on stage a wholly different creature from the frail, white-clad angel of the morning, now in black clothes and low-brimmed bowler hat, feral, prowling and unpredictable; Lenny, a leggy chicken-boned guitar-wielding giant; Ivan Kral, bassist-cum-lead-guitarist with Eastern European cheekbones, deploying a classy selection of traditional rock poses; Jay Dee, his hands wrapped for protection in trailing white bandages, playing like a soldier in a fire-fight, punishing his drums as if the music meant life or death; and the whole they added up to – a bristling totemic countercultural poetry-fuelled garage rock band.

And like all great bands should, the PSG looked and moved like a gang. They were Patti's droogs, clad in sharp, colourful clothes and longer-than-punk hairdos that suggested their communal fashion clock had stopped the day in 1968 when the Rolling Stones made their promo film for 'Jumpin' Jack Flash', the *ne plus ultra* of pure rock'n'roll. As for the music, it was seethingly, beautifully, skull-rippingly loud, especially the riffs detonating from Ivan's guitar amp just in front of me. The band performed most of my favourite numbers: 'Set Me Free' (explosive neo-biblical rant-rock), 'Ain't It Strange' (eight minutes of wild, chicken-scratch reggae) and the mighty 'Easter' itself, almost as luminous and transcendent as the record I fell in love with.

There were other people close to me in the shadows, friends of the band or executives from the record company. They looked bored and didn't clap after songs, creating an incongruous dead-zone around the inferno burning on stage. I'd never stood side-stage before and felt self-conscious about clapping; would it distract the band and be a terrible faux pas, or would they welcome a flicker of encouraging energy at the stage's edge? How would I feel if it was me up there? I didn't know, but sacrificed my cool and clapped anyway; I was witnessing my most loved band in performance and I hadn't come 400 miles not to applaud. The band paid no attention.

When the show finished I had to survive on my wits. My chaperone Lenny was occupied with post-gig well-wishers, and I was only one of many hangers-on hanging around backstage. Alone and with no role to inhabit, place to be, or groove to follow, I rootlessly haunted the corridors around the dressing room. And when I saw Lenny leave I followed and attached myself to him, exiting by the same stage door we'd come in four hours earlier and getting into the same chauffeur-driven car.

The car didn't take us back to the hotel but to a basement music club in Covent Garden where a bash was being held in Patti's honour. I followed Lenny in. The place was loud and crowded and Patti was on stage with a reggae band as we entered, sharing the spotlight with a dreadlocked dude called Tapper Zukie whose main riff was to hold his fist in the air and repeatedly holler what sounded like 'Bell!' (When I re-enacted this for certain friends back home they found it very funny and for several years afterwards, whenever we would meet, we'd greet each other with raised fists and pained, intense cries of 'Bell!')

This was my first experience of an after-hours music business party. Free fruit and sandwiches lay on long white-covered tables, and free drink was served at the bar. And there were stars. Phil Lynott of Thin Lizzy, a lanky black Irishman sporting a drop-dead pale blue suit and a wicked glint in his eye, promenaded through the crowd, the tallest and most charismatic person there, looking for all the world like he was on stilts. And Johnny Thunders, a sneer-lipped cartoon Italian-American punk guitarist in black Crombie coat and fedora hat, exuded a malevolent gangster cool. I dug it all, got close to the little stage, saw Tapper Zukie re-christen Patti 'Black Cinderella' during a clanking skanking reggae number, filled my gob with sandwiches, and kept a well-skinned eye on my *passe-partout* Lenny. In the small hours, when I saw him making like he was going to leave, I made a beeline for him, racing through the melee, up the stairs and out of the club just in time to squeeze myself through the closing door of a stretch limousine as it took off.

As my eyes got accustomed to the darkness in the car I saw I was sitting next to Lenny, who was next to Patti, who was next to a good-looking young roadie with chiselled features and curly hair. Opposite us sat an older gentleman in shirtsleeves who looked like an accidental acquaintance swept along in a crazy adventure. In the front passenger seat was Jay Dee Daugherty with a pretty, long-haired girlfriend on his knee. Patti was holding court, addressing the older gentleman, who she seemed to know as 'Flight' and ominously warning Jay Dee's girlfriend not to do a particular something (what, I'd arrived too late to hear) or Patti would have to give her a 'punk-rock haircut'. It was said semi-humorously and there was some nervous laughter in response, but there was an undertow to the comment; Patti's voice carried a subtle, yet pointed, warning tone. The effect was intimidating; the space in the car contracted, a sense of claustrophobic pressure descended and everyone except Lenny, Patti's nearest equal in the band's hierarchy, grew silent and uneasy. Whether she was aware of this atmosphere or not, Patti didn't stop and continued to hold court, dominating, aggressive and scary. I was witnessing what happens when a star performer, the centre of attention, high on the residual energy of the show, lets that energy spill over into their offstage life and their interactions with others. With Patti it was like being in the presence of a capricious, haughty queen toying with her subjects.

Several years later I learned how hard it is to manage the forces that flow constantly into and through the person playing the role of star. These forces manifested through me in different ways than through Patti, at least on the evidence of that car journey, but the principle was the same: receiving powerful energies of enthusiasm or devotion from an audience, small or large, is an experience that changes the recipient. Quite how depends on their character and degree of self-mastery, but the common outcome is one of being pumped-up, gratified, excited and reaffirmed in one's sense of self; *all these people love me so I must be OK*, which can quickly and easily spill over into: *all these people love me so I must be as special as I've always hoped/thought I am*. Without a mediating dose of humility or gratitude, the star mistakes this condition for reality and begins to think and act from it. Soon he or she displays egotism in action, with all its familiar hallmarks: an inflated sense of one's importance, a lack of awareness of other people's feelings or perspectives, a reluctance to bear criticism, the expectation that one's desires and needs, however trivial, are justified and will be unfailingly met. At its worst, unchecked over time, and encouraged by the fawning and lying of sycophants, this process turns sane, talented, loving people into vile monsters.

Patti wasn't at that stage, nor, I think, would she ever be, but it was still an uncomfortable group of passengers who drove through a deserted London in the pre-dawn hours of the morning, along Bayswater Road and Notting Hill Gate, finally turning into the familiar street of stucco-fronted houses. The limo pulled up at the Portobello Hotel and we tumbled out and up the entrance steps. In the lobby, to my terror, Patti loudly exclaimed: 'Where's that Scottish boy?' I presented myself at her side, making myself as small and neutral as I could, while her eyes, with all their piercing regal curiosity, fell upon me. She instructed me to go back to Scotland and 'tell the kids about the show.' None of the intimacy and fragility of the morning apparition was present. Patti's post-show energy was too strident, too out of her personal control, for her to express the same gentleness, or to sheath her power so people could feel safe around her. She left in the direction of her room, chisel-cheeked roadie, the night's prize, in tow.

In my little top-floor room I slept deep and I slept long. And the following lunchtime, packed and ready to leave, I went in search of Patti to thank her. I found her in the bright little hotel bar adjoining the dining room I'd waited in the previous morning. She was talking with a bespectacled Irish rock journalist. Reggae music was playing. I sat discreetly at the bar and waited for my chance to talk to her. Then a phone rang and one of the hotel staff came over and said to Patti, 'A long-distance call for you.' She picked up an extension phone on a table next to her, put the receiver to her ear and started to talk.

Instantly the atmosphere changed. It was a serious phone call and clearly, from the tone of Patti's voice and her choice of words, she was talking with a lover. At first I thought she'd take the call in her room, or else ask the rock journalist and myself – the only other people in the bar – to leave. But she proceeded to talk, hunched over the phone, wild hair in a curtain over her face, with the journalist and myself still present as she explained to the person on the end of the line why a male voice had answered the phone in her bedroom. 'We're all doubled up in the rooms at this hotel,' she said, not convincingly. I sat frozen with embarrassment, listening to my rock'n'roll heroine lying to a lover across a transatlantic phone line. I saw the veils fall away and reveal her as a flawed, card-carrying, mistake-making, bullshit-capable human being, just like anyone. 'You *know* my life begins when I hear your voice,' she said pleadingly into the phone. I looked round at the journalist. We made eye contact for the first time and an agreement passed between us. We stood up simultaneously and left Patti to her man troubles.

I left a few minutes later to catch the train back to Scotland and never got to thank Patti Smith for everything she did for me. Organising and paying for my hotel room, taking care of me and fixing it for me to see her show were more than I had any right to expect – but what I really want to thank her for is the fast-track education I received; a series of priceless advance insights into the complexities of a life I'd lead myself a few years later.

CHAPTER 4

A FRIEND CALLED Z

The car stops and the engine switches off. Slowly I lift my slumbering head and open my eyes on an entirely unexpected sight: half a mile away, set against a green landscape is a vast, hulking grey structure. The thing is familiar, full of evocative power, stirring my imagination and emotions, and something more; a kind of racial memory. For even before I am conscious of what it is, I'm aware I'm looking at something familiar to every Briton.

All this dances through my mind in the brief, beautiful moment before my brain catches up with my eyes and I realise that I'm looking at Stonehenge. I've seen a thousand pictures of Britain's most famous ancient monument, but to come upon the real thing suddenly and unexpectedly for the first time is magical; for a few seconds I've witnessed Stonehenge in all its enigmatic glory with my mind a blank slate, no preconceptions or expectations. Then a secondary realisation hits: my friend Z, sitting next to me, must have deliberately stopped the car without alerting me so that I'd wake naturally and encounter Stonehenge in this delicious way. He didn't shake me by the shoulder a mile back and say, 'Oi, if you don't wake up you'll miss Stonehenge!'. No, he allowed something else to happen and by doing so gave me a rare gift.

Z and I met at Edinburgh University in the autumn of 1977. He was just plain *Ed* then and we were new boys, freshers living in Pollock Halls, a sprawling student village beneath Arthur's Seat, that curious elephant-shaped mountain that broods on the Edinburgh skyline. I noticed Ed one afternoon, a slouching, interesting-looking character in a shapeless sweater making his way across the lawn below my window, a punk rock album under his arm. Within minutes we were friends.

He came from a small town called Langholm in the Scottish

border country, which accounted for his odd accent with its thick vowel sounds and melodies that curled playfully up and down over the course of each sentence. We had musical tastes in common and I enlisted him to write reviews for my homemade fanzine. Soon we were inseparable, going to every punk and New Wave gig that hit Edinburgh. And the timing was perfect for at that precise moment of the twentieth century, punk was exploding.

Edinburgh, with its castle, cobbled medieval streets and gothic monuments, was an unlikely backdrop for touring punk rock bands. The great gobby snarlers like Joe Strummer or Johnny Rotten belonged in gloomy Soho alleys, or under yellow-lit London motorway flyovers, or leaning against brick walls in graffiti-blitzed housing projects. Strummer, lurching unhealthily up the steep hill of ancient Cockburn Street on his way to an album-signing session in one of Edinburgh's record shops, the green vista of Princes Street Gardens stretching airily behind him, was an incongruous sight indeed. Leather jacketed, grimacing, one shoulder hoisted insolently in a well-practised pose of defiance, brightly-coloured zips mysteriously sewn all over his trousers, and denuded of the camouflage of his native habitat, Strummer looked like a homicidal hunchback who'd found a sewing manual in a landfill.

Likewise Johnny Rotten. The Sex Pistols couldn't play in Edinburgh because they were banned throughout the UK, but they came for radio interviews and to make an appearance at the local Virgin Records shop. Word spread like wildfire, even to Pollock Halls where Ed and I dropped everything and rushed downtown. Virgin was on Frederick Street, a noble thoroughfare just off the main drag of Princes Street, in the shade of Edinburgh Castle. Luck was with us for as we turned the corner there was Rotten crossing the road in black coat and flat Chinese straw hat, his lips grotesquely puckered outwards according to the strictures of punk fashion, his eyes narrowed into snake slits. But the apparition of Johnny Rotten and the tableau of Scotland's capital didn't go together; he looked like he wasn't really there, as if someone had drawn a crude cartoon of him onto a colour postcard of the city.

Edinburgh nurtured a peculiar intellectual variation on punk. The best local band was The Rezillos, a shrieking gang of rubber-faced pop-art terrorists with great choruses and sheet metal guitars. And like the rest of Britain in 1977 Edinburgh was riven by the cultural war between New Wavers who understood punk and Old Wavers who didn't and obstinately stuck to the 'dinosaur' bands like Genesis and Led Zeppelin. Even in the sheltered world of university the schism was starkly visible. Ed and I wasted no opportunity to wade into this conflict and to airlift people stranded in the Old Wave across to the New. Usually all we needed to do was take a university mate – a degenerate Eagles fan perhaps or a stubborn Tull-head – to a half-decent punk gig. Suddenly they'd get it: the excitement, the raw power of the music, the sense of everyone in it together, and hey presto – another convert.

Not all our efforts were so coherent. One of our favourite pastimes was to stand on the roof of the Pollock Halls refectory while our fellow students were passing in their ragtag hordes, and loudly sing 'How Much Longer', a punk anthem by a London band called Alternative TV. We altered the words to make reference to a randomly-chosen victim in the crowd, like this:

How much longer!
Will that guy wear! *(the two us pointing gleefully at our victim)*
Dark blue anorak! *(or whatever our victim was wearing)*
And normal hair! *(or Old-Wave hair, or soul-boy hair, etc)*
Well you don't know nothing!
And you don't really care, do ya?
You just don't care!

This afforded us hours of moronic fun and somehow no one beat us up for it.

Before long I discovered that Ed was a resourceful chap with a knack for getting into bands' soundchecks or the backstage areas of Edinburgh rock venues. This talent comprised persistence, brass neck and an easy affability; Ed could talk to anyone. Together we sought and found ingress to behind-the-scenes action at shows by The Clash, The Boomtown Rats, The Tom Robinson Band, The Skids, The Stranglers and many others. If it moved, Ed and I were there. By the time we were blagging our way into Joe Strummer's hotel or Bob Geldof's dressing room, however, I'd given Ed a punk name, Z, pronounced like the letter 'Zed'. He reciprocated – amused by the pseudonym I'd assumed for my fanzine writing, Velvet Lanier, he unfailingly referred to me as 'Lainay-er'.

Thus appellated we went on our myriad expeditions. We hitchhiked to concerts in Glasgow and St Andrews and expanded our operations to include lightning trips to London, where we learned how to get into the press offices of record companies by brandishing copies of our fanzine and saying we wanted to write articles about their acts. Rich pickings awaited: places on concert guest lists, snippets of privileged information, glossy photos, free singles and albums. Through all of this Z was the main instigator, the canny operator with a eye on the main chance, for the way in, behind, or through. No surprise then that when it came time for me to become a professional musician myself, I knew who had to be my manager.

And Z had other talents that qualified him as a rock Svengali. He was incredibly tight with money. In that first year at university he once took it upon himself, as a kind of ideological challenge, to live for a week on eighteen pence. I don't know why specifically eighteen pence but I kept tabs on him through the seven days, and he really did it. He bought some cheap fruit and made it last all week, walked everywhere, contrived to get in free to any concerts that were happening, didn't drink (or at least didn't pay for his own) and ate only the meals that were provided free at the university halls of residence. And not only was he canny with money, he had willpower of iron. Indeed, he *had* to be my manager. What's more, he was forthright and fearless. Some might have classified this as rudeness, for example the American punk rocker Richard Hell, who'd been famously fired from the band Television by his ex-friend, now sworn enemy, Tom Verlaine. But this didn't perturb Z who sat in Richard's hotel bedroom the night we interviewed him, vehemently pronouncing Verlaine's album *Marquee Moon* 'a great masterpiece'.

Others might have thought him aggressive, like the queue jumpers in the overnight line to buy Bob Dylan concert tickets in Glasgow in the summer of 1978, at whom he snarled, 'Oi! Cut the crap!' Yes he *had* to be my manager! And soon he was.

We went to see Dylan play at Earls Court in London. Bob transcended all the Old or New Wave stuff just like David Bowie, and nothing would have kept Z and me from attending his first British concerts in twelve years. And somehow, despite having been way back in the queue for tickets, we'd scored front-row seats for the first night. Only we didn't know it. The tickets said 'Row A', which we took to mean something like the first row of the third upper circle in some dim distant balcony of the arena. But when we arrived at the vast barn of Earls Court, Bob already on stage and into his first number, the steward walked us to our seats not up the metal stairs or round the cavernous flanks of the venue but straight down a wide walkway through the middle. We followed him, getting ever closer and closer to the front, our disbelief and delight growing with every step. Finally he indicated our seats in the first row, *right in front of Bob.*

To two young sprogs from Scotland, being so close to Dylan performing on stage was like being in a beautiful, impossible dream. We copped every grin and gurn Bob pulled, hung on his every tattered poetic word, dug his band, grumbled to each other about his backing singers, got the goose bumps when he sang 'Just Like A Woman', and looked in mystification on the cabaret-style lightning flashes embroidered down the sides of his out-of-fashion flares. The show was slick, good rather than great, and a long way short of the brilliant Rolling Thunder shows he'd played in America a few years previously (which we'd heard on bootlegs), but it didn't matter; we were seeing Dylan!

After the show we decided to try our usual meet-the-band tactics, though we knew Bob's security arrangements would be a little different from those at Edinburgh punk gigs. We waited outside Earls Court as close to the artists' entrance as security would allow. Soon a great wheezing steel gateway opened and a single-decker bus rolled out. Its inside was lit and we could see members of the band, their heads framed in the windows. And there was Bob! He had shades on, looked just like one of his mid-sixties album covers, and was looking round quizzically. We waved to him and he waved back. Z wrote 'Good luck Bob' on his concert programme and held it up. Bob waved again, with a nod of thanks. The bus wheeled past us and out onto the streets of west London. We stood dazed, recovering from the shock of having communicated, even wordlessly and through glass, with Bob Dylan. Then we looked at the disappearing bus and noticed it was moving slowly; the streets were jammed with all the cars leaving the concert. The same thought struck us simultaneously – we could follow the bus on foot and see Bob in his hotel!

This unlikely plan worked. The bus proceeded, mostly, at such a snail-like pace that we were able to always keep it in sight. Forty minutes later, out of breath and with very sore legs, we saw it come to a definitive halt in the semi-distance outside a massive brightly lit building at the far end of Kensington High Street. A few minutes later we caught up and discovered this was the Royal Garden Hotel, a swanky joint on the corner of Hyde Park. And there was the bus outside, now empty. We ascended the steps to the hotel doors, suddenly conscious of our ragamuffin appearance (both in punk uniform of motorcycle jackets and ripped jeans), wondering whether we'd be allowed in.

We found ourselves in a cathedral foyer of glass and marble. Looking up and down its length we saw the open doors of the hotel bar and headed towards it, feet sinking into the plush carpet. We peered in: the bar was full of wealthy-looking people enjoying shorts and cocktails at low-lit tables, jazzy music playing over a hubbub of conversation. Our hungry eyes scanned this tableau and swiftly found their quarry. Bob was sitting, hunched in conversation, with a few people at the far end of the room. As if drawn by a magnet our feet started moving towards him. We drew closer and closer. We were going to meet and shake hands with him!

Two thirds of the way across the room, a couple of dark shapes sprang from either side of us, barring our way. One of them, a heavily built bearded gentleman in a black bomber jacket, said to us with a kind of pleading sadness in his voice: 'Bob's done his job. He's given everything. Let him relax now and have his peace.' Z and I, though sympathetic to this argument, still thought Bob might have just enough time and energy left to say a short hello to us, but there was no dissuading these guys. The game was up. As they escorted us out of the bar I asked the bearded man if he was one of Bob's roadies, but he just shook his head sadly and ushered us out of the bar. In the corridor two silent security guards took over and deposited us back on the pavement where we belonged. A few years later I saw the burly gentleman on TV. He was Harvey Goldsmith, the biggest rock promoter in Britain – and I'd asked him if he was a roadie!

A week before the Dylan shows I'd left university, dropping out after a first year spent attending almost zero lectures and countless punk gigs. And the following autumn, still in Edinburgh, I started my first serious band, Another Pretty Face, which comprised myself and three pals, all veterans of my teenage bands in Ayr: John Caldwell (talented, dour, handsome guitarist, and my co-writer in the band), Jim Geddes (still a scarf-toting Stones fan) and Crigg (still a wiggy mod drummer).

As I'd intended, Z became our manager and quickly succeeded at his first job, finding us a rehearsal room. Well, it was a cave really – a rectangular cube hewn from damp stone in the maze of medieval catacombs under Edinburgh's Royal Mile. The place was run by an owl-faced entrepreneur called Ian McCain who lived, unbelievably, in a flat in the catacombs with his wife and kids. To get to our cave we had to haul our gear along numberless fetid tunnels, past the sounds of a dozen other bands rehearsing in the same subterranean purgatory as ourselves. It was Dickensian, unhealthy and probably illegal, but we didn't care. It was where our music lived.

Then Z started booking us shows. He was good at it from the start, finding it easy to be business-like with agents and promoters, securing us support slots at the Edinburgh venues of the day like Tiffany's Ballroom or sending us further afield on jaunts to Glasgow and Aberdeen. Next he formed a record company for our first single, a piece of spunky doggerel called 'All The Boys Love Carrie'. He named the label after a Richard Hell song, 'New Pleasures' (reparations, perhaps, for his *Marquee Moon* gaffe), and by the spring of 1979 our little record was being played regularly on the John Peel radio show and was Single of the Week in the *NME*. We were off!

The next six months were exciting. Doors opened and obstacles crumbled, local audiences grew and the world, it seemed, was ours for the taking. In the wake of the 'Carrie' single we were wooed by several record companies, and after our first show in London that September a number of A&R men sidled up to us and spoke sweet nothings in our ears. My tendency to be argumentative with these guys, especially when they got our song titles wrong, was compensated by Z's diplomatic skills and soon he'd sewn up a tidy eight-album contract for us with Virgin Records, at the time an edgy, hip and newly chart-successful label.

And then he walked out on us. On me. The ink on our contract was still glistening when Z announced out of the blue that he was giving up managing to spend a year going round the world with his girlfriend, with no promise that he would come back to the job after that. I was shocked and could do nothing to change his mind, but I'd found the Achilles heel of Z's managerial skill set. He got bored quickly. Eager to keep our momentum going, we hired a fellow traveller on the Edinburgh music scene, Johnny Waller, as a replacement. Johnny was a great character and a good friend but a terrible manager. He specialised in unpredictable, shit-stirring wind-up antics, such as getting a skinhead haircut with the band initials APF shaved into the side of his skull the night before we left for a tour. In the 1979 Britain, a couple of decades before a number-one crop became the norm for footballers and businessmen, this was a seriously anti-social statement. A shaved head meant only one thing: *bovver*, and Johnny's fashion statement resulted in us being instantly banned from hotel after hotel by terrified staff.

Added to this was the band members' not inconsiderable youthful arrogance, with myself the prime offender. Always convinced of the rightness of our actions, and without Z's ameliorating influence, we led our genial and decent Virgin A&R man, Arnold, a merry dance, ganging up on him and generally reacting to his perplexed ministrations as if he worked for an evil empire. Our attitude was based on the absurd premise that despite giving us money, wanting to release our records and trying to make us successful, the record company was our enemy. We played silly psychological games with Arnold, for example ensuring a different band member or my punkette girlfriend Mairi answered the phone every time he called so he could never progress in whatever the argument of the day was. We were a regular group of horrors and unsurprisingly we fell out with Virgin and were kicked off the label, one not-quite-finished and not-very-good album later. This taught us tough lessons about the consequences of our actions as well as the capricious nature of success – having lost our record deal, no one was interested in us anymore. I returned to Edinburgh to contemplate my follies, lick my wounds and, soon enough, make another more effective and sustained assault on the mountain of stardom. Meanwhile Z was in East Africa. Our paths didn't cross again until two years later.

In the autumn of 1982 I'd moved to London and was living in a basement flat off the Portobello Road. The area that had seemed so exotic to me six years earlier, when I'd mistakenly turned up at Island Studios for my recording session, was now my neighbourhood. It was the freest I'd ever been; living on my own, writing songs all day. Another Pretty Face had split that spring and with no bandmates to compromise or argue with I could follow my muses wherever they led. Thus I found myself in the middle of a writing explosion that yielded most of the first two Waterboys albums, and in September I went to New York, for the first time, to record some of my new songs with Lenny Kaye, my friend from the Patti Smith adventure.

I'd just checked into the Chelsea Hotel (my only night there on account of cockroaches in my room) when I got a call from Z. To my amazement he'd arrived in the city that day, also for the first time, and was preparing to hitchhike across America on his way to a teaching job in Mexico. We spent a couple of days together rekindling our friendship and found that all the things we'd liked and enjoyed about each other were still the same. We spent hours in the Grass Roots Tavern on St Mark's Place, a funky basement bar and perfect venue for soulful conversation, then went exploring in Coney Island, remapping the broad spaces of our shared brotherhood as we walked along ocean highways and across green parklands, never quite finding the fabled Coney Island fairgrounds. At night, back on Manhattan, we re-enacted the punk wars, cheekily heckling intellectual art-prog guitarist Arto Lindsay at the Irving Plaza Theatre by calling for the kind of songs Arto was least likely to play: dumb-ass numbers like 'Louie Louie' and 'Hang On Sloopy'. Our friendship was intact, the same as it ever was.

Even so, it was another eighteen months before we met up again in London in 1984. By this time I'd formed The Waterboys and we were beginning to make a name for ourselves on the London scene, though I felt like a musical alien. The popular sound of the day was all synthesizers, clicky bass drums and mechanical pomp played by angular-haired people with tablecloths round their necks who sang in portentously deep faux-Germanic voices; the purgatorial heyday of the New Romantics. With my dreams of acoustic-guitar walls of sound I was a thousand miles out of step with the times. The nearest kindred spirits were Echo & The Bunnymen and The Smiths, but they were in other towns, other dimensions, far from London pop city. No, I was deep behind enemy lines in the domain of Spandau Ballet, Modern Romance and Bananarama, none of whose manifestations appeared to admit of what I considered the foundation stones of modern music: Dylan, The Beatles, the Stones, punk, soul, Chuck Berry and the counterculture. Either they were all insane or I was.

The only people who seemed to share my ideas of how rock'n'roll should look and sound were the Johnny Thunders clones who hung out on a retro glam/punk scene that festered round some of the city's music pubs, and for a while I was so lonesome I even took comfort there. Thunders himself, the Italian-American guitarist and ex-New York Doll who I'd seen at the Patti Smith bash years before, was the god of this scene despite being a notorious junkie who played only one good gig in every six or seven. My first sighting of him on stage was at Dingwall's in Camden Town. The act playing that night was Sylvain Sylvain, another ex-Doll, and a rumour spread that Thunders was in town and would make an appearance. I was eager to see him so when the doors opened I got down the front and stayed there all evening. After the support act, Sylvain and his band entered by the main door, pushed through the crowd and trooped across the stage into the tiny dressing room at its rear (there was no other artists' entrance) and I resigned myself to a Johnny Thunders non-appearance. I'd been there all night and he hadn't come in.

Sylvain's set was a master class in dumb rock'n'roll. During the encore he started strumming a Bo Diddley riff, leaned into the microphone and introduced a 'friend'. The dressing room door opened and rock'n'roll walked out.

Clad in black cloak, scarlet waistcoat, white dress shirt, flat black Spanish matador's hat tilted insolently, his lips curled in a sneer that made Elvis look like a pretender and Billy Idol like a gnat, Johnny Thunders strutted to the microphone, no guitar, and started to sing in a cartoonish, sleazy voice like Bob Dylan, had he been born in Little Italy instead of Hibbing, Minnesota: 'Ah said ah was layin' in a hospital BEDDDDD ...' with a ridiculously exaggerated lift on the 'bed'. It was the greatest stage entrance I'd ever seen, and I realised that to ensure its impact Thunders must have gone into the tiny dressing room before the audience arrived and waited there all night, an incarceration of over five hours. That was dedication.

A couple of nights later he did his own show at the Hope & Anchor, a basement club in Islington I'd played myself a few times. I got close to the front again so I could study Johnny's moves. Fortunately this was another night when Thunders was 'on'. I've never witnessed a sharper guitar player. He'd deal out a lazy blues riff, one hand contemptuously fingering the guitar neck while with the other he pulled a steel comb from his jeans pocket and fixed his hair, preening for the girls in the front row. Then he'd swing full circle on one boot heel and as he came face-on to the crowd again crack out a machine-gun riff in perfect sync with a drum fill before swinging into another beatifically brilliant dumb chorus. He was *outrageously* great and no other flash rock guitarist, not Keith Richards, not Jimmy Page, not Jack White, has ever come close. But the next time I saw him a week later he was so out of it on heroin he had to be carried into the venue flaked out between two roadies, belly distended, eyes rolling and legs like Plasticine. When they propped him up on stage he couldn't even play in time. He'd morphed from the sharpest man in the universe to the saddest, and I didn't have time to stick around and watch his decline.

Another junkie, the rock journalist Nick Kent, lived a few doors up from me and I'd often see him standing in his garden, slightly dazed as if he'd just woken up, watching the world pass him by like a horse looking over a hedge. Further down the street a gang of truants sniffed glue every afternoon, holding plastic bags to their noses and staggering around cross-eyed. Each summer, as August Bank Holiday weekend approached and brought with it the Notting Hill Carnival, massive sound systems appeared on every street. Monolithic speakers emblazoned with the names of Brixtonian or Jamaican DJs blocked the roads, and the neighbourhood would shake to loud, feral Rasta music, its supersonic bass tones rattling the foundations of the Victorian houses.

Most days I'd step out wearing a cowboy hat I'd bought in New York with a couple of feathers in the brim, a pair of striped trousers, a black jacket with the sleeves rolled up, and jingly boots from Johnston's on the King's Road. As often as not I'd have my acoustic guitar with me, slung over-shoulder or carried under-arm ready for action. I'd stroll down Portobello Road digging the bustle of the market, buy bootleg albums and second-hand books, then go to Mike's Cafe on Blenheim Crescent for lunch. Lots of musicians ate in this semi-legendary greasy spoon; I'd bumped into Mick Jones of The Clash here several times and the luckless A Flock Of Seagulls, whose notoriously over-the-top haircuts were just as mad close up. And once, the gay punk rocker Gene October, leader of perennially unsuccessful punk band Chelsea. I'd actually bought one of Gene's records in 1977, a thug-like dole queue rant called 'The Right To Work'. He sat down opposite me in Mike's one day while I was eating my lunch, leaned across the table and in a conspiratorial cockney voice said, 'You look like a muso. Wanna be in moi band?' I was being invited to join Chelsea! It took me about one and a half nanoseconds to inform Gene I was already gainfully employed, thanks mate.

Then Z walked back into my life, turning up at my flat one March morning in 1984. He'd heard my Waterboys records on the radio and fancied working with me again for a while. Not as manager – he had no intentions in that regard anymore, but as an assistant, and strictly temporarily. I needed a road manager to organise and drive the band on our first tour, which started in a couple of weeks, so I had a word with my financial backer, Nigel Grainge, in his office on nearby

Westbourne Grove. Nigel was a London music biz man, something of a maverick, and he'd taken a shot in the dark by signing me to his Ensign label in 1981 when no one else was interested. He'd funded my musical explorations and encouraged me in what he felt were the right directions for me to go. And sometimes they even were. Happily, he agreed to bankroll Z for a hundred quid a week. We were off again.

Z moved into a flat on the same street as me and I introduced him to the four other Waterboys. Saxman Anthony Thistlethwaite was a beatnik character and former Paris busker. He'd been in my last combo, an outfit called The Red And The Black that had gigged round London a couple of years earlier. When Anthony played he turned into a human saxophone, and the mighty Promethean wail of his horn provided most of our solos. He also played mandolin with the exquisite tenderness of a lover. Our drummer was an unusual player called Kevin Wilkinson, a mate of Anthony's with a pointed chin, a craving for Frank Zappa music, and a penchant for rearranging hotel furniture upside down. Keyboard player Karl Wallinger was a gifted, complex Welsh Beatles fanatic who'd answered my musician-seeking ad in the *NME* nine months earlier. And the bassist, a quiet cerebral fellow called Martyn Swain, was a friend of Karl's.

Another Pretty Face had been like a gang, with a group mentality, and Z was one of that gang. But now there was a different dynamic. The Waterboys was indisputably my band, and the others, at least at this early stage, were hired guns with different degrees of empathy and involvement. I half-expected therefore that as soon as Z stepped in, the fact of our history would mean we'd reprise the two-man force-of-nature mentality we'd had in the past. I was wrong. Perhaps because our lives had been on different paths for so long, or because Z wanted to keep his options open, this didn't happen. Nevertheless, it was good to work and travel with my old friend again, to feel a familiar hand at the wheel and once more witness his ability to deal well with business people. This came in particularly useful with one of our booking agents, a smooth young persuader named

Steve, with short, smart hair and alarmingly blue Teutonic eyes.

Steve had strong opinions regarding what we should do, which concerts we should play, which groups we should open for. But if I didn't agree immediately he seemed to regard me as an irritating obstacle. *Why, oh why,* I imagined him wondering, *does Mike have to think about things so much? Why can't he just say yes to the gigs I've worked hard to secure?* Of course, I had my own sense of what was right for my band, though not as yet the ability to articulate it in a way that an agent or anyone else could understand. Consequently I always felt Steve to be impatient with me, and all the band perceived his presence at our shows as a pressure. Yet Z remained aloof from this feeling and he and Steve developed an understanding which allowed our train to keep rolling.

These were rough beginnings for The Waterboys. Though we'd been on radio and TV and were getting known in London, we were a long way from being established nationally. Many of our early concerts were poorly attended. We stiffed in Bournemouth and Folkestone, battled with the potted plants and disco lights of Busby's nightclub in Redhill, and finally met our nemesis at the New Ocean Club in Cardiff, a vast hangar of a place populated at show time by all of six fans. By some miracle this event turned into that rare but blessed phenomenon that every up-and-coming band experiences once: the scantily attended gig that turns into the greatest night of everyone's life. Those six guys came down the front and danced unselfconsciously to our rough but enthusiastic set like we were the best band in the world. And for those sixty minutes, I guess we were. They were certainly the greatest audience.

Things revved up when we were booked as support act on a twenty-date European tour with The Pretenders, then at the peak of their popularity. But when I turned up to meet everyone at the Westbourne Grove cafe that served as our touring departure point, the others had all got themselves variations of the dreaded then-fashionable angular haircuts, rendering me a long-haired stranger in my own band. Kevin had a new-romantic wedge with a fringe that jutted several inches from his brow, curly-locked Karl looked like a pruned bush, while Anthony had been to a trendy Kensington salon called Antenna where apparently a trainee had gone experimental on him, resulting in a look halfway between Billy The Whiz and a Mohawk. All my ideals of what a rock'n'roll band should look like were severely challenged. But at least Z was still his usual scruffy self and with my mate reassuringly at the controls we drove off, angular haircuts and all, on our greatest adventure thus far.

Touring as a support band is a fantastic way to see the world. We played nineteen towns in nine countries in a month and only had to play forty minutes at each show, leaving plenty time to hang out and explore the great cities of Europe. And because we drove everywhere the journey had an epic, real-time quality. Then there was the onstage education: as the tour moved across the continent I began to understand the differences between the audiences, and therefore the national characters of the various countries. Nordic punters were earnestly soulful, signifying appreciation by applauding in slow communal handclaps (a phenomenon deeply unnerving at first, for the same thing means impatience and contempt in Britain); the French were hard to please but passionate once roused; Italians were combustible, like dry tinder ready to be sparked.

In these pre-euro times, we had to change money every few days – lira to kroner to marks and so on – and generally had no idea of the value of what we were spending. It quickly became confusing, and in a fateful motorway service station on the Swiss border, hungry but with no usable cash, Karl Wallinger pushed it too far. He complained bitterly to Z that he had no Swiss francs, with the whinging implication that it was all Z's fault as usual. Z, stretched beyond all reasonable limits after three weeks in foreign countries with Karl, blew his Scottish gasket and in one athletic movement spun round and landed a wild haymaker of a punch on Karl's protruding jaw, knocking him, poetically enough, into a rack of Europop cassettes.

From Switzerland, and despite Karl's punctured but soon restored dignity, we continued to Berlin, where Thistlethwaite smoked so much reefer his head changed shape, clockwise through Italy and France, and finally to Ireland. After our performance in Dublin, during the intermission before The Pretenders' set, I was ushered by a red-haired roadie into a dark and cordoned-off projection room. There U2's Bono awaited me, wishing to proclaim himself a Waterboys fan and talk with me about C.S. Lewis. Seemingly too famous already to stand among his home crowd, secreted in a hidden corner with a man to do his fetching, Bono struck me as a kind of benign rock emperor – a mixture of fervour, self-import, curiosity and a mannered humbleness that felt about seventy per cent genuine. We hung out with each other for half an hour and shared a bottle of champagne, beginning an occasional friendship which flourished for six or seven years. And in the dim room, with the hubbub of the waiting audience roaring like a restless sea in the background, I sensed Bono was sizing me up, measuring my energy and intensity, my charisma and desire, like a tiger sniffing out territory, to see if I was a dangerous competitor with my eye on the same prize as him. And at that moment, before I discerned other more distant and mysterious mountain peaks to shoot for, I was. What's more, I was measuring him up too.

A week later the second Waterboys album, *A Pagan Place*, came out and we played the Glastonbury Festival for the first time. On our way there Z stopped to give me the gift of looking on Stonehenge with pristine eyes, and a few miles further on came another striking vision, our first glimpse of the fabled Glastonbury Tor, which rose ship-like on the horizon, its tower-crested profile Calvaryesque against the morning sky. I already knew the spiritual tradition of Glastonbury, of how it was said to be 'the holiest earth in England', and I couldn't wait to play the festival that bore its name.

The gig was a shock. We were the first band of the festival, a thirty-minute performance on Friday lunchtime. When we walked up the slippery earth-encrusted ramp to the rear of the Pyramid stage and stepped out into the light, there before me was the biggest audience I'd ever seen; fifteen or twenty thousand punters arrayed from skyline to skyline, most of whom hadn't the foggiest idea who The Waterboys were. With no containing roof or walls, how was I to project my voice and songs into such a vast space and to so many faces? How could our presence fill this stage, this spectacle? By the time we returned to Glastonbury two years later, with the wind at our heels and victory in our grasp, I'd have solved these problems, but for now we were neophytes, dwarfed by the occasion, and played a blustery set that left the audience unmoved. Crowning our disappointment, half an hour after we came off stage an impatient Z, with some pressing but undisclosed London business of his own, announced he was leaving immediately in our van. For the band this meant leave now or stay and be stranded, but this was my first-ever rock festival and I wanted to soak it up. So drummer Kev and myself stayed and embarked on a sleepless twenty-four hour marathon of high jinks, reefer smoking and general wide-eyed and ecstatic exploration of the festival's parallel universe. We also witnessed the greatest show I've ever seen at Glastonbury.

It was late at night and all scheduled performances had finished. Six lads who'd brought their instruments to the festival were playing an impromptu set at the side of one of the rough thoroughfares. A small crowd had gathered around them as they played a homespun mix of dixieland-cum-swing with guitars, sax, trombone, percussion and a stand up bass. Their name, The Forest Hill Bums, was proclaimed on a piece of cardboard propped up in front of them and their songs were catchy, good-natured and innocent. I don't know whether they intended to be humorous, but the little crowd found them so, especially the exertions of the hard-puffing trombone man whose eyeballs swung from side to side as he blew, grunted and grinned. As we watched, the crowd's mood began to shift from amusement to affection and then to deepen into something bordering love. This feeling spread and radiated itself to the band, who could feel it even if they didn't know what it was. Before our eyes, raised by the surrounding audience's emotion, the little band grew as performers, relaxing into their stride, sensing what was funny about themselves then subtly emphasising it, joining in with the gentle joke and hitting heights of confidence and excellence they hadn't known they had in them. The love was thereby radiated back to the crowd and, now flowing both ways, lifted us all in a sweet and heady atmosphere. At the end of the set, as Kev and I walked off into the Glastonbury night, we felt as if our souls had been cleansed.

The next day we blagged a lift to London with some friends and a week later regrouped with Z and The Waterboys for a tour of the UK. As we criss-crossed the country we were at first blighted by the same poor attendances as before, but after three or four dates I realised we were also suffering from a more immediate malaise: Z was burned out. The poor fellow was beginning to visibly wither, his skin grey and eyes bloodshot, and had taken to spending much of the day asleep in the parked van, neglecting his duties and leaving the band to fend for themselves. The solution, clearly, was to bring in an experienced tour manager who did this job for a living, and after a quiet conversation with our soundman, a stalwart Brummie called John who gave me the phone numbers of some likely candidates, I found one. Proving the truism that people who want to be successful will even fire their best friends, I sacked Z in the car park after a tough gig in a Preston disco full of oblivious soul fans. Next day his replacement turned up, a professional tour manager called Chris Rowley, and that evening we played what I still remember as the first truly great Waterboys show, in a tiny Manchester club called The Gallery. We were off again.

This time it was Z's turn to retreat to Edinburgh to lick his wounds. He knew I'd done the right thing and we remained friends but I was to see him less and less from here on in: his global wanderings would take him to Madagascar, Brazil and the Far East. Whatever lay in wait for me on the road of rock, I would meet it without my old mate and fellow dreamer.

CHAPTER 5

THE BLACK BOOK
AND THE MOON

It's a wickedly cold January evening in New York and my Canadian girlfriend Krista and I are walking arm in arm down Lexington Avenue. As we cross Twentieth Street she asks me, 'So, is it easy to write songs?' The correct answer is, 'Yes, no, kind of, sometimes, but it depends and every song is different,' though that won't win me any kudos with my girl. But a demonstration might. So I say, 'Of course it's easy. I'll write one now,' and pluck a pen and a three-day-old envelope from my pocket.

I look around for inspiration. A luminous full moon dangles in the New York sky, the frayed edges of clouds streaming through its aureole like witches' rags. On the envelope I write down a title – always a good starting place – 'The Whole Of The Moon', then a hook line pops into my mind: 'I saw the crescent, you saw the whole of the moon.'

Nothing more comes but it's sufficient to impress Krista, who squeezes my arm and gushes, 'Oh, that's wonderful! I hope you'll finish it.' Well, we'll see. It has a ring to it all right, and I can hear a hint of a melody dancing around the words as I spin them in my mind. I need my guitar. Fast. I fold my arm round Krista's shoulder and hasten us back to our hotel.

A few days earlier, on a shadowy New York backstreet, I'd discovered the most curious shop I'd ever seen. It was a witches' store, its shelves filled with potions, grimoires, scraps of wood, bark, root and numberless weird things I had no words or names for. As I explored this strange grotto my eye was attracted by a massive, enigmatic-looking black-bound book. I drew it from the shelf to find it was full of blank white pages. Mystified, I asked the man behind the counter, a lantern-jawed fellow with an air of brusque authority, what it was for. He told me it was a 'Book Of Shadows' in which witches wrote down spells, rituals and accounts of their experiences. I'd heard of such things, but the idea immediately struck me that the book was perfect to write my lyrics into – and lyrics, with their intent to enchant and transport the listener, were a kind of spell anyway.

Back at the hotel the beginnings of 'The Whole Of The Moon' were quickly etched into the newly purchased book, with a couple of added lines establishing the theme of the song's hero seeing or experiencing more than its narrator. When I got back to London a few days later, I wrote into the Black Book all the other songs I had in progress, forty or fifty of them, the repertoire for the third Waterboys album, *This Is The Sea*.

Having all my songwriting in one volume instead of on a hundred scraps and sheets of paper had an unexpected effect, for within a few days of using the Black Book I found that by simply opening its pages I entered the flow and absorption of my writing; a feeling like switching on a light. It may only have been a conglomeration of paper, cardboard and binding thread, but once filled with songs the Book was alive, a thing of power, a gateway. And it would accompany me on every step of the making of *This Is The Sea*; spread open on the floor as I wrote for hour after hour, next to me on the seats of a hundred black cabs as I travelled to the recording studios of London through the spring of 1985, laid open on the mixing desk, instructions displayed, while the album was being made, and doubling as a table top as I wrote out track sheets in the studio or rolled myself a reefer.

Alongside each lyric, and covering the page in slithering hieroglyphics of tiny handwriting, were lists of rhymes and instruments, plus notes describing the recording process of each song and how I imagined the sound, sometimes accompanied by drawings: cartoonish electricity volts bursting from twin speakers with notes like 'fades up then explodes' or 'shining trumpet against cloudy backdrop'. The Book was also filled with unused song titles, stray verses, poems, dreams, future concert set lists, potential album running orders, musicians' phone numbers, artwork ideas and all manner of notes to myself, such as:

Create new acoustic electric cold-country rock/folk music, jagged or rolling as the land (remember folk music corresponds in shape and form to the land it springs from), five string acoustics (no 'G'), droning electrics, pagan drum grooves like the bass drum on 'Be My Baby', the sound of rocks, caves and hard places. Lyrics: resurrect the narrative in poetic wild impressionistic form. Express and use my own language and do not simplify for all.

I lived in those days in a flat on St Mark's Road in Notting Hill, where I wrote in a long sitting room with a velvet-curtained sliding door at one end, opening onto a little garden. The walls were decorated with photographs of American Indians and rock'n'rollers – Sitting Bull brooding, Iggy Pop snarling, Bob Dylan grinning over his guitar – and books lay everywhere. The mantelpiece supported a teetering cliff face of Waterboys cassettes and my record collection was stashed in rows on the floor, hundreds of vinyl albums propped against the wall. Aside from writing songs, my favourite pastimes were lying on the floor listening to *Astral Weeks* by Van Morrison or turning out all the lights, sticking on Steve Reich's album of sacred music, *Tehillim*, and letting its swirling mosaic of female voices dance like illuminations in the darkness of the room. I call it a sitting room but it had no chairs. I'd crouch on the floor, guitar by my side, poring over the Black Book, working on 'The Pan Within' or the Thatcher-era protest song 'Old England' or 'This Is The Sea' itself, a coming of age folk/soul ballad with twenty verses, which I intended to whittle down to five or six. Or 'The Whole Of The Moon', for which I drafted dozens of couplets developing the saw-more-than-me theme.

As each song evolved it took on a life of its own and I'd be swept up in its flavour and personality, a feeling like being enfolded in a heady scent, or like being in love. Whether the soul of a song existed in some ineffable realm of music before I wrote it I neither knew nor truly cared, but at some stage in each song's composition it would become a thing with its own distinct identity and take hold of my imagination. For days I'd live in the song's atmosphere, and when I ventured out to the world to buy bread and milk at the corner shop or further abroad to Ladbroke Grove, I'd do so inhabiting 'The Pan Within', perhaps, or 'Medicine Bow', the song's melodies and lyrics running ceaselessly through my head, new ideas flashing into my mind at any and all times so that it was essential always to have pen and paper with me. I restructured my life and relationships so I could work like this perpetually and it became my norm.

Soon I began to notice that rather than making decisions about a song's content I was following instructions; the music was telling me what to do. It was like being tuned into a wavelength containing the DNA of the song, and the wavelength was informing me. I'd recognise the authority of each instruction: make the melody do *this*, create a middle eight *here* – by getting a 'go' feeling in my guts, a kind of flavoured certainty, every time an idea was right. And if I didn't get this feeling I'd keep trying different things till I did. I came to look on my role as being a kind of translator, discerning the will of the music and transforming it into sound so the listener could tune into the same wavelength. My absorption was broken every now and then by Anthony Thistlethwaite, who'd turn up in his car and whisk me off to the pubs of Chelsea or Primrose Hill (and once for a day in the country) because he thought I needed to get out more. Or by my fortnightly visits to Karl Wallinger, who had a home studio in his West End flat. Karl would patiently record me exploring my guitar and piano soundscapes, usually adding contributions of his own; a slinky synth bass line or a glittering keyboard backdrop. Many of the sounds that would define *This Is The Sea* had their sonic dress rehearsal at Seaview.

When I'd arrived in London a couple of years before, I'd done my recordings in an eight-track studio in Islington called Redshop (actually in the back of an empty red-painted shop) where I developed the sound journalists called 'the big music', after one of my songs. The core of this sound was two twelve-string rhythm guitars. I discovered that when I played the second one immediately after the first, I could remember every nuance of the playing on the first one, and could match those nuances or, better still, play subtly different to them, with little rhythmic comments and echoes. When these performances were split into opposite speakers it sounded like two musicians incredibly in tune with each other, and with the fullness of the twenty-four strings the soundscape was broad and rich. When I added rolling piano and a hatful of reverb I had a shimmering wall of music. I fell in love with this sound and used it as the springboard for The Waterboys' style. And when Kevin Wilkinson's epic drums and Anthony Thistlethwaite's sax were subsequently added the musical picture became huge.

By 1985 I'd graduated to twenty-four-track studios and heard the songs full-blown in my head before I even started. But with *This Is The Sea* expected to be our breakthrough album, Ensign's Nigel Grainge insisted I work with a co-producer. Nigel didn't think I was ready to produce a hit on my own – he was wrong, as things turned out, and I agreed to work with the guy he suggested. John Brand was English, easy-going and mad about The Waterboys; I could feel his belief in me every time he walked in the room and I felt good about playing for him. Best of all there was no conflict between our agendas: far from imposing his own vision on the music, John was happy to create an atmosphere in which I could follow my 'instructions'. He booked a studio called Parkgate on the southeast coast, an hour from London, and because we planned to record solo demos of the songs first, the two of us travelled a few days ahead of the band.

The studio was in a converted barn, a vast high-raftered space with a spectacularly good grand piano. John set up microphones, I propped the Black Book open on the piano top and we turned the

69

lights down. Then I spent two days and nights singing everything in the Book, including 'The Whole Of The Moon', which now had several verses set to one of my lop-sided teenage piano grooves, still played with one finger on the low notes and three fingers for the chords. John and I listened back in the control room and I imagined the song's eventual sound: hurdy-gurdy carnival music with colourful flourishes weaving through it. But it wasn't finished; it needed a chorus, and when we began recording the album proper with the band a few days later 'Moon' wasn't even on the shortlist.

The band at this juncture was Anthony and Karl plus a doleful session drummer called Chris Whitten. We set up as a four-piece, with Anthony on bass, and began knocking out numbers. Listening back to the band through the speakers I realised something wasn't right. John's sound was too *indie*. I wanted a powerful mainstream sound with no limitations on its potential audience, and we weren't getting it. I was reluctant to split with John because his heart was in the work, but the music came first. So I phoned Nigel Grainge to ask if we could replace John with Mick Glossop, an engineer whose work with Van Morrison I admired. Nigel drove down from London that afternoon and to my shame I bottled out and let him tell John he was fired. They had the discussion in the control room and emerged after ten minutes. John looked glumly at me, shoulders drooping, and said, 'Oh, *Mike*!' in the saddest voice, a lover jilted. I felt one inch tall, and fair enough. But I was right to make the change. Glossop arrived next morning, cranked up a slick sound, and the game was on. Yet there was a trade off; I got the sonics right with Glossop but I lost the sense of empathy I'd had with John. Mick and I never perceived Waterboys music the same way; he understood the mechanics of the music but not, I think, its drama and romance. And though we successfully produced half of *This Is The Sea* together, including powerful recordings like the title track, when the time came to record 'The Whole Of The Moon' I cut loose and defected to a north London studio where I produced the song myself.

In fact, even as spring laid its benediction on London and pink blossoms burst on the trees along Ladbroke Grove, 'Moon' was still being written. Finally in mid May I completed it with a chorus hook of 'too high, too far, too soon' and, though still only imaginary, a Beatlesque trumpet solo.

Just as I was closing the Black Book on what I thought was another finished song I got a kind of itch in my soul telling me something else needed to happen, some kind of lift-off after the last chorus. I reopened the book, knuckled down and tried out numerous ideas: double-length extra verse, coda, instrumental bridge, all the tricks I could think of, before finally, in a moment of clarity, I got it: *a list of all the things the song's hero has seen.*

The phrase 'unicorns and cannonballs' was first and the rest came quickly, almost fully formed. Only the penultimate line 'carriages and cars' got changed later to 'scimitars and scarves' when I remembered from my childhood a book about the medieval crusades, with a picture of Saladin, the Saracen lord, slicing a blue scarf in the air with his scimitar. When I sang the 'list' back in my head I noticed that by raising the emotional heat of the song it created the necessity for a final heightened chorus. And just repeating the earlier chorus wasn't sufficient; I needed to tweak the words to build on the heat the 'list' had established. So instead of 'you stretched for the stars and you know how it feels', which had featured in the first two choruses, I stuck in 'you came like a comet, blazing your trail', which supplied the emotional pay-off.

There was another surprise to come. Three weeks later I sat in the recording studio, Black Book open on the mixing desk, as the newly recorded song crashed out of the speakers. My piano and a drum loop grooved beneath a carnival of trumpets, candy-flavoured 'la-la' backing vocals and Karl Wallinger's masterful synths. I was leaning back listening, eyes closed, when as the last chorus rocketed by I got the itch in my soul again. Every time the words 'like a comet' jumped out of the speakers it seemed some final touch, some coup de grace,

71

wanted to happen. When the idea dropped into my mind it was beautifully simple: *add the sound of the comet*. I found a firework sample on a BBC sound effects record, had my engineer Felix send it through a super-powered echo unit, then inserted it one beat after the word 'comet'. No sooner was it in place than the final unforeseen part of the whole puzzle was revealed: *have a sax solo explode out of the comet*. I'd been wondering how to get Thistlethwaite onto this song. Now I knew!

CHAPTER 6

DON'T FORGET TO GET ON THE BUS

A quiet London pub on an autumn afternoon. I'm standing at the bar with two men, one of whom is The Waterboys' booking agent, a silver-haired, silver-tongued trickster called Ian Flooks. Flooks likes to introduce me to other musicians and today he's brought me to meet Jackie Leven, the singer with a band called Doll By Doll, a gently spoken long-haired fellow eight or nine years my senior. When Flooks goes to make a phone call Jackie asks how I'm doing. Because he's older than me and a fellow Scotsman, I find it easy to confide in him. There's always been something about older Scottish men I find comforting, as if they're the big brothers I never had.

I tell Jackie I'm OK but under a lot of pressure. The new Waterboys record has just come out and I need to find and rehearse two new band members for a tour starting next week. Meanwhile there are demands on me to sign contracts that will commit my future five, six years down the line, to make this or that video, do interviews, go to meetings, agree merchandise and publishing deals. It's good to be wanted but I feel pulled every which way. Managers, agents, record company men, even band members and my forceful American girlfriend all want me to do what they think I should do – and they all want me to do different things. The clamour is driving me nuts and it seems like ages since I had the space to just hang out and have some uncomplicated fun. 'What I'd like,' I tell my patient listener, 'is to be on the top deck of a bus in Edinburgh, looking out the window, just taking it all in.' Flooks comes back and the conversation turns to other things. When I get up to leave forty minutes later, Jackie walks me to the door. As I shake his hand he leans forwards with a glint in his eye and says, 'Don't forget to get on that bus.'

In the summer of 1985, with The Waterboys' third album *This Is The Sea* set for release, word was we were the next band likely to explode out of rock'n'roll and break America.

America! Its music had cast a spell on me since I was a child. I dreamed and breathed its sound, its energy. I wanted to plug my soul into its motherlode and send my records crackling across its sweet airwaves. And so did my record company bosses, Nigel and Chris. At the thought of breaking The Waterboys in America they'd come over all intense; their voices would get louder as if someone had pumped gas into them, they'd slap their knees, talk in big numbers, quote the names of US promo men like they were holy talismans, and break into impromptu hollerings of the *Dallas* theme music as if to affirm 'Yes! We're coming to the party!'

Meanwhile the music press was talking, though I had mixed feelings about what they said. When *Rolling Stone* headlined me as 'rock and roll's poet laureate' or *NME* called me the latest 'god-like genius' I appreciated the enthusiasm but mistrusted the hyperbole. It wasn't so much that they were likely to knock me down six months later, it was that the blunt sloganising of the headlines made me cringe. Why couldn't they just say what they felt about the music without hanging weights around me? But they couldn't or wouldn't and the dramatic press coverage, fusing with the publicity machinations of the record company and the organic word of mouth that surrounded Waterboys shows and records, created a powerful sense of expectation and presumption.

I could feel this power collecting round me like a breeze that blew when I walked, a beam of light that shifted direction when I turned, an edge that entered a room when I did. It was a powerful, almost hallucinatory stimulant, and for the moment I was comfortable within its gravity. I'd been dreaming and working towards this breakthrough since I was a teenager, and to feel the wind of momentum at my heels was part of the script I'd planned. I believed in myself, and though I had an uncertain relationship with my new American manager, a tough, gruff man called Gary Kurfirst, who managed several top bands I admired, and though there were fault lines in the personnel of my band, still my feet were steady on the rock of the music itself.

I'd hired Kurfirst to make The Waterboys a success in America, and to stop Nigel and Chris interfering while I completed *This Is The Sea*. My two backers had championed and nurtured me as an artist for four years but we'd begun to disagree more than we agreed. Nigel had lobbied me to drop several of what I felt were my best songs, 'Red Army Blues' and 'Old England' among them, and putting my music through the filter of his judgment, which usually resulted in one of two pronouncements, 'It's genius' or 'It's shit', had become confounding. I got a sore head trying to figure out why some of my songs were shit while others were genius, and knew that if I wanted to make the records that were in my heart I needed to forestall Nigel's influence. Kurfirst had achieved that for me. As for his effectiveness in America, that remained to be seen.

Against this backdrop, and in perfect timing for the coming campaign, I found the final element of The Waterboys' sound: The Fellow Who Fiddles. One night in his flat, Karl Wallinger played me a demo he'd just recorded for a new singer called Sinead O'Connor. Sinead was sixteen and Irish, a discovery of Nigel's, and she had a great voice, but what caught my ear was the violin player behind her. I'd toyed with adding fiddle to our sound for ages and had already tried three fiddlers: a Polish session guy, a Liverpudlian squaddie, and a Marble Arch busker called Frank, but none of them provided the alchemy I was looking for. The player backing Sinead was rootsy and edgy, passionate and exciting; here was the sound I wanted. His name was Steve Wickham and I tracked him down through the Dublin recording studio Windmill Lane. He accepted my invitation to add fiddle to a song on *This Is The Sea* and two days later, on a hot July afternoon, he flew to London and came straight to my Ladbroke Grove flat. When I opened the door I found a cheerful gypsy-eyed ragamuffin looking back at me. He came in, lay on the living room

75

floor with his head propped on an elbow and proceeded to tell me his life story with endless diversions, ruminations and meanderings, all in the most charming Dublin accent. After a few hours of tales populated by charismatic characters with names like Clancy, Cooney and O'Kelly, I made Steve some ham sandwiches and tomato soup. Then we picked up a couple of guitars and bashed out the Waterboys song 'Savage Earth Heart'. By the way Steve played it, and though he hadn't even picked up his fiddle yet, I knew we were going to be musical brothers.

Next day we went to a studio where he played on 'The Pan Within', giving a masterful performance that exceeded my expectations; bright, gossamer-thin shards of melody that curled around my voice like a spell. I knew then that if I had Steve in The Waterboys we'd be the best band in the world. Steve was already in a Dublin group called In Tua Nua but I invited him to guest on the Waterboys tour due to start in six weeks' time, and foolishly they allowed him to do it. Once ensconced in our rehearsal room with his electric violins to hand, a bank of effect pedals at his feet, and the sound of The Waterboys blasting around his ears, The Fellow Who Fiddles never fiddled with In Tua Nua again. Now I had a killer album, a tough manager and a new star instrumentalist. The only thing missing from the mix was that most dangerous of rock accoutrements, the manipulative girlfriend. And lo and behold, along she came.

In late July I went to New York to meet with Kurfirst and the American record company. Someone had the idea of doing a TV film about The Waterboys and so I was introduced to a director called Kate Lovecraft. I knew Kate by reputation: she'd worked with artists I admired, including Dylan and Patti Smith, and she understood rock'n'roll. I'd also read she had a deep interest in Eastern spirituality, and this intrigued me. But nothing prepared me for the reality of Kate. Within minutes of our meeting she was flitting around her bright studio, sassy, lithe, petite and pointing a video camera at me while exclaiming in an adorable cartoony little girl voice: 'Oh my *God*, you should see how *great* you *look* in this *camera!*' Ten years older than me, she'd been a young adult in the cultural explosions of the sixties and seventies, and the mark of those fateful days was upon her. She burst on my consciousness like a love grenade and seemed to my impressionable eyes to be everything I looked for in a woman.

Next day we met at her studios again. This time she was wearing a sweet, lacy white dress. She took me on the roof and as I stood being filmed, the Manhattan skyline shimmering behind me in the summer heat, a profound feeling descended on me. I suddenly felt heavy and awestruck as if my soul had received some great news. I looked at Kate pointing her camera at me, white-clad, her reddish-gold hair blowing in the rooftop breeze, and I began to fall in love. There was an old upright piano in a room of her studio and when we came in from the roof I sat down at it and poured out my feelings in deep, long rolling chords. Kate came into the room without a word, placed one delicate kiss on my cheek, and stepped out again. Filming finished, we walked up Sixth Avenue together in the early evening light, she still in white, wheeling a bicycle, me floating by her side, aching to get close to her. Outside a deli store, watched by a hard-eyed Chinaman on a stool, Kate turned to face me and we kissed properly for the first time. A few blocks later I left to catch my plane and we said goodbye, promising to get together on my next trip to New York.

Back in London, ecstatic and excited, I booked plane tickets for a week hence and four nights in a New York hotel. I called Kate to tell her, expecting her to be thrilled. 'A hotel?' she exclaimed in an outraged voice, startlingly different from the sweet tones I'd heard in New York. 'Are you crazy? Don't you know how short life is? Why aren't you coming to stay with me in my apartment?' In these few words were contained impatient summons, spiritual rank-pulling and offended generosity. Quite a cocktail. But all I knew was that I had got it spectacularly wrong. I found myself spluttering, backtracking and agreeing to stay with her, apologising for my thoughtlessness and thanking her profusely for her gracious invitation. I was falling all right, not just in love but into Kate Lovecraft's power.

Four days in her own domain with Kate turned out to be a white-knuckle ride. We weren't in a studio now, no longer potential client and director; we were would-be lovers, with distance and privacy removed and any prospect of our love affair progressing in a gentle or cautious manner utterly gone. And in the quiet studious atmosphere of Kate's living room, with its African art and ceiling-high bookshelves, I realised something shocking: the gulf in power between us. Quite apart from our age difference and her confidence as an established world-class artist, Kate was like no other woman I'd known. She was supremely wilful: dramatic, intense and unpredictable. She changed moods from baby-voiced bunny to drama queen to frosty critic faster than the weather on a Scottish holiday. She coined a term, 'Dreamboy', an ideal she required me to live up to, and to which she consistently referred, as in 'Dreamboy wouldn't say that' or 'Dreamboy wouldn't do that to me'. I was expected to upgrade my behaviour to 'Dreamboy' standards. This made me feel constantly inadequate, but so in thrall was I to the force of Kate's personality and so glamoured by being her boyfriend that I kept trying to please her. What she probably needed was an older man with ice in his veins, a thick hide and bottomless wells of patience, and that wasn't me. Still, it was exciting to wake with Kate in her wood-panelled bedroom, thrilling to walk with her late at night through the heady swirl of the East Village with its hipsters and hustlers and all the debris of the counterculture strewn across its Babylonian pavements. In such moments I imagined us as golden – destiny-crossed lovers from another world on our travels through this one.

When I flew back to London we continued our affair by transatlantic phone calls. The safety of distance afforded me the illusion that the relationship could work and with renewed vigour I stepped back into the fast-moving river of Waterboys business: press interviews, record company meetings and auditions for new band members.

I was becoming one of the world's great audition experts, hosting a stream of bassists and drummers in our rehearsal room in North London. It had got so I knew within the first ten seconds of the first song whether a player was right or wrong. I'd welcome the guy, give him a minute to adjust the drums or amplifier, then crash into a Waterboys or Dylan number with a simple chord sequence so we could play without having to stop for instructions. 'Be My Enemy', with its recurring blues pattern, was a favourite and its breakneck tempo soon sorted out the contenders from the pretenders. If I wanted to really put a player through his paces, we'd play 'Enemy' for ten or fifteen relentless minutes, a serious test for drummers. One afternoon a cocky skin-basher showed up and commented that I looked worn out. This injudicious remark condemned him to a rip-snorting twenty-minute blast through 'Be My Enemy' till his arms and legs were bursting and his breath came in shuddering gasps. Despite all the effort expended, and all the faces that passed through the portals of our rehearsal room, a new rhythm section proved elusive, and all the time the clock was ticking and the first dates of our tour drew closer.

Then like a gathering storm Kate came to London in the last days of August to stay with me for ten days. And her schemes left me standing. She'd decided we'd buy an apartment in London's Docklands; she wanted us live together in New York; we were going to have children in a few years; I was to stop being friends with a top rock manager who'd supposedly snubbed her. She took over my little flat with her papers covering every surface and the ever-changing weather of her moods filling every space. I began to feel like an extra in the all-encompassing drama of Kate Lovecraft's life and when I finally saw her back onto the New York plane at Heathrow, I felt as if I'd been dragged cross-country by a wild horse, one of my feet caught in its stirrups. After she left I wondered why she was with me. Was it my youth, or for the energy of potential rockstar glory? And why was I with her? I no longer knew. The attraction had given way to a weird defensive desperation: being with Kate made me feel deeply insufficient but only by her approval could I transcend this condition and feel good about myself.

Yet my affair with Kate wasn't compromising my work: the music was flourishing. I may have been feeling gauche and inadequate in the relationship but she dug my music and that meant a lot, and when Kate wanted to be, she was a great encourager. What's more, having a New York heavyweight like Kate as my girlfriend did a lot for my artistic confidence. Being in her life felt like entering a higher, quickened echelon of popular culture. I stood a few inches taller when I strapped on my guitar.

And the songs were coming too. In the first flush of love I'd written several romantic numbers with titles like 'Higher In Time' and 'Born To Be Together'. And even now, as things became more difficult, a stream of edgy, perplexed songs like 'We Will Not Be Lovers' were tumbling out of my head. Even a doomed love affair was healthy for the muse. In September *This Is The Sea* came out, its songs indeed crackling across the American airwaves though not yet in enough volume for the breakthrough everybody wanted. I started to come under pressure to sign extensions to my recording and publishing deals, for as the prospect of success grew closer, the investors – Nigel and Chris's label Ensign and their paymasters Island – wanted to ensure that if things went sky high they got the maximum payback. But different parties wanted different things and as the one person whose signature on a piece of paper determined how matters would resolve, I was caught in the crossfire. Gary Kurfirst would advise me one way, while Nigel and Chris would advise the opposite. I was constantly pulled, each camp trying to sour my view of the other. To Nigel and Chris, Gary Kurfirst was a shark, an opportunistic Johnny-come-lately who hadn't done any of the hard work building up the Waterboys, while Gary thought Nigel and Chris were 'small-time guys', 'scumbags' without a classy idea in their heads.

The murk deepened when I learned Island wouldn't fund a proper advertising campaign in America unless Ensign guaranteed them more than the two further albums on my contract. I was loath to sign away more; I was fond of Nigel and Chris and appreciated all they'd done for me, but they were like a suit that had grown too small. I didn't want to be making records with them five or seven years down the line. A solution was to move directly to Island but, close to a commercial breakthrough after years of financing, there was no way Ensign would let me go. The arguments ran for months. And because people in the music business usually tell artists no more than what they want them to hear, I probably knew only the half of it. Yet what all this meant was that there was little prospect of a major campaign with the cash support for extended touring that would give *This Is The Sea* its shot at success. If my instincts had been attuned to the pursuit of success at all costs, I'd have signed whatever I needed to guarantee the push for my record, and hang the consequences. But my instincts were for the courses of action that would let me keep making the music I chose, to continue following my 'instructions'. That's what I trusted and Faustian bargains weren't on the menu.

There was conflict around the choice of singles too. Everyone knew 'The Whole Of The Moon' was the potential hit on the album. But this was a demanding song and the lyric was crucial to people's appreciation of it. The Waterboys weren't yet an established band and we couldn't expect our singles to automatically chart, so I suggested we release a rocker like 'Don't Bang The Drum' or 'Medicine Bow' first, then follow up with 'Moon' when the public's attention was aroused. But no one agreed. 'Moon' was thrown away sacrificially as the first single and sputtered like a damp squib. I'd made the right record but almost as soon as it was out, it seemed, its stars were crossed. All I could do was hope the pieces would somehow shift themselves on the chess table and set off into the maelstrom of our three-month concert tour of Britain, America and Europe.

On stage, at least, the music was exploding. The addition of Steve Wickham was as great as I'd hoped: a one-man artillery battalion. He played rock and blues on his fiddle, all bendy notes and gravity-defying harmonics, and these were the product of his fingers, not added effects. But he had effects too: echo, fuzz, and a gizmo that made his fiddle sound like three or four Steves playing at once. He linked up with the Human Saxophone, Anthony, whom he nicknamed 'Anto' after the Irish fashion, to create a two-man orchestral section that made a monumental banshee roar. And best of all Steve was the perfect onstage foil for me, dancing across the stage with rubber legs in baggy trousers, a good-natured Elvis sneer on his lips and strands of gypsy-black hair sticking out through the top of his holey hat, star quality bursting from him like a thousand sparks of lightning.

After the summer auditions we'd settled on a bass and drum combo, Sara Lee, lately of the British post-punk band Gang Of Four, who would have been the first Watergirl, and a drummer called Mike Osborne. But at the last minute they threatened to walk out unless they got higher wages and were fired, not unreasonably, by Gary Kurfirst. Coming on the eve of the tour, though, this was a disaster. So doleful drummer Chris Whitten was recalled, while Kate Lovecraft suggested a bassist from New York. Marco Sin was a gentle-hearted, roly-poly man, and the best bass player I'd ever worked with. He was also an alcoholic and former heroin addict, which, if she knew, Kate neglected to tell me, with near fatal consequences a few months later.

As well as suggesting musicians, Kate had inevitably begun to advise me about my career. This advice, usually opposite to the counsel of my manager, was given with a dramatic spin of, 'If you don't do what I suggest, you're insulting me and choosing Gary Kurfirst over me.' This pressure did nothing to foster my ability to discern whether Kate was giving good advice or bad, and several times I went to Gary and robustly told him that Kate had suggested such-and-such and that I agreed with her. He would be pissed off, his street-fighter's nose knocked out of joint, and the wheel of our artist-manager relationship would slip a few degrees further into the mud. I'd stumbled into a classic rock'n'roll trap: the powerful girlfriend who countermands the influence of the manager and so comes between manager and artist. At one point Gary's assistant Andrea phoned me and said, 'This is an important time for you. What are you *doing* with her? She's a neurotic New York nut!' This, of course, only made me more stubbornly loyal to Kate.

Meanwhile the tectonic plates were shifting under the band. Karl Wallinger had grown resentful of my leadership and, perhaps, the attention I was getting. This came to a head at a soundcheck in Birmingham when I noticed Karl's keyboards taking up approximately half the stage front, relegating poor Marco Sin to a shadowy rear corner. When I suggested we move his gear a few degrees westwards Karl erupted, accusing me bitterly of thinking I was Bruce Fucking Springsteen and that the musicians were my personal E Street Band. I may not have wanted to be Bruce, but this was my group and the vehicle for my songs, and if Karl, the veteran of one and a half albums, couldn't deal with it, that was for him to work out. But I didn't want one musician's personal drama causing the stage to mutate into a fiefdom, and the keyboards were moved. I resisted the temptation to emulate Z's right hook and Karl contained his impatience until after the show in Detroit, three weeks later, when he announced his departure to the rest of the band in a motel bedroom.

Karl and I had been friends, often hanging out smoking reefers, listening to music and talking till dawn. He'd brought a lot to Waterboys recordings, especially *This Is The Sea*, but dealing with him in the daily life of the band had become a burden. Every time we came off the road I swore to myself I'd never tour with him again, but because he was such a good player – and because in a corner of my heart I loved the guy – I didn't follow the promise through. Now Karl had made the decision for me and his news came as a mighty relief. That night I went for a long walk with Steve Wickham through the moonlit Detroit suburbs, past flat-roofed houses and the churches that stand like sentries on every corner of that city, enthusing about what we'd do with The Waterboys from here on in. For the way was clear for Steve, myself, and Anto to emerge as the three-man soul of the band.

Karl stayed on till our final American concert in New York a week later, but as we burned the miles the vibes in the band were weird. Everything was splintered. Some people on their way in, others on the way out. Karl wasn't the only one splitting: Chris Whitten would be leaving after New York too. When we returned to London we'd have to audition and rehearse new players all over again for the next leg of the tour starting ten days later. Between Chicago and Detroit we fired our tour manager, a hapless ex-pat Englishman called Biff, Kurfirst's man, whose levels of ineptitude were matched only by his good nature. Biff was demoted to humble roadie, a position in which he seemed far happier, and our usual roadie, a taciturn Brixtonian called Jim Chapman, was elevated to tour manager. Kurfirst didn't like it but, trying to keep my ramshackle tour rolling somewhere in the freezing Midwest of America, I was past caring whether my manager blew his top in the comfort of his Broadway office.

In mid November we flew from the Midwestern snows into the mellow balm of California and in L.A. we stayed in a motel where oily-furred rats scurried round the bottom of a dried-up swimming pool. At night we played two sets at the famous Roxy club, a funky, dark neon-crusted shebeen of a shithole on Sunset Strip. The guest list was a roll call of L.A. scene-makers and punk rock aristocracy; someone told us Bob Dylan was coming and there was a seriously buzzing atmosphere in the joint. Our trumpet player, Roddy Lorimer, a wire-haired Glaswegian with the purest, most soaring sound in rock, had joined the tour and somehow all seven of us fitted on the egg-box-sized stage. Dylan didn't show but his rumoured presence added an extra edge to the performance. We would encounter him for real, soon enough.

After the show in Berkeley the band went sailing on San Francisco Bay with the crew of a Greenpeace boat, but I flew on ahead to New York, scene of our final American concert, to stay with Kate Lovecraft, a moth to the flame. Our love affair had been flickering on and off. We'd split up transatlantically a couple of times during The Waterboys' British dates, then got back together in New York at the start of the American stint. We were 'on' now, but only just, and the final drama was about to play.

On the early morning of the show, lying in Kate's bed and drowsing in the hinterland between sleep and waking, I became aware of sounds penetrating my dream. Then I heard footsteps approaching, bare feet slapping on a wooden floor. The bedclothes were ripped off me. My skin felt the cold rush of air as Kate's voice, in one of its high-pitched cartoon manifestations, burst on my consciousness: 'Ha! I *found* it! I saw it in my *mind*! I knew it *psychically* and *here's* the evidence!' I rolled over and looked up. She was standing over the bed, an explosion, hair piled high on her head, holding something in her hand and waving it triumphantly. I squinted until the thing came into focus. A notepad. *My* notepad, from my inside jacket pocket. She started to quote from it in a singsong voice: 'Do I love Kate or do I love Krista? I probably love neither.'

I couldn't remember writing these words, but as she thrust the notepad an inch in front of my face I saw them there in my own once private handwriting, incontrovertible evidence of ... what? Not infidelity, certainly, but of confusion and uncertainty, yes. Guilty as charged. I felt in my guts I didn't love Kate but my desire to please her and hold onto my illusions wouldn't let me admit it: the incriminating words had been written in a rare moment of self-awareness. Krista was my Canadian ex-girlfriend, the one who'd asked me if it was easy to write songs, sparking the writing of 'The Whole Of The Moon'. She'd turned up backstage at the Berkeley show and had fatefully found her way into my journal musings. Before I could respond Kate threw the notepad at me, swivelled on her heels and vanished into the bathroom, slamming the door and locking it from inside with impeccable dramatic timing. Within seconds I heard the rush of water hissing from the shower and then another sound, her voice, now blithe and carefree, singing a familiar old song, 'I'm Gonna Wash That Man Right Out Of My Hair'. I sat up, horribly awake. I had a drama-queen eruption of the first order to negotiate my way through but what really worried me, what shook me to the core, was that Kate Lovecraft appeared to have clairvoyantly seen something I'd written days ago in my notepad, something I'd even forgotten I'd written. How else could she have known to look for the evidence in my pocket?

It didn't occur to me, nor would it for some years, that she'd simply been snooping in my garments and when she found something incriminating, made up a story about being psychic in order to mask her actions. To my twenty-six-year-old self, it appeared alarmingly clear that this powerful, unpredictable woman who over the short months of our relationship had shattered every personal boundary I had, had just breached the last one. *She could see into my mind!* Kate eventually emerged from the bathroom and after apologies and self-abasements on my part we negotiated a truce. She came to the concert that night and all, briefly, was sweetness again. But I was desperate to get back to London to regroup my thoughts and emotions.

I say she had broken all of my boundaries, but before I left New York the next day she made an assault on one more.

In the late morning Kate and I went to a café on Columbus Avenue. Having seen The Waterboys perform for the first time the night before she had some feedback on the show for me. She took out a sketch pad covered with her handwriting and began reading aloud instructions regarding the songs that worked and the ones that didn't, what I should say on stage and what I shouldn't, the good moves I made and the bad ones, how I should have ordered my songs, and so on. She was telling me how to make my music and present it to the public. I sat and watched, as if from some great distance, as this woman pushed her way with absolute entitlement into the most intimate relationship of my life – the one between me and my music. I heard her once-devastating voice fall away like a murmur. I saw her face, pinched and sun-shrunken, and it held no more power over me. My authority over my music was one boundary she would not cross and in a moment of clear, crystalline certainty my mind and heart were made up. At last I had found the bedrock of my self-worth. There would be no scene – a phone call or letter from the removed calm of London would suffice – but Kate Lovecraft and I were indisputably over.

I'd seen Gary Kurfirst in New York too but by now we were strangers to each other. He hadn't been able to shift the business impasse between the record companies, and the promotion of *This Is The Sea* was still gridlocked. Though word of mouth would turn it into a gold record over the next few years, its campaign was stillborn. So, it seemed, was Kurfirst's management of The Waterboys. I couldn't figure out what the guy did for me at all. His dismal prognostications – 'You have no touring prospects' – offered no sign of light at the end of the chaotic tunnel, and when I boarded the British Airways flight out of JFK I knew that this relationship, too, was in terminal decline. I wanted out. Squeezed into seat 31F next to The Fellow Who Fiddles, I wrote down my feelings in verse on the back of my boarding pass, the beginnings of a new song called 'Fisherman's Blues'.

In London I checked into a hotel in Bayswater – my landlord had sold my flat six weeks earlier – and began to get ready for the next round of auditions and our subsequent European tour. Then I got a call from an American lady I knew called Rovena Cardiel, a tenacious and pretty hustler who ran the London office of Geffen Records. She was buddies with Bob Dylan's girlfriend and rang to tell me Bob was in town and that having heard and liked 'The Whole Of The Moon' he was inviting me to come and join in a recording session. I asked Rovena if I could bring Steve and Anto. She checked this out and the answer came back yes. So on a bleak November afternoon as the wind raced through the streets like a league of phantoms, the three of us jumped in a black cab with our instruments and headed up to north London.

The studio was a converted church in Crouch End. We buzzed the doorbell and climbed a flight of stairs, emerging into what was once the vaulted nave of the church, now the studio's live room. At the far end was a row of soundproofing screens and sticking up above one of them was a tousled head of curly hair. Yup, it was Bob, and as I crossed the floor this time there were no bouncers or Harvey Goldsmiths to block the way. We walked round the screens into an enclosure filled with enough instruments for a large band, and in the middle Bob was sitting on his own. His face, so familiar from film and photograph, looked more Eastern in real life, as if he were an inscrutable Chinaman or a Zen Master. He was dressed in jeans and red shirt with a blue scarf, and having shaken our hands (he seemed genuinely pleased to see us) he reverted to his afternoon's pursuit, playing ceaseless lead guitar, coaxing burbling, bluesy sounds from a Fender Stratocaster.

The rest of the band came out of a nearby control room and introduced themselves. The only ones I recognised were Clem Burke, the drummer from Blondie, and Dave Stewart of the Eurythmics, a gangly, nervous chap who functioned as ringmaster, cajoling everyone along and suggesting each next musical activity. We found spaces to sit and joined in on what turned out to be a slow, sexy instrumental. To our disappointment Bob didn't sing, just kept playing that burbling guitar, even in the breaks between takes. In one such break Bob had a short word with each of us. He'd met Steve when In Tua Nua had played support to him in Ireland a year earlier and so he genially, if tactlessly, asked Steve, 'How's your band doing?' For me he had some kind things to say about 'The Whole Of The Moon', and there was an encouraging word for Anto too.

When we were all in the control room listening to the instrumental we'd recorded (except Bob, still in the studio playing lead guitar), Dave Stewart asked me if I had any tunes we could do. I scratched my head and went out to the piano. Bob stopped playing and came over. Several tunes came into my mind, but I had them all earmarked for new Waterboys songs and I wasn't giving them away, Dylan or no Dylan. Then I remembered one that didn't figure in my plans, a reggae-cum-jazz number called 'Say You Will' about my travails with Kate Lovecraft. Of all the songs I ever wrote it was not the most auspicious one to play as a demo for Bob Dylan. I sang a verse or two, the band joined in and Dylan played yet more burbling lead guitar. When the song finished he leaned over and said in a kindly tone, 'You can keep that one.'

There's a legend that the day we jammed with Dylan we were meant to be performing 'The Whole Of The Moon' on the British TV show *Top Of The Pops*, the implication being that I'd sooner fool around on guitars with Bob than shoot for success by playing the biggest music show in the UK. It's a great story, but it isn't true. By the time we jammed with Bob, 'Moon' had already had its brief run in the lower echelons of the charts. It would return in greater style six years later.

The Dylan session was followed by several more trips to North London for our latest auditions. These yielded a veteran punk drummer called Dave Ruffian and a young piano player, Guy Chambers. Thus re-constituted we flew to Rotterdam and began our final tour of 1985, a winding crawl through Holland, Belgium and France opening for Simple Minds. Halfway through the tour I started to notice Marco Sin taking whole bottles of vodka and whisky back to his hotel room after shows. I'd never been around an alcoholic and didn't understand what this behaviour signified, but in the French town of Brest, a couple of days before tour's end, things got serious.

After the concert a French cocaine dealer came backstage and invited us to a nightclub. We went along, partook of his wares in the toilet, and felt jolly pleased with ourselves. Back at the hotel I was lying in bed when I heard a terrible coughing from the room next door. It was Marco. I thought to myself, *ah he'll be OK*. He'd looked pretty stoned earlier but I didn't think there was cause for alarm. And sure enough the coughing subsided. I fell asleep. Suddenly I was torn awake by urgent banging. I jumped out of bed and opened the door to find Anto and Steve, white-faced, frantically telling me that Marco had overdosed: apparently the dealer had had heroin with him and Marco had taken some. They'd bust down the door to his room. Dave Ruffian was crouched on the floor cradling Marco's lolling head, its eyes two sightless white ovals. Anto, a fluent French speaker and the angel of the hour, had called an ambulance. We slapped Marco's face, punched him, tried shouting at him then speaking in tender whispers, but nothing would bring our friend back from the far off zones where his consciousness was roaming, perhaps for good.

The ambulance arrived and two medics put Marco on a stretcher, pronounced him stable and took him away. Luckily they'd got to him in time. When we visited Marco next morning he was lying sheepishly in his hospital bed, a black tube stuck down his throat. He couldn't speak but wrote 'I feel so foolish' on a piece of card and held it up, the sweet, silly man. He was repatriated to New York a week later and never touched heroin again. Shell-shocked, we played our last couple of shows with Anthony deputising on bass, then broke for Christmas.

As I didn't have a flat in London anymore I went to Scotland to spend a week with my mother. How strange to be suddenly back in my teenage bedroom with its punk rock posters still on the wall. But the ground was moving here too. My mum had sold the house and would be leaving it in a few weeks' time. My ties to both the recent and the deep past were being broken. Standing at this crossroads, scorched earth and the wreckage of my rock dreams behind me, the vague horizon of the unknown ahead, I took Jackie Leven's advice and got on the bus. Except it wasn't an Edinburgh bus, it was a Dublin one.

I flew into Ireland on the fourth of January 1986 to visit Steve Wickham for a weeklong trip that turned into six years. He was waiting for me in the arrivals lounge of Dublin airport, a purple scarf round his neck and a grin on his face. We hugged, picked up our non-stop conversation where we'd left off a few weeks earlier, stepped outside and got into a minicab. 'Lennox Street, by the canal,' Steve told the driver as we sped off. The radio was announcing the death of Phil Lynott of Thin Lizzy. With sorrow in his voice the DJ was playing all Philo's old songs: 'Don't Believe A Word', 'The Boys Are Back In Town', and there was a fatefulness in the air as we hurtled through the winter's evening past long avenues of old-fashioned shops and pubs. In Steve's basement flat I was introduced to his wife Barbara and shown the guest room, a tiny chamber with a narrow single bed and a window onto a grimy backyard. Then we went out into the soul of the Dublin Saturday night, found a bar, Cassidy's on Camden Street, and drank to Phil Lynott, friendship and new adventures.

Finding myself in Dublin was like going through the back of a Narnian wardrobe. I was in a convivial parallel universe, led by The Fellow Who Fiddles down colourful streets into dusty cafes where roguish men with scarves and glass eyes said things to each other like, 'I hear you're playin' chess for money these days.' Or archaic newsagents' shops with fifties décor, which sold Irish cigarettes – Major and Carroll's Number One – and whose magazine shelves contained little songbooks with titles like *A Collection Of Sea Ballads* or *Sing An Irish Song*. I gathered this strange new world around me like a fog, quickly realising Dublin afforded me space and distance. The wilful voices of agents, managers and record companies were out of hearing. And after the shock of discovering, as I believed, that Kate Lovecraft could read my mind, Dublin was a safe haven. Even if Kate really was psychic the Irish cultural fabric was a hazy, mysterious domain of which she had no experience and couldn't penetrate. She didn't know where I was, didn't have my phone number or a mental image of my whereabouts. I felt secure.

I set about enjoying myself, regrouping my band and planning my next assault on the citadel of rock'n'roll. I wrote to Gary Kurfirst and split with him, hired a solicitor-cum-big-brother called John Kennedy, and found myself a flat, a bright little cave on a leafy lane a mile from the centre of town. And that would be the end of one part of the story, and the beginning of all the others, but for this epilogue:

91

Six months later I was in Frejus, southern France, where The Waterboys were to play in a Roman amphitheatre. I got a message at the hotel telling me someone called Kate Lovecraft would be at the concert and wanted to see me afterwards. When I walked out on stage I saw her immediately. She'd positioned herself on a platform next to the sound desk, elevated above the rest of the audience, straight ahead of me where I couldn't fail to see her. There she sat, cross-legged, wearing shades, watching me intently. I played the show with Kate in my line of vision at almost every moment – not a comfortable experience. I didn't know what she wanted, but I expected the old cocktail of drama, accusation and power. After the show I asked our tour manager to hold the guests till I'd eaten. Withstanding bad vibes is easier on a full stomach and I wanted all the protection I could muster. Finally I gave the OK and the tour manager brought Kate into the backstage enclosure, an English girlfriend of hers reluctantly in tow. The friend waited some distance away and Kate sat down beside me.

She cut straight to the punch and told me she'd been diagnosed with tuberculosis and had less than two years to live. She'd wanted me to know so she'd come to Frejus from London, where she'd been visiting her friend, especially to tell me. What a complex of emotions moved through me as I heard these words! Suspicion that she was lying, swiftly followed by shame and embarrassment that I could think such a thing; guilt for having been churlish and mistrustful enough to seek to protect myself from her only minutes before; compassion and alarm for her condition; readiness to make reparations and remain in contact with her; desire to be a friend to her in her time of need. But no romantic attraction. That, for certain, was gone. I gave her my hitherto-secret Dublin address and phone number and told her she could call anytime. When she stood up to leave I hugged her and felt very sorry and very ashamed indeed.

Two months later I'd been in London on musical business, and, returning to Dublin on an autumn afternoon, I found in my mailbox a letter with a New York postmark and the sender's name: K. Lovecraft. Guts tight with apprehension, wondering what awful news it contained, I tore it open. It said: 'I lied. I don't have tuberculosis. I don't even know if I can spell it correctly. Just because I make a joke, doesn't mean I think what I did is funny. I am truly sorry.'

As I read these words I felt eviscerated, as though a rough hand had forced its way into me and torn out my guts: tricked, relieved, confounded and assaulted all at once. I laid the letter down, walked to the window, drew the curtains and lay down on the sofa. I wrapped my arms round my head and lay in darkness, neither weeping nor sleeping, deep into the evening till a friend knocked on my door and time began again.

CHAPTER 7

YOU GUYS ARE THE WHIZZ!

Dublin, Valentine's night 1986, the back room of a city bar. I'm strumming and singing an old country song called 'The Wayward Wind'. To my right Steve is drawing lazy western chords from his fiddle and on my left, conjuring luminous flashes of sound from his mandolin, is Anto. People cluster round: my new Irish girlfriend, Irene, Steve's wife Barbara, various mates, musicians, onlookers and scene-makers. For tonight is a Happening, a rumour-turned-manifestation of The Waterboys, currently the musical talk of the town. We can fill Dublin's concert halls but here we are where we shouldn't be, playing in a tiny bar.

Sitting as close to us as he can physically get is B.P. Fallon, an Irish disc jockey and star-fancier in his late thirties who once worked as PR man for Marc Bolan and Led Zeppelin and who seems to have been present, Zelig-like, at every significant moment in rock since 1965. B.P. is wearing drainpipe jeans, teddy boy jacket and a bootlace tie. What hair he has left is slicked back from his gnomic face while his eyes, ravenous black jewels in which desire, humour and wickedness dance, are locked intently on the musical action. He leans forward, rapt and shining as if he is both feeding our energy and feeding on it like some kind of semi-depraved human transformer.

Next to B.P., sitting on a low stool, is a very different beast altogether. This heavily bearded American looks like a mountain man or an intrepid hunter. Long Viking hair, broad shoulders, thick plaid shirt and brown jerkin. His expression is a mix of intense concentration and grave emotion, and he's aiming a little cassette recorder at us as if getting our ragged performance on tape is the most important work in the world. Three days in town, his name is Bob Johnston and in his golden late-sixties heyday, as staff producer for CBS

Records, he made album after album with Bob Dylan, Johnny Cash and Leonard Cohen. Now he's wooing my band, seeking to be our record producer.

As the song ends and the room of listeners claps and cheers, Bob slaps his knee, guffaws heartily, and leans over to me. Shouting over the noise he yells in my ear, each word louder than the last as his sentence rises to its climax: 'Man, you guys should do that on the GRAND OLE OPRY!'

Yes indeed, we are in a different landscape now.

By the time I moved to Dublin I'd taken the rock sound of the first three Waterboys albums as far as I could. After *This Is The Sea* – the song itself, with nine acoustic guitars simulating an ocean and an accompanying soundscape of brass and string orchestrations – I stood on top of the sonic mountain with nowhere else to climb. I'd finally learned how to reproduce on record the sound in my imagination and somewhere deep inside me a bus-riding, foot-stomping schoolboy was happy. But already the music in my head was changing and I was falling in love with older styles like country, blues and gospel. Frustrated that I couldn't reproduce the full-blown sound of Waterboys records on stage, I envied these forms of music their simplicity. At the same time I was keen to depart from the formula-repeating script that managers, agents, record companies and even Waterboys fans were imagining for me. I didn't want to keep repeating myself like some kind of hack. I remembered the stylistic turns Dylan and The Beatles had taken in the sixties, or Neil Young and Bowie in the seventies, and that was my model of how an artist should evolve.

So when I discovered that Anto's mandolin, my guitar and Wickham's fiddle added up to our own style of acoustic music, the gateway to the new swung open. And paradoxically, it required us to travel some very old paths indeed. The three of us immersed ourselves in roots music, listening to albums of twenties gospel singers on tiny labels then reworking their songs for our set; and initiating ourselves into the mysteries of Woody Guthrie, Little Walter, the great Hank Williams, colourfully named Cajun bandleaders like Rockin' Dopsie and Dewey Balfa, and the Irish gypsy singer Margaret Barry. We poured our music into the forms we learned from these artists then reshaped it into something of our own.

This sound, primed and honed in hotel bedrooms, backstage jam sessions and Dublin bars, emerged fully formed on our first visit to Windmill Lane Studios in January 1986. Joined by Trevor Hutchinson and Pete McKinney on bass and drums, a pair of Belfast lads befriended by Steve who sounded from the start like they'd been with us for years, we recorded a dozen tracks in one myth-like day. A motherlode of originals and newly learned Hank Williams songs and gospel spirituals seemed to tumble out of the air like magic. Everything we tried worked, and a new Waterboys identity was born. Two of the songs recorded that day – 'Fisherman's Blues' and a version of Van Morrison's 'Sweet Thing' – would be key tracks on our next album. But that album, though we had no idea at the time, wouldn't be completed till almost three years and several lifetimes later. Along the way we would be changed and changed again by music, events, places and people. And not the least among these was Bob Johnston.

Johnston had got in contact with me through a San Francisco-based agent called Kathy Bishop, one of several allies I had in the American music business at the time. He called me, unbelievably, at my mother's house in Scotland during the 1985 Christmas holiday. He'd heard *This Is The Sea* and wanted to work with us. 'You guys are the whizz!' he exclaimed and my heart, an easy conquest, was won. I knew his work. I'd been listening to Dylan's *Blonde On Blonde*, which Johnston had produced in Nashville in 1966, since I was twelve years old and it had always sounded divine to my ears, a transmission from some secret higher realm, with its stream-of-consciousness lyric play and semi-improvised country rock music. That the man who'd overseen and produced this masterpiece, who had *enabled* it, now wanted to work with me and my band was like a heady dream. A few weeks later, by which time I'd gone to Dublin and it was clear I was going to stick around for a while, I called Bob and in early February he flew into Ireland from California. He booked into a hotel close to where I was staying and I went to meet him with Steve, Anto and our latest friend, the ever-present B.P. Fallon.

It was early evening and Bob was waiting for us in the hotel bar, a Texan in his early fifties with the charismatic southern accent of a defrocked preacher. His stocky frame contained a raging storm of compressed energy that might erupt at any moment and frequently did, in laughter, whoops and sudden exclamations. To listen to Bob was to enter a world of true-life music mythology. 'I HAD DYLAN IN THAT ROOM!' he'd begin in a voice loud enough to carry across a ship's deck in a storm, and then enchant us with a tale in which Dylan (always presented as quiet-voiced and shy, but, as each story would reveal, with a will of absolute iron) would ask Johnston to organise a tuba player for a recording session at three in the morning.

We were thrilled and flattered that this legendary operator wanted to work with us and that we were to enter the rarefied pantheon of artists he'd produced. We left the hotel and crammed into a taxi, Bob in the passenger seat, B.P. and the band squashed in the back, and drove to B.P.'s flat where we spent the night talking and listening to music. We nervously played Bob a tape of the country and gospel songs we'd just recorded in Dublin, including a couple of Dylan covers, the originals of which he'd produced twenty years before. He sat and listened to these, roaring enthusiastically, exclaiming 'Oh, man!' and 'Dylan would dig that!' and other encouragements that put us at our ease. Next day I called B.P. and asked him what he thought of Bob. His reply: 'A mainline viber.'

That lunchtime we met Bob at Bewleys restaurant on Grafton Street. Bewleys is a Dublin institution, a bustling dining hall with a vaulted ceiling and fantastical stained-glass windows. Ideal circumstances in which to eat egg and chips and hang out with wild

Texan record producers. Johnston sat close to us like we were conspirators and talked about all the stuff he was working on, how he was going to set up a 'Children's Foundation' in every major American city to help get kids off drugs, how Bob Marley, Willie Nelson and Dylan were visionaries, and how the world would soon go through great changes of consciousness. This was exciting stuff. Our mainline viber was a philosopher too.

He stuck around for another couple of days and was with us for several of our impromptu music jams, which happened at the drop of a hat, usually Steve's. And as I got to know Bob I discerned a greatness about him. It wasn't the Marley-as-visionary, new-day-coming stuff that got to me, though. What impressed me was the residue from his sixties glory days that lingered about his persona. He'd been no small participant in a historical era, and the dust of those golden days gathered in the lines on Bob's face, the contours of his voice and the creases of his mind. And from the way he talked to us I could tell this was a man who knew how to inspire musicians; who had fine-tuned to a science the Zen-like art of allowing them to reach their peak potential, then get it down on tape. I wanted to experience this art in action. I also asked myself why, out of all the upwardly mobile mid-eighties rock groups, Bob chose to work with us, and I figured it was because of two things: we worked in the lyrical song-based tradition he knew and understood, and I was known to be a Dylan fan.

And The Waterboys were hot. If Bob was looking for a way back in we were as good a bet as any. Yet I wondered what he'd been up to since the early seventies and why, if he was still a good producer, I hadn't been seeing his name on any records. I guessed that like many sixties survivors he'd found it hard to find a place in the changed landscapes of the following decades, and I was cocky enough to imagine my band and I might be able to help him on that score – that while he would use his veteran skills to draw the best out of us, our modern edge could rekindle the best in him and return him to

98

prominence. A further sense of headiness was fostered by Bob's penchant for slapping me on the back and shouting, 'I had DYLAN, I had CASH, and now I've got SCOTT!' I didn't think of myself as the equal of Dylan or Cash but if Bob thought I was, that meant a lot, and added a degree of strut to my walk as I rambled the streets of Dublin, a new silver earring dangling from my left lobe and a pair of pointed leather boots on my feet.

On Bob's last night in town he took us for a meal with our girlfriends, wives and B.P., and afterwards we had a celebratory party in Wickham's flat. In the wee small hours Bob said his goodbyes. Standing at the door he pulled Steve, Anto and myself into our first communal hug and told us he believed in us and was going to do great things with our music. As he climbed the steps and headed into the Dublin dawn I felt we'd found a great soul who could bring the magic through us. The shivers ran up and down my spine. I turned to look at my two bandmates and they just said 'Wow.'

Before he'd left, Bob had invited us to come and stay with him at his house in Mill Valley, a fabled hippie enclave near San Francisco, where Janis Joplin had lived and where Jack Kerouac had written *The Dharma Bums*. I fancied an adventure, so a week later I flew out to visit him. He met me at the airport with a friend and we drove to the port of Sausalito on San Francisco Bay. There they left me in a waterside restaurant while they went off excitedly to get 'buds'. This was a mystery, but when they came back for me and we piled back into the car I soon realised what 'buds' were. They were ultra-potent reefer-making clusters of freshly cut marijuana leaves and Bob was a serious aficionado. In a pungent cloud of smoke we drove on into Mill Valley and up Homestead Boulevard, a grandly named dirt track winding through the forested hillside, finally arriving at Bob's two storey frontier-style wooden house, set amid eucalyptus trees like something out of an old sepia photograph, a huge American Flag draped over its upper deck.

This was all wildly enchanting, especially after smoking reefers with the producer of *Blonde On Blonde*. As we stepped out I noticed a couple of neighbouring houses through the trees. I asked Bob who lived there. 'Hell, I don't know WHO they are or WHAT they do!' he yelled with a loud laugh. I thought it was strange he didn't know who his neighbours were, but what the heck – maybe it was a Californian thing. In the house I met Bob's wife, Joy, and his two grown-up sons, Bobby and Andy. A meal was on the stove and Bob showed me to a little bedroom they'd prepared for me at the back of the house, futon on the floor, trees outside the window. I dumped my bags and guitar case and followed Bob into the upstairs living room. This was a vast open space with a long wooden dinner table, a grand piano on a raised podium, a giant sound system with towering speakers that looked like the monolith in *2001: A Space Odyssey*, a couple of leather sofas and a fireplace big enough to hold a tree trunk. The walls were festooned with the largest collection of framed gold discs I'd ever imagined, let alone seen, and a double door led to a wooden balcony that ran round the house, overlooking Mill Valley. The piano, Bob explained, came from CBS studios in Nashville and had been played by no less than Hank Williams himself. I had arrived in American music heaven, just in time for dinner of sweet potatoes and chicken.

In the evenings, as lights flickered on the other side of Mill Valley, Bob played me country records: Hank, The Nitty Gritty Dirt Band, Willie Nelson, Rattlesnake Annie, Doug Kershaw and Carl Perkins. We listened to the album of Johnny Cash *At San Quentin*, which Bob had produced, and he talked me through everything that happens on (and off) the record as a live commentary, bringing alive visions of the condemned men from death row whooping and cheering when Cash sang 'their' song, the blackly humorous execution ballad '25 Minutes To Go'. I received the finest country music education right there in Johnston's house, first hand from one who knew, with a log fire roaring and reefers perfuming the air. Bob also sang me his own songs. These were written in slow gospel/blues style and sung with a 'voice of the rock' tone, but with spacey lyrics. One was about how the rock'n'rollers of the fifties and sixties were aliens sent down to change the world. Another was about California breaking off and becoming an island after an earthquake. He would sing one, finish it, then get up from the piano laughing heartily, waving the song away with his hands as if it were a folly.

I stayed at Bob's for four or five days and we set a date to do some recording the following month. But I was torn between working in San Francisco with Bob's team and working in Dublin. After the successful session in Windmill Lane I trusted the sound engineer there, a talented though delicately strung character called Pearse. I should have kept the two worlds separate, done some recording with Bob in California, and some without him in Dublin, but - and this proved an epic mistake – I merged the two worlds and asked Bob to work with us in Ireland.

Four weeks later he flew back into Dublin. He didn't book into a hotel, but stayed instead in the spare bedroom of my flat. I figured this was because he wanted us to be close friends – it never struck me he might be broke – and it was a thrill to have this inspirational man lodging with me. One afternoon Bob called me into his bedroom and asked me to think about what his royalty rate, his percentage of the earnings, on the finished records should be. 'How much do you want?' I asked him. But he wouldn't say and told me to decide how much he was worth to me. I looked at him and noticed there was a tear in his eye. He saw me watching him and brushed the tear away, saying, 'Ah'm just a foolish ol' man.' I was distressed by this. A business decision had just become an emotional one and I found myself in a position of not wanting to let down an older man I looked up to, whose approval and belief meant a lot to me. By my choice of what to pay him, it seemed, I would be worthy of his mentoring and affection, or not. The matter perplexed me for several weeks until I bit the bullet and instructed my solicitor to pay Bob a percentage in the upper strata of acceptable producer royalties.

Meanwhile we were ready for the studio, Bob revving us up,

shouting, 'Ah'm gonna git that sound WIDE OPEN and you can do anything you WANT!' We were inching towards experiencing the old master at work and seeing what musical wonders would come through the gates he opened. And at first the sessions were a success. Bob mixed the recordings from the day we'd done *Fisherman's Blues* and made them sound great. He knew how to use tone to heighten the sound of Steve's fiddle, Anto's electric mandolin and my voice, and his deployment of echo and reverb was exquisite: old school and classic, with a freshness akin to the great Elvis Presley Sun recordings. B.P. Fallon turned up in the midst of the work, his antennae twitching at the prospects of a 'vibe'. B.P. had once done an interview with Leonard Cohen, during which Cohen had waxed lyrical about Bob. B.P. brought the tape of the interview to the studio, fast-forwarded to the relevant comments, placed the cassette player on Bob's knee and pressed play. As Bob guffawed to hear Cohen describing him, B.P. sat with his camera a few inches from Bob's head and, like an American Indian counting coup, took photographs of Bob Johnston listening to Leonard Cohen talking about Bob Johnston to B.P. Fallon.

B.P. was conscripted to add handclaps to our hoedown version of an old black spiritual song 'Meet Me At The Station'. Bob balanced the sound and played it back to us at full volume, yelling, 'THIS IS A WORLDWIDE NUMBER ONE SMASH!' above the din. In fact he had both sets of speakers – the massive industrial ones built into the wall and the regular ones on top of the mixing desk – running at full volume plus a set of headphones, also at full, wrapped round his ears. Bono dropped by from U2's management offices upstairs to see what the commotion was. To his great credit he gamely withstood the volume levels, sent for a bottle of champagne (these seemed to follow Bono around) toasted us all and shouted, 'Congratulations!' But when we started to record things began to get weird.

The Waterboys' method of recording at the time was to set up all together like at a show or rehearsal and play for real. I'd have a sheaf of papers with songs written on them which the band might or might not have heard before and I'd whip them out as the mood took me. Or I'd write songs on the spot and trust the band to pick them up fast and come up with hooks and parts in real time as the tapes rolled. This was absolutely against the run of recording techniques in the mid eighties, an era of structured and tightly controlled recordings heavily dependent on technology and drum machines.

With all his experience of producing musicians in the days when playing together was the norm, Bob was a natural partner in this, and he encouraged me to take risks, to compose out of thin air, to arrange music from scratch in the studio. When successful, like on the *Fisherman's Blues* day, this method produced recordings with a fresh, spontaneous sound and a spirit that shone through the music. When it didn't work, when the on-the-spot songs weren't of the highest standard or the band chemistry took a vacation, the results could be terrible. Our debut recording with Bob was a bit of both … and then some. As we soundchecked, first one piece of studio equipment then another broke down. Then the headphone system wouldn't work. Then a microphone blew out. Then several channels on the mixing desk malfunctioned. Poor engineer Pearse, mortified that this should happen on the day the legendary producer was present, ran around desperately trying to get the gear going. Meanwhile Bob, just being himself, was loudly asking when we were going to start, pacing the studio impatiently like a great brooding cat. His strident Texan voice lacerated Pearse's gentle Celtic sensitivities. As Pearse became progressively more terrified, Bob got more cantankerous and displeased, and as the relationship between these two broke down, so more and more gear started to malfunction. It was as if Bob's frustration and Pearse's terror were short-circuiting the studio equipment, or maybe the wild mismatch of their diametrically opposed personalities had triggered an energy malfunction in the bones of the building.

The band played on regardless, pulling our music round us like a circle of wagons. Drawing on the atmosphere, I pulled out a song I'd written six months earlier that seemed to harmonise with the sense of gathering doom, the appropriately named 'We Will Not Be Lovers'. The other musicians hadn't played it before but they joined in. Steve and Anto hit an insistent fiddle and mandolin riff that channelled the fractious mood, and for nine minutes we dealt out the ideal soundtrack to the day: a pummelling wild groove teetering on the brink of chaos.

But this was as good as it got, and the rest of the music we managed to record between equipment breakdowns was disappointing. Bob tried his best, coming into the studio and yelling and swinging his arms round like a mad conductor as we played, but there was no more magic in the box. As the day whimpered to its close Bob walked round muttering, clearly unhappy with the experience, and, though he didn't say it, surely feeling he hadn't been given a fair shot and would have been better served with his own engineer and studio. After all the high promise of our first meetings, we were banjaxed. And at what a cost. Apart from the dashing of our Johnston hopes, poor Pearse was never confident on a Waterboys session again and the dread memory of the 'Bob Johnston day' would loom like a spectre over his future work with us.

When I said farewell to Bob next morning an awkward feeling hung in the air between us. Was this the end or would there be more? We promised to stay in touch, that was all, and I waved him off at Dublin airport. A few weeks later I discovered he'd left a bunch of records in a corner of my flat. They were acetates: one-off test pressings of old sixties recordings by Dylan, Johnny Cash and Leonard Cohen, eight discs in all, many of them live and each one shockingly rare and very valuable. I wondered if Bob had deliberately left them as a surprise for me, intending that I'd listen to them and be inspired. Or might he have been short of money and brought them to sell in Ireland if his funds ran out? But this was too embarrassing a question to ask a man like Johnston, and with The Waterboys about to tour again I had other things on my mind anyway.

The tour was a four-month roller coaster through Ireland, Britain and Europe, our chance to introduce audiences to our new rootsy sound. First we needed a manager and I knew who I wanted. I'd got to know Paul McGuinness when The Waterboys had supported U2 on some shows eighteen months before. He'd given me good advice and was everything I thought a manager should be: cunning but honourable, close with his band, imaginative, realistic and powerful. So when things didn't work out with Gary Kurfirst, inviting Paul to manage The Waterboys seemed the obvious move. The only problem was his availability. 'My hands are tied,' he replied ruefully when I popped the question to him over lunch in a smart Dublin restaurant.

I took this to mean that his deal with U2 didn't allow him to manage other acts, let alone competitors like The Waterboys, but Paul was willing to get involved through the back door. 'I've got a manager for you to meet,' he told me on the phone a few days later, 'if you think you can work together, I'll oversee him for you.' It turned out to be a fellow who managed a top Irish band, some of whose members I was friendly with. But the way the guy stood in McGuinness's living room, a glass of apple cordial in his hand, blithely assuring me he'd gone as far as he could with his band and was ready to drop them for The Waterboys, didn't exactly fill me confidence. Apart from their being friends of mine, I knew that if he was able to dump this band, he'd dump me just as easily when something else came along. I declined. McGuinness didn't give up and, offering the same 'overseeing' situation, set up a meeting with Fachtna O'Kelly, former handler of The Boomtown Rats and future manager of Sinead O'Connor. But Fachtna struck me as a troubled soul, uncertain about both the meeting and his future. The chemistry was wrong, and I said no again.

Paul gave it his last throw and suggested a third surrogate. This was a chap I rather liked, a red-cheeked, shamrock-faced Irishman called Slim Doherty, but Slim had the persona of an enthusiastic yet unrealistic chancer and had approximately no management experience. I wasn't betting on those odds. So we headed out manager-less on our tour, which turned out to be that marvellous moment in every band's route to success when its reputation catches fire and its audience suddenly multiplies. And it happened for us just as the music hit overdrive. Promoters kept having to bump us up to bigger venues to keep up with ticket sales, extra shows were added every few days, and from Glastonbury to Jerusalem we were ablaze. Between April and July 1986 The Fellow Who Fiddles, the Human Saxophone, Trevor Hutchinson, Dave Ruffian and myself were the greatest band in the world.

I wasn't even thinking about Bob Johnston when he turned up unexpectedly at our London concert in May. The show was at the Hammersmith Palais, a famous dancehall, and Bob had flown in from America. After the show I got back to my hotel to find this note: 'I came eight thousand miles to see you guys. I'm at the Portobello. Kick Steve and Anto in the ass for me.' I rounded up the band and we caught a taxi to the trusty Portobello Hotel to be reunited with our wild friend. As we all squeezed into one of the Portobello's tiny rooms, drinking and laughing, it was clear Bob had forgotten or put out of his mind the semi-disastrous session in Dublin and was keen to go ahead with new recording plans – but on his turf this time, he made that clear. I agreed to go and visit him again in San Francisco and check out the local studios when our tour finished.

It was a re-run of my first visit except this time, tired of smoking reefers, I told Bob when I arrived I wouldn't be doing any of that. To my surprise Bob foreswore his beloved 'buds' and we settled into a week of hanging out together with no artificial highs, the happiest days of our relationship. Bob gave me driving lessons on a piece of Mill Valley waste ground, cajoling me gregariously to drive much faster than was reasonable or safe. We went sailing motorboats on San Francisco Bay, traded songs in Bob's living room, and we looked round potential recording studios like Record Plant in Sausalito, an old haunt of Sly Stone's.

One day we were driving in Bob's car, talking about schooldays. 'So,' he said, 'I guess you were pretty crazy at school, huh? What kinda things did you do to your teachers?' 'Well,' I responded proudly, thinking I had a good one, 'once we shut one of our teachers in a cupboard.' 'Hell,' Bob snorted, 'a cupboard? WE SET FIRE TO OURS!'

Bob continued educating me, turning me onto the gospel singing group The Clark Sisters, and showing me old-time films of country artists. On the Hank Williams piano I learned to play 'Lost Highway' and 'Will The Circle Be Unbroken'. We went to see The Charlie Daniels Band at an open-air venue in North California. Charlie introduced one of his songs by saying, 'I hope them evil Russians see the error of their ways,' and then, before singing 'Amazing Grace' at the end of the show – as most God-fearing country singers seemed to do – he added, 'I'd like to thank God who made the Universe.' I turned to Bob and said, 'Someone's gotta tell Charlie that God made the Russians too.' Bob liked that, and laughed loud and long in his Texan guffaw.

I slipped down to San Francisco for a couple of days to visit some musician friends, and when I came back to Mill Valley Bob cracked out the 'buds' once more. As soon as we were high, all the old Children's Foundation and 'Bob Marley was a visionary' stories, which I now realised had been absent for the previous week, started again and it struck me that Bob's dreams were intricately interwoven with how he felt when he smoked pot. Suddenly I saw him as a once-great man, perhaps still a great man, but one out of time, his dreams rendered hazy and out of reach by decades of reefer smoking. I still wanted to work with him but I decided to cover my ass too; I would bring the band to California to record with Bob in his own world, giving it the maximum chance of succeeding, but I'd also pursue recording without him in Dublin, where I'd produce the music myself.

I found it hard to explain this to Bob. He was fond of saying to me, 'You just call me from anywhere in the world and I'll be there, and

I'll have that sound WIDE OPEN.' I began to feel, ridiculously, that if I did recordings without Bob present I'd be betraying him. For my own peace of mind I had to tell him how I wanted things to be. We drove out to a beach on the far side of Mount Tamalpais, the green Olympian hill that dreams over Mill Valley, and as we walked along the sand with the sound of the Pacific surf in our ears, I outlined my plan. Bob, canny southerner that he was, understood the dynamics of the situation immediately and told me whenever I was ready to come to California and do some recording, to let him know. I flew back to Dublin with an easier mind.

The moment I got back I brought the country songs I'd learned in Mill Valley into the Waterboys repertoire and booked studio time in Windmill Lane. Our relationship with the still-traumatised Pearse was shaky so a procession of prospective new sound engineers passed through the studio portals, each for a day or two of recording. Most, having done their homework and listened to *This Is The Sea* before arriving, expected a serious, furrowed-brow session of making big-scale layered rock music. Instead they encountered a gang of ragamuffins who wanted to play live in the studio and sound like Hank Williams and his Drifting Cowboys circa 1951.

Most of these knob-twiddlers, trained in the era of overdubs and click tracks, looked at us as though we'd just teleported from the moon. I was hoping for one guy, just one, who had an intuitive rapport with me and a feel for the music we were playing, but none did. Though we made some some good recordings, almost as an aside, I found no engineer/collaborator. Sitting on top of a whole lot of nothing I began to wonder if working with Bob Johnston was what really needed to happen here. I contacted him to say we were ready to come to California.

Bob booked us six days in Fantasy, an old-fashioned studio across San Francisco Bay in Berkeley, and in late November Steve, Anto and I flew into California. Bob picked us up and, as before, we drove through the woods, past the eucalyptus trees crackling in the rain, up

Homestead Boulevard to Bob's house where the American flag was still draped enigmatically over the balcony. I watched my companions experiencing Bob's Californian dreamscape for the first time, just as wide-eyed and thrilled as I'd been ten months and two visits earlier. I'd figured if we were doing the recordings Bob's way we should ask him to supply bassist and drummer, so during the days leading up to the session he drove us back and forth over the Golden Gate Bridge to a rehearsal room in San Francisco, where he'd organised a selection of top West Coast players to come and try out with us.

Some of them we'd heard of, like Prairie Prince, the drummer with The Tubes, and Willie Hall, who'd played with Booker T & The MGs. And under normal circumstances we'd have gelled with these guys and made sweet music but something seemed to be wrong in the machinery of the band – or with me. Perhaps I was jaded with the catch-lightning-in-a-bottle recording methods. Maybe what I really needed was to deploy some eighties-style planning and get more formal about how we worked, or at least find a balance between deliberation and spontaneity. For though I didn't yet know it the absence of structure was beginning to burn me out, and working with Bob Johnston wasn't the solution. We rehearsed for hour after hour, blasting through our massive floating repertoire of songs and jams, but didn't chime with any of the players. In the end, pressured by Bob to make a decision, we picked Prairie Prince and Ross Valory, bassist with eighties pomp-rock band Journey.

But before we hit the studio I needed to move out of Bob's house. I couldn't face the intensity of recording with Bob all day – a wild enough experience in itself – then going home with him at night. A doom was gathering over this project and the strain was beginning to show between the two principal actors. I told Bob I needed to stay in a hotel. He wasn't happy about it but the southern gentleman in him wouldn't let him refuse, so he reluctantly drove me to a couple of desultory highway-side motels in the middle of nowhere. I can still picture him stepping out of the car glum-faced, showing me these places with a doleful demeanour as if no one could possibly want to stay in them and the most natural thing in the world to do was return to Johnston towers in good ole Homestead Boulevard. But I didn't wanna. And so I did what any sensible bohemian rocker in search of a bed would do: consulted the Californian version of the *Yellow Pages*. I found a little place in Berkeley itself called the French Hotel, a couple of streets from the studio. I booked myself in, got a piano delivered to my room, and that was that. And with Steve and Anto still billeted at Bob's we entered Fantasy Studios on the second of December and starting running down the clock on the incineration of all our dreams.

Fantasy was a good studio, stuck plumb in the middle of an industrial part of town, still decorated in its original seventies tat, blue carpet on the walls and wood everywhere; a warm and lived-in creative environment. Bob installed his own engineer, a quiet bespectacled genius called Tom Flye, then unleashed his most fearsome voice to terrorise the assistant, a long-haired young cove named Ralph, who sat quivering in a corner of the control room the entire week, taking note in a log book of everything that happened. Under coloured spotlights out in the studio were my electric piano, a drum kit in an alcove, and a Hammond organ, all close together for musical camaraderie. To the left and right of the piano were microphones for Anto's sax and Steve's fiddle. As soon as we were soundchecked I hit the ground running, vamping the piano and leading the band into a composed-on-the-spot song. As improvised songs often will, and ideally should do, this one caught the mood in the air – the awkward dynamic between Bob and myself – and turned into a rollicking kiss-off called 'Ain't Leavin, I'm Gone'. Sample lyrics: 'You're always right, baby when I'm wrong' and 'Your beauty is legend, your face is like the dawn,' each repeated then capped by the resolution of 'Well, I ain't leavin', I'm gone!', which didn't do much for the already strained studio vibes.

After that we jammed for several hours and tried unsuccessfully to get magic to flow. Clearly I needed some fresh inspiration and on the morning of day two I found it. Before the session I took a stroll through the Berkeley streets and noticed a dog-eared book in a junk shop window. It was titled *Folk Song Jamboree* and according to the cover contained 'songs from many lands'. I bought it and started flicking through it as I walked to the studio. On page fifty-seven was a song called 'When Will We Be Married', apparently from South Africa. I couldn't read the music but I liked the words. I took the title and a couple of lines, added some more of my own and by the time I got to Fantasy I'd fashioned it into a lyric. As chance would have it, Steve was in best Fellow-who-Fiddles mode that morning, cheerfully skirling out rustic jigs and reels as we warmed up. I tried singing my new concoction over one of these and to my delight it fitted. Prairie Prince joined in with some Scottish-style military drumming, and suddenly we'd made something special.

But it was an oasis in a musical desert. The rest of day two, and all of days three and four, were spent in vain pursuit of alchemy. I tried some new songs but they were unfinished, and the extra lyrics they needed didn't flow into my imagination on the spot like they usually did. I tried plucking favourite oldies out of the air like Bob Dylan's country waltz, 'Wallflower', and the old Irish ballad, 'When I First Said I Loved Only You Maggie', but nothing caught fire. We replaced Prairie and Ross with another couple of guys but were still becalmed.

Meanwhile the studio had calcified into two sharply delineated territories: the control room was Bob's domain and I hardly ever went in there (and took a deep breath for courage before I did), while the live room was the band's domain, which Bob rarely entered. The two camps existed almost independent of each other, a wall of glass and a thousand miles separating us. We played with no direction from Bob and he worked on the sound and recorded the music with no involvement from us. On the rare occasions Bob approached me in the studio I could feel a raw aggressive energy radiating from him, which I interpreted as frustration directed at me. And I began to

111

object to it. Though nothing was said, I started to feel he was blaming me for the sessions not taking off. It was no one's fault. The situation was beyond our control because our different worlds were too far apart. A band from the eighties couldn't merge with a producer from the sixties anymore than oil would mix with water. The Waterboys needed the kind of pro-active production guidance – input on arrangements, song selection and performance – that Bob didn't or couldn't give, while he needed from us the discipline and maturity a band achieves only after years of playing live together in studios. Our shared musical endeavour had been doomed before we'd recorded a note, and the dream of making something great together was a delicious unattainable mirage.

To confound things further, none of us was thinking or feeling clearly, for Bob had brought the dreaded 'buds' with him and the reefers were passing round till the air turned purple. What's more, the tapes were rolling non-stop, capturing every blip and doodle we made, the worthy and the worthless, with no quality control whatsoever. By the end of day four we'd gone through a cool *fifty* fourteen-inch master reels and counting, with nary a releasable musical moment to show for it. That night Bob suggested we try yet another rhythm section. He recommended a young bassist called John Patitucci, who we liked the sound of, and the veteran drummer Jim Keltner. I knew Keltner's name from many of my most beloved records including John Lennon's *Imagine* and George Harrison's *Concert For Bangladesh*, but I fancied working with someone our own age and said so. Bob looked at me like I'd grown horns and put the argument to bed, saying simply: 'Jim Keltner is a motherfucker drummer.'

And he was. Next morning, day five, we reconvened with our new guests. Patitucci was nineteen, fresh as a lamb, golly-gosh happy, and played like a funky angel. Keltner was cool, dressed in dark blue jeans and denim shirt, black waistcoat, frontiersman's beard and impenetrable shades, which he never took off. He had that slow-talking, word-weighing American style familiar from Clint Eastwood movies and I loved him instantly, recognising my resistance from the night before as the absurdity it was. And when Jim started playing, a different wavelength of musical reality opened up. His grooves, his drum fills, his timing, his sound and his radar – the ability to intuitively discern the direction of the music as we played – were from another universe. Patitucci, addressing him as 'Uncle Jim', slotted in sweetly on bass. Suddenly we were on the move.

Except for one thing. My songs were still uncooked and I was exhausted after four days of diminishing returns, frazzled by the vibes with Bob and spaced out by the prodigious reefer intake. And a strange thing: I felt so in awe of Keltner's greatness that though I could still play my ass off I could hardly sing. I felt unworthy. But the show had to go on, and so we tried two half-written new numbers, 'Blues For Your Baby' and 'Lonesome Old Wind'. These were good ones and we played them for hours, turning them inside, upside, backwards, forwards, extending them into twenty, thirty-minute improvisations, exploring every nuance and possibility in the music. Keltner powered us like a musical buffalo god, his shoulders heaving in the drum booth, sticks blurred, drum-skins and cymbals reflected in his shades, maracas and shakers bound to his arms and legs with gaffer tape, creating a choogling sonic aura around his beat.

When Keltner played a crack opened and the soul of America shone through. All the wild untamed land that once was the American continent was invoked in his crashing, rumbling, unstoppable groove: prairies, cattle drives, mile-wide rivers, the spirits of great Indians, buttes and canyons, rattlesnakes, badlands and the heavy boom of distant thunder. His drumming expressed a sense of space, sacredness and power as great as the great land itself. Patitucci's warm, human bass playing, full of the nuances of jazz and pop, ensouled this sonic landscape with the beating heart's pulse of steamboats and gamblers, street processions and Mardi Gras, the chorus lines of Broadway musicals, flappers, gospel-hollerers and churches in the wildwood.

And though at the end of the fifth day we had captured nothing that came close to a record radio-friendly rock single, nothing that harmonised with the sounds or styles of the time, and nothing sufficiently structured to put on a record, nevertheless The Fellow Who Fiddles, the Human Saxophone and I had had the most profound musical experience of our lives.

On the final day, like a defeated army charging into a valley for one last vainglorious hurrah, we played almost non-stop for nine hours. I pulled out every new composition I had floating around my head and a slew of classic country and gospel songs. We fused with Keltner and Patitucci and expanded the music to awesome proportions, reconfiguring songs on Olympian scales. We played a forty minute blow-out of 'Sgt Pepper's Lonely Hearts Club Band', a half-hour improv on the spiritual 'Soon As I Get Home', and mighty moss-gathering tumbleweed journeys through Hank Williams's 'Honky Tonkin'', The Carter Family's 'Will The Circle Be Unbroken' and Blind Roger Hay's 'I'm On My Way To Heaven'. We reinvented classic American roots music that day and recast it as a single sacred flowing river of power.

After one extended workout I asked Keltner, 'what's the longest you've ever played non-stop?' 'Uh, well, Michael,' came the answer, 'I think it might be the one we just played.' And when the last chord of the last song died away there came the sweetest of all moments when Jim stepped out from behind his drums and walked quietly to the piano. 'You guys,' he said slowly, with unimpeachable coolness, 'are serious groovers.' Yet still, *nothing we could put on a record*. I knew it, Bob knew it, Steve and Anto knew it. No one asked them, but I'm sure Keltner and Patitucci knew it. We'd gone on a mighty journey but brought back nothing we could show to the world.

For our last night in California I moved back into my old room at Bob's, our relationship restored to cordiality now the pressure of recording was off, and in the morning he drove us to San Francisco airport. We all knew the experience was over, that there would be no more, but neither Bob nor we had the heart to say it. I promised him I'd listen through to the music when I got home, with a view to selecting stuff for our album, but it was a hollow promise. I would listen, yes, but as soon as I could, I'd move on and finish the record in Dublin without Bob. At the airport Bob helped us lift our bags from the car. We piled them onto a couple of trolleys, each of us gave him a hug, then we headed down the concrete tunnel into the airport. We turned halfway and waved back to him and Bob called out, 'Thank you for your music!', his Texan voice echoing after us down the tunnel and down the years.

CHAPTER 8

THE POWER OF THE MUSIC GIVES EVERYBODY WINGS

It's midnight on International Aids Day, the second of April 1987, and Edinburgh is hosting a series of concerts. Two hours ago The Waterboys came off stage at The Usher Hall and now Wickham and I are in the Assembly Rooms on George Street where the rest of the night's shows are taking place. We're in the backstage artists' hangout, a long grand hall with ornate wallpaper and dark velvet curtains. Half the bands in Edinburgh seem to be here, sitting round drink-filled tables in their own little camps, looking warily and competitively at each other, trying to be cool. Most of them have already played, a few are awaiting their stage calls. Billy Mackenzie of The Associates lounges on a sofa wearing a sailor's cap, a couple of dolly birds on his arm. The frosty atmosphere between the Edinburgh bands hasn't changed much since I lived here in the late seventies. How different it is from London where bands want to be cool but at least appear to wish each other well, or friendly Dublin where the inter-band philosophy can be summed up in six words as, 'sure, we're all in it together!'

I'm musing on why this might be, when a familiar sound brushes my ears. It's The Fellow Who Fiddles easing into a slithery Irish jig with no respect whatsoever for the cold-war conventions of the Edinburgh music scene. After a few beats he's joined by Aidan, the suedeheaded mandolin player from We Free Kings, and the two of them jig merrily away in a rough but passionate approximation of Irish traditional music. Their little corner of cheerfulness is a lone flame in an arctic snowfield. The Edinburgh bands either ignore this outlandish development or watch it stony-faced. But wait, another fiddler is

116

joining in; a thin-faced character with a pompadour haircut and a cagoule. And here's Geoff Pagan, the splendidly named We Free Kings violin player, grabbing himself a seat and lashing into the tune with them. The two have become four and the flame is now a fire.

Another couple of Kings pick up their instruments – a mandolin, a tin whistle – and feeling the impulse too I pull my guitar from its case and join in. The music is flying now, a heartily-roaring blaze of sound, and the Edinburgh bands are presented with a conundrum: do they attempt to stay cool in the face of an overwhelming and superior counter-attack by the forces of merriment, or do they surrender and join in the fun? While they're wrestling with this philosophical issue we're joined by yet another fiddler – a chap with a gold-painted violin no less – and Wickham propels us into a shit-kicking set of reels, the temperature rising by several degrees. This is too much temptation for a couple of Edinburgh bandsters who grab their guitars, join the expanding circle and start blasting away. Now we are ten, or eleven, and our booted feet are stomping in rhythm on the wooden floor like jackhammers. Non-musicians are beginning to gather round, clapping and yelling as indeed they should, and the next time I look up there are several new musicians in the circle: a bequiffed gent with banjo and tartan cape, and a couple of the formerly stoniest-faced coolest-of-the-cool Edinburgh dudes, strumming along on guitars self-consciously but thawing fast.

We sound like a cross between a Scottish fiddlers rally and several rockabilly bands all playing at the same time, and the music is now a rip-roaring furnace of sound, a mighty and communal explosion reaching every corner of the great room. The Fellow Who Fiddles has pulled it off: he has brought joy and brotherhood down from the realm of dreams and made them hard reality. With no greater weapons than a wooden fiddle, a horsehair bow and the spark of his good nature, he's triggered a chain of events that has united a room full of strangers, turning thousand-yard stares into whoops of excitement and celebration. Verily, the power of the music gives everybody wings!

We'd arrived in Edinburgh the night before and checked into the Carlton Highland Hotel, a rambling Victorian eyrie perched on the North Bridge where, in what now seemed a previous life, Z and I had once tracked down the American punk rocker Richard Hell. But now I was the star flying in from another land and it was sweet and strange to arrive in the city of my birth accompanied by my Irish entourage and see the old town through their eyes: a dark northern fastness, impossibly atmospheric and romantic, like something from a book by George MacDonald or Edgar Allen Poe.

Steve and Anto were there and Trevor the bassist looking like the handsomest man in Ireland, and Trevor's drumming mate Pete McKinney with his blade-sharp Belfast accent. There was B.P. Fallon in his teddy boy finery along for the ride in the exalted role of 'viber', and our Irish road crew: Jimmy Hickey, John Dunford and Steve Meany, three dark warrior gods from some ancient Celtic myth who'd been shot forwards and transplanted into the twentieth century. Wickham had introduced me to them a year earlier, regaling me with tales of Jimmy Hickey – 'the world's greatest roadie, man!' – who could re-string a bouzouki while Donal Lunny of Moving Hearts was still playing it. We called them the Brown Brothers because they all wore the brown distressed leather bomber jackets popular at the time, and Dunford, the canny, bristle-jawed soundman, was their unofficial leader.

We'd been recording in Windmill Lane for two months and hadn't played a concert since the previous July. So we were excited, almost demob-happy, to be out on the road, even for a one-off. Or a two-off – for on the night of our arrival we were invited to play unadvertised at a place called Calton Studios, halfway down the Royal Mile in the heart of old Edinburgh.

The gig was with We Free Kings, a Scottish band formed by a friend of mine called Joe Kingman. Joe was a tousle-headed punk rock barker and he'd gathered round him a ragtag band of misfits, seven in all, with a weird but brilliant sonic mix of cello, fiddle, flute, accordion, guitar and drums. They played Woody Guthrie numbers at breakneck pace, wrote their own urchin anthems and gleefully deconstructed old folk songs, putting everything through a punk thresher. The result was fantastic: seven characters in search of a comic strip, playing mad swirling music with a righteous intensity and a sense of mischief. They'd toured Ireland the autumn before, camping in tents, and Wickham and I had tagged along with them.

Calton Studios turned out to be a dingy but funky little cinema hidden down an alley. Word of mouth had produced a big crowd and the place was hopping. We threw in songs we'd never played before, like the ancient 'Raggle Taggle Gypsy', with its fateful tale of the bride who leaves wealth and status for the charms of the 'yellow gypsy's lips', and gospel oldie 'I'm On My Way To Heaven', transformed into a bloodthirsty hoedown. We played for thirty minutes and afterwards everyone in the place wanted to talk to us, a barrage of bright, enthusiastic, sweat-glistening Edinburgh faces crowding round. I recognised one guy from my early days, a shop assistant from Phoenix Records, a tiny prog-rock cave on the Royal Mile which Z and I had often sneered at during the punk wars. In fact when they'd declined to stock my first record back in '79 I'd indulged my jilted feelings by anonymously letting off a stink bomb on their floor.

Next evening we played our main concert at the Usher Hall, a domed orchestral palace shaped like a jelly mould in the shadow of Edinburgh Castle, where, aged twelve, I'd sung in the school choir at a Christmas concert. I remembered thrilling sense of imminent event as the audience gathered, the hubbub of their voices merging with the sound of the orchestra tuning up, a sense of awe sparked by the plush grandeur of the Hall. I felt the same now, except instead of an orchestra it was The Fellow Who Fiddles and the Human Saxophone tuning up as we stood in the dark corridor, hearts beating, waiting to go on. We were part of a four-band bill and played a forty-five minute set. Most of it was from our unfinished new album and despite the absence of familiar songs the show was a success. Yet as I sat on the plane back to Dublin the following day, it was the Calton Studios performance and the post-gig bash in the Assembly Rooms that reverberated in my memory. I felt as if something new was trying to be born; that a promise had been vouchsafed in those unscripted moments of what The Waterboys could become.

By stepping out of the music business machinery at the end of 1985 we'd established our independence, but I'd felt for some time The Waterboys should evolve into something more organic than just another rock band putting out albums and touring in the prescribed way. Now suddenly I knew how it would look. I leaned back in my seat high above the Irish Sea and imagined The Waterboys recast as a colourful travelling musical explosion, rooted in the magical folklore of the British Isles and Ireland and expressing a holistic non-dogmatic spirituality, becoming legendary not through studio trickery or the artifice of promo videos but through what we wrote and played and by connecting directly with the audience. And all this while having a damn good time.

Back in Dublin the events of our Edinburgh jaunt receded into the background as we re-immersed ourselves in recording. The first opportunities to develop this new vision came soon enough. Six weeks later the Greenpeace boat *Sirius* docked on the Liffey, a few hundred yards from Windmill Lane. All the band were Greenpeace members or supporters and Robert Hunter's book *The Greenpeace Chronicle* had been a Waterboys bible, passed around on tour from bandmate to bandmate till it was falling apart. The idea struck several of us at once – why not play a free gig on the ship's deck to an audience on the quayside? We could drum up a crowd by word of mouth and create some Irish publicity for Greenpeace. We sent a diplomatic delegation to the ship. Anto, frock-coated and skinny-legged like the footman in Tenniel's illustrations for *Alice In Wonderland*, and Jimmy Hickey, as red bearded and broad-chested as a Viking chieftain, presented our compliments and the offer of a free gig to the captain. This was a gaunt Dutchman, with a face out of a

Rubens painting, called Willem, who accepted the offer and proposed to repay us with a meal in the ship's cabin after the concert. The next afternoon our crew drove to where the ship was anchored on the quays and hauled the band's gear on board.

Someone phoned the national radio station and a DJ announced the show. By five o'clock a crowd of several hundred had converged on the docks, including every busker in Dublin and the ever-alert Bono. What they found was a gaily-coloured ship resplendent in the late afternoon sun, a black-and-silver whale painted on the forecastle, and amps, microphone stands and drum kit set up on deck. From the PA system Hank Williams music floated sweetly across the quays, warm and rustic, a startling sound in those dog days of drum machines and arena rock.

At five-thirty we walked up the rear gangway, plugged in and blasted into an hour's worth of songs, including nautical-themed numbers like 'Fisherman's Blues' and 'Strange Boat'. The band was augmented by two new Waterboys: a Dublin drummer called Fran Breen with a Yosser Hughes moustache and a habit of jerking his head side to side with every beat like a robot, and a young Irish piper called Vinnie Kilduff, a friend of Wickham's. Vinnie was that rare beast, a trad musician who could play rock'n'roll. And when the wild bluesy howl of his pipes, with all their evocation of the Irish soul, merged with the swoop and staccato of Steve's fiddle, the music hit a whole new level.

And there was a mighty thrill to playing on the ship. Partly this was the novelty of discovering that its deck, raised in the water a few feet higher than the audience on the quayside, provided an ideal stage. And partly it was the pleasure of playing on sloping wood among the capstans and hatches, the smell of the river in our nostrils, teenage fans sitting crowded on the quay's edge, legs dangling over the water. But the biggest thrill was that we were playing for Greenpeace, connected to a world-spanning cause we felt was a wave of the future, and this put fire in our bellies. It put helium in our dreaming too; for weeks afterwards we mused on the possibilities of a Waterboys and Greenpeace tour of Ireland, sailing the circumference of the country, playing shows in all the harbours; Belfast, Derry, Galway, Cork, Waterford. And if we could do it in Ireland, why not Britain? But we didn't have the resources to realise this dream, and the crew of the Sirius had more pressing matters than jollying round Irish ports in search of good vibes. Still, the concert achieved what we wanted; as we'd hoped, the press were lured to the scene and next morning we saw photos of ourselves and the boat on the cover of the *Irish Independent*. We'd done it – Greenpeace was front-page news in Ireland.

A few days later the ship sailed off to keep appointments with whalers in the North Atlantic. And we were travelling too, by plane to Scotland to play at something called The Pictish Festival. This was run by a friend of We Free Kings called Robbie The Pict, a tall sandy-haired Scotsman, a principled activist and scurrilous hustler with a dash of wizard thrown in. He'd founded a 'Pictish Free State' on an acre of land he owned, and spent his time campaigning for independence from the British crown. I liked Robbie and loved how he always responded to the question 'How are you?' with the reply 'Brand new!' The Festival was his annual hoolie, held on the anniversary of an obscure seventh-century battle between Picts and Teutons.

We arrived at our hotel, an ancient commercial travellers' stopover in Forfar called The Salutation, to be greeted in the foyer by a grinning Robbie and sidekick in homespun Scottish revolutionary kit: 'Pictish Free State' t-shirts, leather flying jackets, paratroop boots and kilts. They piled us into a Land Rover festooned with Pict logos and whisked us off to the venue, five miles away. Letham Village Hall was a lonesome-looking redbrick building on a hill overlooking a tiny hamlet, not much more than a crossroads. A gaggle of rural punk rockers festered round the entrance while inside was a spartan auditorium, like a school gym, filled with feral highlanders out of their skulls on a homebrew administered by Robbie and his minions,

122

plus a smattering of intrepid Waterboys fans who'd made the trek from Edinburgh or Aberdeen. At one end was a stage, and for a backdrop someone had improvised a Scottish flag out of a wodge of blue cloth with strips of white gaffer tape stuck diagonally across it.

The concert had been going all day and was running hopelessly late. We Free Kings were on before us and when their fiddler didn't turn up, Wickham stepped into the breach and played their whole set. The Waterboys finally took the stage shortly before one in the morning and the atmosphere was dense; thick with drunkenness and excitement, a wild tartan bacchanalia. We poured our music into this atmosphere, playing till almost 4am. We closed with 'A Pagan Place' and during its extended outro, with Roddy Lorimer's trumpet soaring and Vinnie's pipes wailing, several members of other bands on stage with us, and a freight-train mother groove roaring around our heads, a critical mass of musical wildness was achieved. With a sudden 'Pop!' I felt us come into alignment with a down-flow of power, some bright shard of the Celtic soul, wild and ecstatic, that flowed through us and into the audience like a rite.

When we stumbled outside for air, dawn was softening the sky and the birds were singing. I stood, ears ringing, feeling the breeze on my skin. Something had just happened, some piece of the new Waterboys vision had slotted into place and it had to do with the Celtic. I *was* Celtic, and so were most of my band. But it was something I'd never consciously thought about before. What did it mean to be Celtic? I would find out soon enough, in a new and magical landscape that was about to open up before me: the West of Ireland. *The West of Ireland* means Ireland's great Atlantic seaboard: from County Donegal in the north, southwards through Sligo, Mayo, Galway, Clare and Kerry to the western parts of County Cork. I'd been there a few times: a childhood holiday in Sligo, a couple of concerts in Galway and some brief trips with The Fellow Who Fiddles or my girlfriend Irene. But it was during a trip to County Kerry a week after the Pictish Festival that I began to comprehend what was special about the west.

B.P. Fallon had been raving about an upcoming festival called the Cibeal, held in Kenmare, close to the Cork and Kerry border. It sounded magical indeed; a little market town taken over for the weekend by music and high spirits, with festivities in the street and an influx of trad players, gypsies and rock bands. 'It'll be shaking, man!' said B.P. in his hushed, intense voice. Anto and I decided to go down with him.

The drive from Dublin was a hundred and eighty miles southwest across Ireland, and when we came into County Kerry the fields and low hills of the midlands gave way to sharp noble mountains and blue lakes, a landscape of the gods. Kenmare was in a lush valley, resplendent in late spring abundance, and as we drove through the toy-like streets of brightly coloured houses to the town square all my expectations were realised. It was like a frontier town in the Wild West or an olden gypsy fair. Covered stalls and marquees occupied the pavements while festive strings of bunting hung from one side of the town's broad main street to the other. The pubs spilled clouds of revellers onto the sidewalk and convivial music, a bright mosaic of whistles and fiddles, flavoured the air. Dark-eyed black-bearded men and thin lawless women who looked like they'd come down from the mountains hung out in every doorway, smoking, drinking and dancing. A long flat truck with a stage set up on it stood ready for action on the square. High trees and church spires shaded the scene while a backdrop of mountains brooded in the distance. It was like stumbling on a hedonistic Shangri-La. I wanted to be in every part of it at once.

There were concerts and events all round town, in school halls, hotels, even churches, and B.P. quickly vanished in pursuit of some scene or other. Anto and I rambled around the town square and somebody told us that a band we knew, a Dublin country-rock combo called the Fleadh Cowboys, were playing right now in a hotel on the outskirts of town. I had my guitar and Anto had his sax, so as we walked to the gig through the cheerful streets we started playing. A small crowd gathered round us and we made our procession through town. Finding myself in the role of pied piper, I made a medley of songs last for the twenty minutes of our march while the Human Saxophone blew loud solos that reverberated off the stone fronts of the houses. Finally we came to the edge of town where the stately pile of the Park Hotel stood amid trees and meadows. There we found the Fleadh Cowboys hanging around, smoking and talking on a patio outside the ballroom, their performance just finished. The Cowboys were led by two Stetson-wearing Dublin characters, Pete Cummins (tall, rangy, always looked like he'd just climbed down off a horse, nasal singing style) and Frank Lane (charismatic, testy, with a Hank Williams fixation and a helium voice). We'd guested with them a few times before and they invited us to form a one-off band to play that evening on the truck I'd noticed in the town square. Bingo! We'd scored ourselves a gig in paradise.

Down at the square an hour or so later word had spread and a rowdy audience was gathered. We climbed onto the truck and soundchecked in twenty seconds flat. B.P. Fallon appeared bang on cue with The Pogues' accordion player, James Fearnley, who was quickly hauled up to join us. We struck up a boxcar-train groove and lit into a set of country songs, all rattling Tennessee Three drums and slide guitar licks punctuated by Anto's rasping sax breaks, while I traded lead vocals with the two Stetsoned Cowboys. Between numbers I heard the unmistakeable sound of someone shouting for 'Red Army Bluuuuuues'. This plaintive holler, a plea for the least-played, most-requested Waterboys song, our own personal 'Freeeeeebiiiiiird', had followed us on tour from L.A. to Tel Aviv and someone was even shouting for it in this mad Irish mountain fastness. Halfway through the gig I noticed Liam Ó Maonlai, the young singer from The Hothouse Flowers, in the crowd. I loved his bluesy swagger and deep voice, and with his floppy fringe and piano antics he was like an Irish Jerry Lee Lewis. I reached down and pulled him up from the crowd and asked if he'd sing a song I'd heard him do a couple of times. He agreed, I gave the band a signal, and we smashed into Iggy Pop's mighty 'Cock In My Pocket', with its all-time great lyric, 'I've got my cock in my pocket and I'm rootin' down the old highway!'

Rootin' … I loved that! It conjured up an image of Iggy or Liam slouching down the road, fist in the air, on the scout for mischief, sex and trouble, and it was a perfect punk rock note to sound on a truck in Kenmare to an audience of wild Kerrymen and lawless women. Except for one thing: the Fleadh Cowboys couldn't play punk rock, so our rendition of 'Cock' was closer to an Allman Brothers' Southern-fried boogie than the metal mayhem of The Stooges. His song well sung, Liam jumped back into the audience, and a few numbers later we finished our set. We wrestled our way through the crowd, crossed the square and ate a quick meal in a teeming bar. And there was no time to waste, for the musical worlds weren't done colliding yet.

My girlfriend Irene, who'd come with us, wanted to take me to the late-night show at the Park Hotel to see a hot trad music supergroup called Patrick Street. Their accordion player Jackie Daly was local and as dusk descended on the festive town a heavily accented male voice crackled through the tannoy speakers that hung from every lamppost, cajoling all and sundry to 'coom and hear Jackie Daly an' his friends oop at the Perk'.

Oop at the Perk the atmosphere was electric and the grand ballroom was packed. I'd heard a lot of trad music on tape and record and I'd gamely played along with The Fellow Who Fiddles when he cracked into jigs at rehearsals, but I'd never seen trad played live by master musicians or heard it amplified through a PA system. A revelation was in store.

Patrick Street looked like the archetype of a folk band: beards, waistcoats, brown tweed jackets and flared jeans, fiddle, accordion, bouzouki, guitar. And when they started playing their nimble jigs and reels it sounded pretty much like all the other traditional Irish music I'd heard, sweet on the ear but likely to leave me as it found me. Then I looked at Irene: standing beside me on the ballroom floor, she was

126

rapt. I watched her and began to see she wasn't listening so much to the tunes, the melodies. She was connected to the *energy* of the music, its rhythm and spirit. And as I observed my lovely Irish girlfriend responding to the sound, whooping spontaneously at a moment of emphasis, swaying like a willow in the wind as the tune picked up rhythm, lifting her arms high over her head in joy when the music revved up a gear, I began to understand and to feel the energy myself. At one point she turned to me with a quizzical look as if to say, *'now do you see?'* And by God, I did. I looked at the crowd and they were all plugged into the music like Irene, receiving its pulse and force in the same way as a rock audience, except this transmission was on a different, finer wavelength. And it had balls – amped up loud through a sound system, trad music packed a serious visceral punch.

After the concert we hooked up with Anto, B.P. and Liam and played music in someone's hotel suite, making up strange songs that were sung once and never heard of again. In the small hours of the morning Irene and I drove twenty miles over the mountains to Killarney where we'd booked a room. As we journeyed the empty road in sweet silence, the events of the day buzzed in my memory and the sounds of trad music echoed ecstatically in my mind. And all around us a mighty Celtic dawn was breaking. The clouds and the high faces of the mountains were burnt scarlet by the rising sun and the landscape on either side of the narrow road looked prehistoric and wild. Nothing would be the same again: I had left one world and entered another.

CHAPTER 9

GO SLOWLY AND YOU MIGHT SEE SOMETHING

It's a blustery day at sea and the fishing boat rocks as we cross the choppy waters of Galway Bay. Anto and I are strumming mandolins on deck, sending up peals of bright music that evaporate like sea spray in the March air while the dreaming hulks of the Aran Islands recede behind us and seagulls chase the boat making their wild cries. The Human Saxophone and I are a long way from anywhere, not just geographically but mentally and spiritually. We have become walkers between the worlds, two of Rimbaud's 'horrible workers' of the future. We have breached the veils of an ancient realm and now, returning, bring with us news and visions.

But for all that, I need a piss. So I lay down the mando, its strings still vibrating, and step down into the shaded hold of the boat. There I find a rough little cubicle with a swinging, creaking door and a toilet. I step in and make my peace with nature. As I'm heading back up the steps to the sunlit world, I notice an old wood-framed mirror on my left. Casually I look into it and to my amazement see a creature who is not me. The god Pan is looking back. How do I know? No one's ever seen a photo of Pan, but the inscrutable goat-like face in the mirror is unmistakeable, a face I've known forever. And yet it's my face too, Pan and myself sharing skin and bone. By what alchemy is this happening? I look into the reflected eyes and with a slow thrill realise (though it will take me years to frame this realisation in words) that Pan is an archetypal power deep inside all human beings, and my experiences in the primeval atmosphere of Aran have called forth this power in me and laid its mark on my face. I stand gazing at the mirror contemplating this mystery, my ears filled with the roar of the ship's engines and the crying of the gulls.

Snapping back to the here and now I feel the boat turning as it comes within the lee of the Connemara coast, and Pan or man, or both, I climb back on deck, stand beside Anto, and turn my eyes to the fast approaching land.

Back in the summer of 1986, around the time I was playing the Hank Williams piano in Bob Johnston's house, my old mentor Nigel Grainge sold Ensign Records and The Waterboys' contract with it. But the decision who to sell to was made by me. Chris Blackwell, the owner of Island, who licensed and released Ensign's output, phoned to tell me Nigel was on the cusp of selling Ensign to Virgin Records. Blackwell explained, however, that neither Virgin nor the other company bidding for the deal, Chrysalis, would buy Ensign if they couldn't also secure the rights to the first three Waterboys albums, which Island controlled. Consequently Blackwell was positioned to decide the outcome of the deal by his choice of which company to sell the three albums to.

'So,' he asked me, 'do you want me to sell them to Virgin or Chrysalis?'

Blackwell was giving me the power to decide my own future, and I was damn grateful. I didn't have to think long about the answer either. I remembered my liaison with Virgin seven years earlier and didn't want to go back there – nor did it escape me that Nigel, doing a deal on the strength of The Waterboys' then sky-high stock, hadn't asked my opinion. I told Blackwell to sell the albums to Chrysalis.

Exactly as he'd forecast, Virgin dropped out and Chrysalis bought Ensign. And because Chrysalis knew they'd sealed the deal through my casting vote, I was in a strong position to have my lawyer John Kennedy renegotiate my contract. Kennedy was a whip-sharp English son of Irish parents. He looked like the sixties pop star Joe Brown, and played the legal side of the music business like a splendid principled game. He took to the negotiations, his first big job on my behalf, with lip-smacking relish, a hound to the hunt, and quickly convinced Chrysalis to flip my royalty rates dramatically upwards from the meagre cut I'd got when I signed as an unknown to Ensign, and to grant me the holy grail of artistic freedom, final approval over my records.

I went to meet the Chrysalis boss in London. Doug D'Arcy was an affable fellow with a sculpted beard and a Yorkshire accent, but he perplexed me. I was so used to Nigel trying to get me to do what he wanted, as if my own ideas about my music were an obstacle to be worked around, that I was confounded by Doug's willingness to listen to me and let me do what I felt was right without my having to fight for it. Like a traumatised dog finding itself in a safe home for the first time, it was a couple of years before I started to trust Doug and use him as the shrewd counsellor he was. The first thing I told him was I didn't want an A&R man interfering with my records. After delivering the goods with *This Is The Sea* I wanted to keep making albums my own way. Doug accepted this and amazingly didn't even ask to listen to what we'd already recorded. Then he bankrolled our Bob Johnston recordings in San Francisco, and with nary a raised eyebrow backed me when the band spent several months in Windmill Lane through the winter and spring of 1987.

In fact we had enough killer music for an album from our Dublin sessions the previous year, only I couldn't see it. I hadn't yet learned that with spontaneous studio recordings it's crucial to accept flaws. All the best records are full of mistakes, as any sixties Stones or Dylan album will attest, but I felt I had to re-record a song if there were slight tuning or timing problems, or when a drummer overplayed or my singing didn't please me, even if the overall impact of the track was powerful and infectious.

And the variety of material was overwhelming. I had dozens of songs in almost as many genres and my usual focus and ability to make hard decisions were undone by the volume of music. As the stack of tracks grew the scope of possible album directions became dizzying and decisions went unmade until it grew harder and harder for me to hear my 'instructions' and locate the inner musical will that had steered me through *This Is The Sea*. Another factor was that we didn't have a full time drummer, so we were forever trying out new guys or bringing back old ones. We outdid *Spinal Tap*: no less than fifteen tub-thumpers played on this one album. And because the sound and feel of a song changes dramatically with each drummer, and because some of our songs were recorded on three, four, or even five separate occasions with different dudes on the drum stool, the range of strikingly different yet usable versions of the songs expanded. How was I to choose between the Pete McKinney version of 'Fisherman's Blues' with its lusty, crashing drums and the Noel Bridgeman version with its subtle groove, both of which I loved? Even as I vacillated the music kept evolving with new sounds and players entering our orbit, like Vinnie Kilduff and his Irish pipes. We fearlessly integrated these new elements with often thrilling results, but with the consequence that songs we'd cut a year, even six months previously now sounded like another group.

By the late summer of 1987, a year after the Chrysalis purchase, I felt like a madman trying to steer a runaway train. If ever I needed a strong hand on my shoulder and some artistic steering it was now, but as a consequence of my own choices no one was empowered to play that role. I was alone in my responsibility for the album, acutely aware that the eyes of the music world would be on its eventual release. Burned out, confounded and with over sixty tracks in various states of completion, I withdrew from the studio. I didn't know whether I'd come back to the existing work after a break, or whether I'd scrap it all, re-gather my energies and quickly record an all-new record that captured the band at its latest stage of development. For out of the studio the changes in the music kept right on coming. The new folkier elements in our sound were integrated during shows in Dublin and Galway that autumn as trad music, which had begun to enchant me in Kenmare a few months before, now cast its whole spell.

131

I'd started hanging out with piper Vinnie who lived in the street next to mine in Ranelagh, on Dublin's Southside. Vinnie was a dapper Brylcreemed fellow with a maroon waistcoat, a headful of craftiness and an insatiable appetite for hedonism – a cross between Brer Rabbit and Mr Toad from *The Wind In The Willows*. He would stand in the middle of his living room, its walls covered with Irish movie posters and dodgy pop pin-ups torn from the pages of *Smash Hits*, a straw-thin reefer dangling from his lips, while holding forth on the stylistic differences between tin whistle players in adjacent town-lands of County Mayo. An ever-voluble font of information on all things trad, Vinnie became my guide, initiating me into the mysteries of Irish music and bringing me to sessions; not recording sessions but pub sessions, the lifeblood of the trad scene, in which musicians sat round a table and played tunes – reels, jigs, hornpipes, polkas and slides – while the bustle of the pub went on around them. To enter a Dublin bar and find a gaggle of musicians firing off joyful, celebratory music is a delightful experience, as any lucky tourist will confirm. And to my ears it was heaven. Here was a wild, articulate music that expressed the soul of Ireland and evoked its landscape, played with power but without machismo, with mastery but without ego. How this appealed to me in my weary and confused condition! The charms of traditional music emerged from the mist as eternal verities to be envied and achieved, emanations from a world far removed from the manipulative, distorted ghetto of the rock business.

Soon this education was expanding my musical consciousness and changing the way I listened: trad tunes flew by so fast I had to sharpen my wits just to follow what was happening, and as I drew closer to the music I discovered sophistication at work – nuance, ornamentation, interplay, the personality of individual players, all of which my ears had to learn to grasp and my mind to process. And the instruments! Dusty bustling fiddles, sputtering banjos, melodeons and button accordions that sounded like trails of winking lights, the primal wail of the pipes, the thrum and plash of the bouzouki, the lonesome purity of the whistle and the warm quizzical burr of the flute all recast the musical colour scheme of my imagination and resonated with new possibilities, the promise of magic. In addition to Vinnie's ministrations, our soundman John Dunford was turning me on with live recordings of the great Irish groups he'd worked with like Moving Hearts and De Dannan, and slipping me preconception-busting albums by The Bothy Band, full of elemental, Promethean music.

The Fellow Who Fiddles and bassist Trevor caught the bug too. Trevor taught himself bouzouki while Wickham got busy learning tunes from the trad player's bible *O'Neill's Music Of Ireland*, an inch-thick yellow tome containing a thousand manuscripted melodies with archaic titles like 'The Fiddler's Frolic', 'The Bashful Bachelor' and 'Banish Misfortune'. As 1987 marched to a close all influences conspired to bring The Waterboys ever deeper into traditional music and the older, wilder world it represented.

I spent that New Year in Scotland and bought some Scottish folk records while I was there. When I listened to them I recognised the music was the same as Irish, only a different vernacular: harder, more angular perhaps, and paradoxically more straight-laced and less free, but as like to it as brother and sister and flowing from the same Celtic wellspring. And many of the tunes I'd been hearing in Dublin, I realised, were Scottish. This was a revelation. As a teenage rock'n'roller I'd considered Scottish folk music a hinterland of kilted buffoonery. Now I heard it anew, and the music I was in love with was the music of my own ancestors. In the bloom of their youth on the Isle of Mull my great-grandparents themselves might well have shaken a leg to 'The Fiddler's Frolic'.

I flew back to Dublin in the grip of a dream, devouring Celtic albums on my Walkman at the rate of nine or ten a day, and having made the decision to go immediately to the west of Ireland, the cradle of Celtic culture. I wasn't up for dabbling; I wanted to step fully into this older world, absorb it, become it and bring back what I found, however long it took. And despite the pressure of the unfinished album, I was relaxed about time. A Canadian band, The Cowboy Junkies, mining the same vein of country and American roots we'd been exploring for two years, had pipped us by releasing *The Trinity Sessions*. That horse had bolted. And with *The Joshua Tree*, on which I heard the spiritual seeker vision and big music of the last two Waterboys albums re-calibrated as towering arena rock, U2 had relieved us of the responsibility of making the follow-up to *This Is The Sea*. I was free to explore, and both the road less travelled and the way of fascination pointed towards the Celtic dreamtime.

And so on a cold, clear afternoon in early January 1988, John Dunford drove me to Ireland's West Coast to look for a cottage I could rent for a few months. We arrived in Galway City at nightfall and checked into an old-fashioned seaside hotel where a wedding party was in full swing: a good omen. Dunford and I spent a week scouting County Galway to the North and Clare to the South, driving under vast ever-changing Atlantic skies through a land of lonesome harbours, wild hills and tiny coastal villages scented by the sweet, intoxicating smell of turf fires. And as we drove, John recounted to me the entire history of modern Irish music while the car stereo crackled to the sounds of Sweeney's Men, Planxty and a hundred more. But as far as finding a house went we were out of luck. Cottages that looked enticing in brochures turned out to be behind petrol stations; others were in lonely depressing spots miles from anywhere; yet more were only available in season, from April to September.

On the seventh day we were in one of Galway's music bars where a session was in progress, five or six players hunched round a drink-strewn table. I knew one of them, a bouzouki-plucking mate of Vinnie Kilduff's called Brendan O'Regan who called me over to play. I sat down and banged away on my guitar, guessing the chords and stomping my feet. Then, gathering my breath between tunes, I fell into conversation with the musician on my left, a cheeky-faced fiddler. He knew I was 'yer man from The Waterboys' and asked me what I was doing in Galway.

'Looking for a cottage where I can stay for a few months and do some writing,' I replied.

'Oh? My old man's got a place, out along the coast. Meet me tomorrow and I'll show it to you.'

I didn't know whether this would turn out be a mirage like all the other leads Dunford and I had followed over the last week, but there was something about my sparkling-eyed new friend, whose name was Sean, that I trusted.

Next morning we met him at a car park overlooking the harbour. 'Jump in your car and follow me,' he called with a grin. We drove out of town by the coast road in the only direction we hadn't yet explored. After a few miles we left the city behind. The full majestic expanse of Galway Bay opened on our left, while to our right lay a strange, rocky land of hills and ancient stone walls. I began to get goose bumps. The wildness of the land and the light on the bay did something fateful to me and I turned and said to Dunford, with a sudden certainty, 'This is the land of my soul!' And it really was. The western fastness of Connemara, into which we were advancing, would become my favourite place in the world and the spiritual home of The Waterboys.

After ten miles of coast Sean turned right and we followed him up a hill road with a kaleidoscope of tiny rocky fields on either side. On the crest of the hill was a modern white bungalow. We parked the cars, Sean opened the garden gate, and I walked up to the house. Standing on its doorstep I looked back downhill over the vastest land and seascape I'd ever seen, laid like glory under immense blue and white skies. My eye tracked far inland to the east where hazy mountains rumbled in the dim distance, then south across the shimmering face of Galway Bay and westwards to where the Aran Islands floated like three upturned boats on the far horizon, the broad Atlantic glistening in the sun beyond them. Peace and stillness enfolded the scene and the only sounds were the birds of the air, cars humming far away on the road below, and the haunting moan of the wind in the telegraph wires. I laughed out loud and rented the house on the spot.

A week later I moved in. I set up the living room, which overlooked the view, as a music space with an electric piano, record player and a low table for the industrial-size acoustic typewriter on which I did my writing. On the south and north walls of the room I stuck huge maps of Ireland and Scotland. In the big country kitchen I pinned up Irish ordnance survey maps, each showing a small part of the country in fantastic detail; houses, towers, old castles and the tiniest country lanes or boreens. I covered a wall with these, creating a montage that showed the whole sweep of the west of Ireland, then spent hours dreaming into the maps as I played my new Irish *bodhrán*, a primeval round drum of goatskin stretched across a shallow wooden frame, which made delicious stone-age *rubdub crackadub thwack* sounds.

On the third night Sean's 'old man' turned up to check me out. His name was Charlie Lennon and he had white hair and a long, serious face like one of the philosophers in *The Crock Of Gold*. He seemed very concerned about what condition I kept the house in and insisted on placing lace covers on the arms of all the chairs. But when Charlie saw the living room arrayed as a musical den he exclaimed, 'How wonderful!' and told me he was a fiddler and composer of traditional tunes. We became friends there and then and he took me to Hughes's bar, a stone-floored tavern in the nearby village of Spiddal. He sat me at a table in front of a roaring fire and made me play bodhrán while he and an accordionist played impossibly complex, almost classical tunes. The locals conversed in Irish around us, a winter wind blew in from the Atlantic and charged up the street outside, and I felt plugged into an older, saner world.

Soon I established a groove in my hilltop house of rising around noon and working through the day, playing and listening to music, writing songs and reading. I'd eat in the early evening – always the three 'b's: boil-in-a-bag braised beef, baked beans and baked potatoes – then work again late into the night, often till dawn. And as the mood struck, I'd cycle into Spiddal and organise a taxi to take me into Galway.

Galway was the port at the last outpost of Europe, at what was once the end of all things, the beginning of the unknown. And how much wonder and mystery still lingered in the first syllable of its name, that profound long 'Gal' with its evocation of distance and immensities. She was a convivial city then as now, but in 1988 Galway had a slow, magical character, mostly lost when it became a Celtic Tiger boomtown in the nineties. It was a cross between an old-fashioned county town and a hip village arts project. The counterculture – or at least a bohemian Celtic version – was a tangible presence, and its actors, poets, philosophers, hippies, writers, students and musicians co-existed happily with the old fishing folk, once the very lifeblood of Galway, and the robust country people of the west: ruddy-cheeked, broad-shouldered men and sharp-eyed queenly women from Connemara, Clare and Athenry. It was common to see wild-looking musicians, parchment-faced fishwives and flat-capped farmers contentedly sharing time, space and conversation in Galway's ancient pubs.

The city was large enough to be cosmopolitan, small enough to be homely. A roaring river, the Corrib, divided it in two and a network of sleepy canals, secret lanes and walkways turned its neighbourhoods into islands. Charming tumbledown streets with satisfyingly logical names like 'Shop Street' and 'Middle Street' were lined with archaic storefronts unchanged since the forties or fifties. Scruffy cargo ships and brightly coloured fishing boats anchored in the bustling harbour, and on the edge of the Atlantic lay Galway's greatest glory: the majestic spaces of South Park, a huge green common, opening onto the Bay and the western sky. I'd make raids on my favourite establishments, Kenny's Books and Powell's Music Emporium, then hook up with friends and join sessions in the pubs. Brendan O'Regan, my closest pal on the scene, was fond of shouting over the music, 'The craic is mighty!' He spelt it 'craic', of course, the ubiquitous Irish word for pleasure and high spirits, but whenever he said it I imagined a thin crack opening in the fabric of the universe and a bright light of joy pouring through.

I'd return to my hilltop eyrie late at night, head full of the evening's fun, arms laden with a haul of books and records to absorb. That winter in a chair snug by the fire I read Daniel Corkery's *The Hidden Ireland*, James Stephens' luminous faery novels, the complete works of J.M. Synge, Liam O'Flaherty's *The Ecstasy Of Angus*, Yeats, Douglas Hyde, Tomás O'Crohan's *The Islandman*, and *The Poems Of Egan O'Rahilly*, the eighteenth-century Gaelic satirist.

Spiddal village was charismatic too, comprising a long main street with a crossroads, three pubs, two general stores and a handsome grey-stoned church I never once stepped into. The residents were characters, one and all, seasoned and shaped by the uniqueness of the place and its raw Atlantic weather, a collection of walking tarot cards: stout, sad-eyed patriarch Festy Conlon; white-bearded American giant Hank, who'd marched with Martin Luther King in the civil rights years; sharp-tongued Celtic Queen pub-owner Brida Hughes; and a hundred other distinct personalities inhabiting an almost Shakespearean tableau of village intrigues and dramas, as if fate had shaken them all down to the end of Ireland to take part in a perpetually unfolding passion play. I was a tarot card myself – the Fool, surely – and entered wholeheartedly into the spirit of Spiddal. And because I'd arrived in the dead of winter, people treated me as a newcomer not a tourist. The O'Flaherty family who lived a hundred yards down the hill from my house kept an eye on me and brought me bags of turf and Polish coal. I had no TV, no radio, no phone, no fax, no email. If I wanted to contact the modern world I had to find a phone box or write a letter. For months the only way Chrysalis Records could contact me was by leaving a message in the Quays bar in Galway and it might be a week before I picked it up.

When a storm struck in February I tasted the full elemental power of the west. Great winds roared around the house for four days creating a wild fantasia of howls, moans, creaks and whistles while the windows bent inwards and pantheons of clouds scudded like chariots across the sky. The storm was all I could think about, all that anyone

I met on rare windblown forays into the landscape could talk about; the experience levelled all differences, humbled us all equally. When the storm finally blew itself out the stillness was like a benediction, as if a mighty god had passed and in his trail the wheels of the world had begun to turn again.

And as I watched the changing tapestry of the days unfolding before and below me I started seeing the world through new eyes. I began to understand the mysteries of landscape: how every bluff, outcrop, hill and promontory had its significance, that each part of the landscape 'spoke' to every other part in a language beyond words. And I became aware of a subtle presence, a lingering sense of the past, which cloaked the west of Ireland like another dimension as if older times were here simultaneously, overlaid one on another like wavelengths. This presence acted on my imagination like a drug and made everything look huge, as if Ireland were as psychically vast a country as America was physically vast. And in these stirrings I found the answer to the question that had assailed me after the Pictish Festival a year before: *what did it mean to be Celtic?* Being Celtic was a way of seeing and feeling, of interpreting and inhabiting the world. The Celtic domain wasn't simply a physical landscape spanning Ireland, Scotland, Wales and other regions on the Atlantic rim – it was a dream-space, a kingdom of the imagination with a coherency, a taste all its own, *room to roam* as the George MacDonald poem said. And this dream-space was inside me too. I was beginning to move at its speed and become a conscious participant in its quicksilver drama.

Yet one mysterious dimension remained out of reach. Spiddal was in the Irish-speaking region, the *Gaeltacht*, and the language, which I heard in the shops and pubs, was a medium through which more of the experience of being in this culture was communicated than ever could be through English. Locals speed-talking in Irish across the counter of the general store were plugged into a communal mind from which I was excluded. Irish was the same language as the Scottish Gaelic my grandmother spoke, and I was separated from it by only two generations, yet it might have been a thousand years. I picked up a few words but the inner life of the language remained secret, a tantalising but unknowable dimension of consciousness all around me.

I wasn't the only cosmonaut heading west into the Celtic mystery. The Fellow Who Fiddles, seeking trad tunes to collect, had lit out for Doolin, a one-street, three-pub village on the Clare coast with a reputation for music far outstripping its size. And Vinnie Kilduff had made for Inishmore, largest of the Aran Islands, a wild outpost on the Atlantic horizon from which he sent me postcards with images of wild goats and the words 'I'm shouting over the bay to you' scrawled in his whistler's hand, cajoling me to visit. And on an early March day I did.

I brought Anto with me. The Human Saxophone had just arrived in Spiddal from London when I whisked him off to Galway airport (two huts and a hangar in a field east of the city) to catch the flight to Aran. It was a gusty day and we flew low in the sky, the little propeller plane bucking and dipping as the ubiquitous landscape of the west, all its mad knot-work of tiny fields and haphazard stone walls, passed beneath us, soon replaced by the grey roiling face of the sea. After only ten or twelve minutes the plane touched down on a grassy meadow in the middle of sand dunes, the propeller engines stopped and we stepped out into the low moan of the wind. Vinnie stood waving to us outside the solitary airport hut, his reddish-blonde hair blown back from his face, and as we approached I saw he was changed. Six weeks in Aran had left its mark: his cheeks were ruddy from the constant wind, but there was something else, a far-sighted look of nobility as if he'd morphed into a demi-god or a Viking, and his eyes were narrow and sharp like a bird's.

Vinnie had hired a minibus, one of only a few vehicles on the island, to take us the three miles to the main village, Kilronan, and as we drove we entered an otherworldly landscape. The colours, grey and green, were similar to the mainland, but unlike Connemara's naturally random tableau, Aran looked *designed*, as by a darker god.

The land rose on our left in a series of scarped stone terraces to a high ridge dramatically silhouetted against the sky. Straight ahead lay a hulking mountain-sized shoulder of rock with no trees or foliage of any kind, only more scarped terraces slanting crazily downwards from right to left. Nowhere was there anything soft or rounded on which the eye might rest, nor any familiar shape or suggestion of conventional beauty. And the scale was all wrong: it was too large, as if a tribe of giants had abandoned the place. As we drove deeper into this domain its personality closed in on us, dense and primal: a strange sensation for me, even after six weeks of cultural decompression in Spiddal, but what must Anto have been feeling? Yesterday he'd been doing his laundry in Hammersmith!

We rounded a bay and approached Kilronan, a cluster of white buildings hunched on a hill round a little harbour. I noted a general store, a tourist shop not yet open for the season with windows full of Aran sweaters, and a sturdy village hall made of the same grey rock as the land. The bus dropped us off by the harbour. Vinnie was staying in a house a few yards away and we threw our bags in then went straight out again to explore. At a harbour-side shed grandly named Aran Island Bicycles we hired bikes and hooked up with a local musician mate of Vinnie's called Sean Watty, a bulky fellow with a World War Two moustache and milk-bottle spectacles. As we mounted our bikes Sean told us, 'Go slowly now, and you might see something.'

I wondered what he meant. The play of light on the land? Glimpses of the inner soul of Aran? Whatever, I took the advice to heart and found myself cycling at a gentle pace alongside Sean in companionable silence, all senses open, a light spring breeze on my face. Across Galway Bay I could see the mountains of Connemara gathered like a cluster of giant buffalos, red and brown in the afternoon sun with slow cloud shadows moving over their flanks. And as we left human familiarity behind and penetrated deeper into the stone landscape, it wove its spell around me, producing a detached, mesmerised mind-set. *Stoned*, indeed. We cycled for several miles until we reached to foot of a hill where we lay down our bikes and began a long climb. After fifteen minutes Dun Aengus loomed theatrically above us, a ruined prehistoric fort, dark against the sky, a hundred yards across with stone walls three times the height of a man. A tiny opening came visible in its side, with a window of blue sky showing cheerfully through, and we squeezed through this, coming into the central enclosure.

It was a sudden clear space; a roofless amphitheatre bounded on three sides by stone-age walls and on the fourth by a shockingly bare cliff edge and the vast panorama of the Atlantic. Far to our left the middle Aran Island, Inishmaan, rose out of the water like a dark snakehead and beyond it the coastline of Ireland tumbled endlessly southwards. I followed it with my eye until deep in the distance the thin faint line of the land faded into curling shapes of horned mountains like wisps of blue smoke on the horizon: the peaks and crests of County Kerry, last outpost of Europe, looking like a domain of magic, the lair of poetry and wizards. Anto and I had brought instruments, figuring that when we got to Dun Aengus we'd have a celebratory tune, but hundreds of feet above sea in a bracing Atlantic wind our hands were too cold to play. We would get music enough that night. Our imaginations satisfied, we descended the hill and cycled back across the island in gathering dusk. We ate greasy fish and chips by the light of the few Kilronan street lamps, then headed into one of the village pubs.

The American Bar was as bright and cosy as the land was barren. Locals sat round the walls and down the length of the bar, all with the same wind-blasted cheeks and sharp, bird-like eyes as Vinnie. A corner was set aside for us where Sean Watty and another local musician called Máirtín were waiting with accordion and banjo at the ready. We squeezed in under the unnerving gaze of the villagers as the pub held its collective breath. Word had spread that there were members of some kind of pop group in the island and by our next actions we would prove ourselves duds or kings. And what would we play? Sean and Máirtín were strictly trad musicians and Anto was a blues man, but we found common cause in an ad hoc repertoire comprising a battery of country hoedowns and robust Irish reels with warlike titles like 'The Silver Spear' and 'The Sailor On The Rock', over which Vinnie shouted chords while stomping his foot on the wooden floor. A slap of the banjo and we were off, with Sean and Máirtín playing like warrior strongmen; Sean ripping wild laughing torrents of music out of his accordion while Máirtín struck notes from his banjo like sparks from a flint. Within minutes we were surrounded by people cheering, shouting and talking unfeasibly fast in Irish.

Towards the end of the night a group of huge dark-eyed young men dressed in tweed waistcoats and flat caps burst through the pub doors. These were the boys from Bun Gowla, westernmost village of the island, a remote storm-battered cluster of cottages seven miles away, who'd heard there were pop musicians on the island and had come to have some sport with us. They brought with them an atmosphere of time unbroken, and as we blasted out the reels they launched into a storm of savage step-dancing, heavy booted feet clattering rhythmically on the floor, grunts, shouts and whoops bursting in the air like fireworks. I'd played on the stages of New York, London and Hollywood, I'd fought in the punk wars and rock'n'rolled from Glastonbury to Glasgow, but nothing had been as wild as this. I looked over at Anto, his strumming arm a blur as he bashed his mandolin. He caught my eye, an understanding passed between us and as the riot of high spirits raged all around we laughed with pure pleasure.

Thus initiated into the community we found next day that, like Vinnie before us, we'd been granted the freedom of Aran. Everywhere we went people smiled and said hello. We'd become part of the local colour, celebrities not because of our status as Waterboys but because we'd participated in an ancient social ritual: playing music for the people at the end of their day's work.

On the morning of the day we left I made for the lonely southeast

143

coast of the island, clambering over cracked stone under warm March sun across the great ridge of Aran until finally I came to the edge of the Atlantic. Huge balls of spray were exploding off the low cliffs, and the sound of the sea battering the island was a continuous roar. Far out on the fringes of the world I stood where the only powers were wind, stone and sea. Looking east my eyes fell on the snakehead of Inishmaan, dark and sullen in the ocean. All its houses were on the sheltered slopes of its northern ridge, facing inland towards Ireland, but on the bare southern side that swept recklessly to the Atlantic there were no buildings at all. Might Pan, the god of the earth and its wild places, I wondered romantically to myself, live on the back side of Inishmaan?

Pan! How much of my journeying, and even of rock'n'roll itself, was nothing more than a search for the spirit of Pan, for the combination of sacredness, wildness and freedom I mused on this for long sweet minutes while absently gazing into the onrushing waves, hearing them boom as they crashed full square into the cliffs below me. Then I turned my back to the wind, flipped up my collar, and made my way across the crackling stonescape, reaching Kilronan in time to say farewell to Vinnie and Sean Watty and catch a ride on a fishing boat back to the mainland with Anto.

CHAPTER 10

MANSION OF
MUSIC

Dunford steers the car through a crumbling stone arch then down a long slope with overgrown woodland on each side. At the bottom we cross a stone bridge and as I look down I see a white-flecked stream rushing underneath. The road rises again, veering left under the eaves of ancient oaks that grow so close they make a green tunnel speckled with jets and darts of flashing sunlight. Looking over Dunford's shoulder, I catch my first glimpse of an enigmatic grey building through the branches. Suddenly we emerge into a sunlit driveway. Before us is an ivy-clad mansion facing a broad lawn. Beyond is a painting-like view of Galway Bay with the mysterious silver hills of Clare in the distance. It is a scene of high magic, private and reserved, as if we've stumbled on one of Ireland's secrets.

We step out. As I turn towards the house its heavy wooden door opens and a woman appears, petite, dark haired, of a certain age as the French say, with a fidgeting Pekinese dog in her arms. Our guide Alec introduces her as Mavis and from her accent and bearing she is one of the old Irish landed gentry fallen on tough times. Traces of beauty linger in her handsome face and as I meet her gaze I look into the flinty eyes of a survivor. She ushers us into the house as the dog yaps angrily at Dunford. 'Quiet, Ambrose!' she scolds.

Inside is a dark corridor with a staircase on the right and a series of rooms on the left, facing lawn and bay, which we enter one by one. Each is a study in faded grandeur; ragged curtains, carpet-less floors and ancient furniture. Alec was right: Mavis could use the money. But the place is full of character and possibility. At the end of the corridor Mavis shows us a long sunlit dining room with chandeliers and wooden floor, large enough for the band. I clap my hands and hear a pleasing natural reverb, then imagine us set up and playing: Anto here, Steve there, drums in the bay window. Dunford and I look at each other and nod. Yes, this is our studio.

Back in Spiddal, with spring in the air and the last of my studio burnout blown away by the blustery winds of Aran, I was ready to go back to work and complete the album. But I was so at home in the west why not bring the band and crew, the whole shebang, and finish the record here? If we were all in this landscape, what music, what magic, might we make? I turned this outrageous thought round in my head for a few days, expelling doubts and conventional ideas one by one, until I recognised it was perfect. I called Dunford and we reprised our two-man travels, looking for a hall where we could set up a studio. We found several unsuitable venues (a damp hotel at Killary Harbour, a too-small country house in the Maamturk Mountains, a cold school hall near Screeb) until once again a meeting with a musician led us to our goal. We'd just returned to Spiddal after an expedition to deepest Connemara and were sitting in Hughes's bar talking to Alec Finn, a curly-haired exiled Yorkshireman who played in the Galway trad band De Dannan. When we told him what we needed he said: 'Why not use Spiddal House? It's big enough.' I'd never heard of this place, but Alec nipped out to the village phone box, made a quick call and arranged for us to see it straight away. It suited beyond our wildest hopes, and Dunford rented it from the owner Mrs Buckley – Mavis – for eight weeks on the condition that she move out. Then we sped back to Dublin to organise band and equipment.

We needed a drummer and Doug D'Arcy at Chrysalis suggested Patti Smith's old skin-basher Jay Dee Daugherty, the chap who'd asked me who I was in her dressing room ten years before. When he arrived in Dublin and walked into our rehearsals Jay Dee didn't remember me from 1978 and it was a long time since I'd listened to any Patti Smith records, but none of that mattered. From the first ear-blistering snare crack his drumming powered our music like a rocket blast.

Two days later we descended on Spiddal House. We commandeered three consecutive rooms overlooking the bay: a snug lounge with wood-panelled walls became the control room with the mixing desk; a large sitting room with French windows, striped walls and an antique piano was our den for hanging out and jamming in; and the dining room, as already decided, was the studio itself. Then we rented several holiday cottages to sleep in because we didn't plan on going stir-crazy by living in Spiddal House as well as working there. Steve, Anto and Trevor were in a house halfway down the hill from mine, Jay Dee Daugherty was shacked up in a one-bed cabin across the boreen, with a turf fire and no phone, probably wondering what the hell he'd got himself into, while Dunford, Jimmy Hickey and our young recording engineer Pat McCarthy were in a bungalow a short walk from Spiddal House.

No band ever worked in more ideal circumstances. Each morning I'd step out my door with plans for the day's music in my head, breathe in the sweet Atlantic air that tasted, as J.M. Synge would say, 'like wine through the teeth', cast my eyes over the awesome view, jump on my bike and swoop freewheeling down the long hill to the main road, then pedal a mile along the seafront, ocean breeze on my face. At the village crossroads I'd hang a right then turn left under the old stone arch, through the woods, across the bridge and finally walk in the door of our mansion of music to hear my bandmates already playing, drums and fiddles echoing through the hallway. As I sat strumming and singing in the studio this is what I saw: Jay Dee in a silver two-tone suit, clattering his drums in the bay window; Trevor Hutchinson standing by his double bass in the far corner, silhouetted against the sunlight; The Fellow Who Fiddles halfway down the room, swaying as he played, a microphone dangling over his fiddle to catch its sound; and Anto on my right, leaning over the keyboard of a Hammond organ like a cosmonaut steering a spacecraft, or crouched over his electric mandolin, absorbed in music.

And we meant business. Having learned from the previous year, I

147

made sure these were disciplined sessions. There were no ten-songs-in-a-day blowouts. We focussed on one track at a time, finished it, then moved on to the next, keeping to a strict schedule: 1pm until 10pm in the evening. These measures restored order out of our creative chaos and in a few days we had our first song nailed. It was one I'd just written called 'And A Bang On The Ear', a nine-minute country-rock romp with six affectionate verses about my old girlfriends, each capped by a request to give the girl 'a bang on the ear', code for 'say hello from me'.

Though I'd often make up joke songs in rehearsals, this lighter side had never percolated to the front line of Waterboys music and made it to a record. I didn't exactly have a rock reputation for humour. But something had shifted since I'd come to Ireland and I'd learned how to take the mickey out of myself without undercutting the point of a song. Polishing off 'Bang On The Ear', with tragicomic lines such as 'It started up in Fife, it ended up in tears', was something of a breakthrough for me, and it felt good. So did the fact that we'd pulled off the gambit of setting up a studio in the frontier wilds of the West of Ireland. With our first master successfully recorded and sounding as slick as if it had been made in London or New York, everyone was thrilled.

We were still dizzy with this sense of achievement when drama struck. Dunford had hired a local Peter Lorre lookalike called Bandy Donovan as our cook and caretaker. At first the arrangement worked well. When the crew were setting up, Bandy was a flash of local colour, handsomely praised for his cooking and made to feel like one of the team. But when recording began, meals became a pit stop and no one had any spare attention to spend on Bandy. Which was a shame because he was gay, not an easy gig in rural Ireland. And being cooped up in the grandest house for miles with a gang of good-looking young men, some of them wearing leather trousers, none of them evincing any romantic interest in him whatsoever, became too much for Bandy's sensitivities.

In the beginning this manifested in odd but harmless behaviour. First he gave us pottery mugs with our names inscribed on them, which we received with bemusement; then he morphed into a kind of loopy butler, emerging suddenly through the studio door holding aloft trays laden with glasses of sherry, a slightly creepy phrase on his lips such as 'I thought you would appreciate some refreshment, boys.' But we never drank alcohol while recording, let alone sherry, and our refusals, however diplomatically given, only increased Bandy's sense of isolation. On the day he got his first week's wages he compensated for his sorrows by downing some sherry himself, followed by several other libations and finally a dose of anti-depressant pills. Then he went and got a double-barrelled shotgun and marched on the house.

The first person he found was Jimmy Hickey. The World's Greatest Roadie was in the kitchen dreaming of spark plugs and gaffer tape when his reverie was interrupted by an agitated Bandy brandishing a shotgun and shouting. 'I'm going to kill you!' Terrified, Jimmy backed himself out of the kitchen into the yard. Bandy followed him, firing a shot in the air. Realising there was no way out of the yard, Jimmy panicked and pushed past Bandy back into the house. He ran to the jamming room where John Dunford was on the floor fixing a broken tape recorder. John looked up to see a Jimmy bursting into the room followed by the gun-waving Bandy, eyes darting in his head, a stream of curses on his tongue. When Bandy spotted Dunford, the man who'd hired him in the first place and caused all his troubles, he forgot about Jimmy and advanced on the author of his misfortunes with gun pointed. But Jimmy, regaining his composure (and courage) crept up behind as if to grab Bandy. Hearing Jimmy's movement, Bandy turned, averting his eyes long enough for Dunford to take his chance, grab the gun and smash its barrel on his knee. When he opened it and found live ammunition Dunford's nerve snapped and he grabbed the luckless Bandy by the throat and dragged him out of the house.

All this time I'd been under headphones in the studio recording a cheery version of 'Spring Comes To Spiddal', oblivious to the unfolding drama. When the song finished I emerged to hear a fracas at the front steps. I ran to the door to find a shaken and very angry John Dunford yelling, 'Just *fuck off!*' at a squirming Bandy who, perhaps not quite grasping the import of what had just happened, was asking whether he should 'go in and make the dinner now?'

As a reciprocal courtesy for recommending Spiddal House we invited Alec Finn to come and play, and on a Saturday afternoon he arrived with two fiddlers, his De Dannan colleague Frankie Gavin and my landlord Charlie Lennon, to record an ancient Irish air called 'Carolan's Welcome'. The track was completed quickly and, though no other song was planned, everyone wanted to keep playing. So I went upstairs to one of the house's several ghostly bedrooms and restructured a song we'd done at Windmill Lane called 'Killing My Heart', giving it a mazy new folk tune and retitling it 'When Ye Go Away'.

Downstairs I played it to the assembled musicians and an arrangement quickly came together, graced by Alec's stream-like bouzouki and Anto's bluesy mandolin. All we needed was a fiddle solo to finish the song but there were three fiddlers in Spiddal House that day, and which should perform it? Like men in a fable each took a shot. First Steve Wickham played a high dreamlike solo, full of sonic swoops and psychedelic murmurings. Then Frankie Gavin overdubbed a robust reel with cunning twists and ornamentations, topped off at song's close, while the tape was still rolling, with a cocky 'How's *that!*' But if these two, respectively Ireland's most famous rock and trad fiddlers, were the hares in the fable, and it was the tortoise, landlord Charlie, whose part made it to the record. While Steve and Frankie were recording their flashy solos, Charlie had been in the garden composing a tune on his fiddle. He cut a strange figure, standing amid spring blossoms, scraps of apparently tuneless melody floating periodically from his bow, his mournful face and white hair crowned by an ill-fitting blue baseball cap, an unlikely accessory which

150

provided some mirth to the onlooking band and crew. But when his turn came Charlie walked in, heedless of our scrutiny, and played a sublime tune called 'The River Road Reel', which sat on top of the track like a jockey on a horse and blew everyone away.

Not every song came together so smoothly. The Waterboys were masters of the great first take but a country waltz called 'In Search Of A Rose' took a prodigious ninety-nine, possibly the greatest number of attempts at any song by any band ever. The recordings absorbed four days, and we *still* didn't get the right version. We tried it slow, fast, with and without drums, with a full band and with nothing but mandolin and fiddle. We even tried the Brian Eno gambit, explained to us by Pat McCarthy, who'd worked on *The Joshua Tree*, which Eno had co-produced. It worked like this: at the end of a day spent unsuccessfully trying to nail a song, instead of simply 'trying it again tomorrow', the band commits to doing five takes first thing next morning then moving on to something else, regardless of how the five takes turn out. According to Pat this method not only focused the musicians but paradoxically defused the pressure on them, usually resulting in the elusive master being among the five morning performances. But while it may have broken whatever creative blocks U2 experienced, even this didn't work for poor old 'Rose', and the song was filed away to be re-recorded for some future album.

Everything else we attempted was successful, and a factor in this was the unseen extra member of the band, the sense of place. When Steve's multi-tracked fiddles blasted out the solo on 'When Will We Be Married', he was mimicking the Atlantic winds that barrelled down the Connemara roads. When Anto struck shards and glints from his slide mandolin on 'When Ye Go Away', he was conjuring the play of light that bewitched the gardens of Spiddal House and the glittering bay beyond. In other ways too location added colour to the work. When we needed extra musicians we sent to Galway for them, like button accordion maestro Máirtín O'Connor, summoned to add flourishes to 'Bang On The Ear'. Or they turned up unexpectedly, like the day Brendan O'Regan materialised at the control room window, waving his bouzouki, and was pressed immediately into service, leading Steve through countless exacting takes of the fiddle jig 'Dunford's Fancy'. And when we couldn't get the groove right on 'Jimmy Hickey's Waltz', Dunford nipped down to Hughes's bar to enlist some dancers. He returned fifteen minutes later with a gaggle of villagers who quickly told us we were playing too slow for them to waltz properly. We sped up and within minutes the master take was nailed, complete with sounds of the dancers' feet and the rustling of their clothes. Likewise, when we needed a party atmosphere for a track late one afternoon Dunford went to the village crossroads and invited a bunch of school kids to come up to the big house and help with the recording. A noisy crowd arrived and we stuck them in the studio, plied them with sweets and soft drinks, blew up balloons, handed round pins to stick in them, then taped the uproar that ensued.

Any place that music happened, in or out the studio, was a recording opportunity. I used to sing my demos into an old-fashioned Nagra tape machine (the one Dunford had been fixing when Bandy Donovan tried to shoot him) and I left it running one night when a gang of Galway musicians came to my hilltop house for a party. Next day I played back the tape and found a joyously ramshackle version of Woody Guthrie's 'This Land Is Your Land', which I half-remembered us doing in the blur of the night before. One section, in which Wickham sang the famous chorus with Irish place names inserted instead of American ones, had a real power to it, and I placed this excerpt at the end of the finished album. If we needed a sound effect – a car driving off or the sound of waves – we went into the landscape and recorded it. And if we fancied playing outside we just did so. For one song I wanted the sound of a distant faery band so we set up on the roof, amid the branches of overhanging trees, and played our bodhráns and bouzoukis into the wind, capturing a hazy, far-off otherworldly music.

Working in a mansion in the charged atmosphere of Spiddal also had a deeper, more personal effect on band and crew. I watched them go through the seasoning I'd experienced a few months earlier, the withdrawal from TV, radio and telephones, the alignment with older ways of seeing and being. I saw my friends develop into archetypes of their own as if the atmosphere was drawing out their essential selves: Wickham a magical clown, Anto a roguish artful dodger, Dunford a merry court counsellor and Jimmy Hickey a warlike man at arms.

Doug D'Arcy came to check out our progress in late May. We played him the work as he sat in the control room, legs crossed, neck stretched forwards and eyes tight shut in an attitude of rapt listening so intent I couldn't figure out whether he was joshing us or being serious. If Doug had come expecting a set of rock songs he didn't let on. He digested our trad and country-rock sounds, pronounced himself happy and we took him off to Hughes's for a celebration drink. In the dark noisy pub, standing squashed between late night revellers, I overheard Doug instructing John Dunford to organise a car to take him to Galway Airport in the morning. In that moment, as I noticed myself bristling and thinking, 'Hey, that's one of *my* men you're ordering,' I realised what tarot card *I* was playing: the Emperor.

As we approached the end of the sessions, spring gave way to summer and a spell of gorgeous weather enfolded the west of Ireland. This and the long light evenings impacted on us like a draught of magic and turned us what in older, more innocent times would have been termed fey. In this mood we embarked on our biggest project, the musical arrangement of W.B. Yeats's faery poem 'The Stolen Child'. The basis of the music was my rolling piano, over which Steve and Anto played long chords and wave-like swells. But for the lead instrument I invited a young Scottish musician to join us. We knew Colin Blakey as the flute and whistle player of We Free Kings, and I loved his Pan-like flute sound. I asked Colin to give 'The Stolen Child' an otherworldly quality and this he did, concocting an exquisite set of melodies that rang like a summons to an older world.

The sense of enchantment deepened when Galway drummer Padraig Stevens came to play percussion. Padraig was an earthy hippie in his early forties who wore hand-knitted pullovers and thick spectacles, lived in a place with the stone-age name of Ugool, and struck me as an Irish version of Stig Of The Dump – a crafty, capable fellow somehow displaced from ancient times into the modern age. Sitting behind drums in the bay window, the sun's rays splitting against his stocky silhouetted frame, Padraig held a string of little brass bells in each upraised hand and at judicious points throughout the song shook a pealing from them like the rustle of tiny silken curtains being parted; the sound, I imagined, of the faeries ushering the stolen child into their kingdom.

Finally we needed a voice to recite the poem. I'd already sung the choruses, with their 'Come away, human child' refrain, but I didn't like the way my voice sounded speaking the verses. In the Spiddal general store a few months earlier I'd bought a cassette by a local Gaelic singer called Tomás Mac Eoin. Tomás, whoever he was, had a Matterhorn of a voice, a sound hewn from rock yet full of a warm broken humanity. I could easily imagine him reciting 'The Stolen Child', and I loved the idea of engaging with the local tradition. According to the cassette inlay card Tomás lived in the village of Carraroe, twenty-five miles up the coast, and one evening Trevor and Anto drove there to seek him out. They tracked him to his cottage where, mystified by these hairy creatures and their talk of 'vocal overdubs' but recognising the famous name of W.B. Yeats, Tomas agreed to do whatever it was they were asking.

If Colin and Padraig brought a tantalising echo of an older time, this guy was the whole symphony. Tomás walked into Spiddal House like a punch line, six feet three inches of Dickensian magnificence, the kind of old world character that has long disappeared in Britain yet lingers in Ireland. He was handsome, with a long-brimmed blue cap, an ambling limp and a quavering high-pitched speaking voice in which he delivered self-mocking statements like, 'I'm nothing but a nuisance' or, running his hand ruefully over his balding head, 'There used to be waves, now there's only the shore!' (This humour could also devastate and deflate. A year later I heard a loud-voiced American boast in a dressing room about how he could, 'git in mah car in the morning, drive for twenty-four hours and *still* be in Texas!' Tomás, overhearing this, interjected in tremulous tones, 'Oh japers, I had a car like that once.')

It wasn't easy recording Tomás – getting his performance on tape was like squeezing the Matterhorn into a jiffy bag. He was willing, certainly, and had the awesome powers of concentration common to people raised in an oral tradition. But because he was a *Sean-nós* singer (a performer of unaccompanied slow airs) and a native Irish speaker for whom English was a second language, Tomás was far from comfortable reciting Yeats's elegant, tongue-twisting lyrics in time to a piece of music.

The session was a spectacular failure. Tomás couldn't find the beat within the music and his pronunciation was poor, with many amusingly mangled words. And he'd never worn headphones in his life. But our new friend was no quitter. He insisted on a second session a few days later and went back to Carraroe determined to practise the poem until he could speak it like a natural. When we tried again there was a huge difference. Tomás had probably been reading the poem aloud every waking moment since we'd last seen him, and he had his delivery nailed. But we still had the timing problem. Dunford and I were racking our brains wondering how to solve this when Tomás suggested a solution – would I sit with him in the studio and cue him for every phrase?

We went into the studio, the rock'n'roller and the *Sean-nós* singer, and sat facing each other across the gulf between our different worlds. I felt like a whippersnapper before this emissary of a venerable tradition, and didn't relish the job of cueing him. But Tomás was putting himself in my hands and I realised that if I wanted to bridge the gulf and bring back the fruits of the older world, I had to stretch out a metaphorical hand and meet Tomás halfway; we had to *be* the bridge. So I bit the bullet and when the music started playing I gave Tomás a gentle signal with my hand a split-second in advance of where I imagined each line of the poem falling. And he responded, his giant of a voice rolling out the rich syllables on cue like an old god pouring wine down a mountainside. Verse by verse, line by line, signal by signal, Tomás delivered and soon we had the poem fastened snugly to the music, worlds merged and job well accomplished. After a celebratory cup of tea in the kitchen, Tomás, his blue cap tilted at a rakish angle, was chauffeured back to his cottage in Carraroe, a relieved and happy man.

The experience of listening to Tomás's voice invoking the haunted islands of 'The Stolen Child', interwoven with Blakey's enchanted flute, hour after hour, day upon day, increased the spell that descended on us that last week at Spiddal House. We seemed to need less sleep, time was slowed down and the playing of the band was shot through with sweet longing. The house itself seemed to have become charged with magic, and walking through its rooms and halls in the long evenings was like passing through gold light. But not everyone was affected benignly.

After eight weeks of being a tarot card in Spiddal Jimmy Hickey was close to snapping point anyway, but the oncoming midsummer madness tipped him over the edge. One night while we were working on 'The Stolen Child', Jimmy got dirtily drunk on whiskey, went into the jamming room, sat behind the spare drum kit and for the first time in his life began to play. The noise was diabolical, like an army of orcs bouncing garbage bins on an iron roof. All work was impossible so our production manager, a mate of Dunford's called Jake who'd been brought in to steady things after the shotgun incident, was despatched to stop it. Five minutes later the din was still going on, only now with schoolboy bass-playing added. I stepped into the room to find Jimmy looking like a distant caveman relation of himself, with bloodshot eyes and blue skin, viciously bludgeoning the drums. I knew Jimmy's nickname among the Dublin roadie fraternity was 'Captain Muck' – *muck* being an Irish term for hedonism, high jinks and the robust consumption of alcohol – but this was Field Marshall Muck, all arms and gangly legs too big for the drum kit, spittle slithering down his chin. The World's Greatest Roadie had reverted to a pre-civilised state. Backing him on bass was Jake, who feebly claimed, 'I thought playing with him was the best way to calm him down.' Only Dunford knew how to play Androcles to Captain Muck's lion, and so he it was who gently coaxed Jimmy into coming out from behind the drums and convinced him to leave the studio. 'He's Spiddalled, man,' was Dunford's expert prognosis, and the next morning Jimmy was banished to Dublin, to the tender attentions of the one person who could soothe him, his patient wife Ceppi.

Two days later, with peace restored, 'The Stolen Child' was completed and on the last night of recording we invited friends for a jam session. There was a feeling in the air that something special would happen; perhaps one of those amazing sessions where the band was swept up in the moment and played one after another master-quality performances in first takes, snatching complete records out of the air. But in fact our last hurrah in Spiddal House was a quiet anti-climatic affair; our energy was spent and the magic, having dwelt among us, had moved on. We drank champagne then made gentle music all night. I remember Dylan's 'Buckets of Rain', some Bo-Diddley-ised Irish reels and a Robbie The Pict composition called 'The Pictish National Anthem', until at 8 am a gang of brawny humpers from Galway arrived to pack up the gear. As they dismantled the mixing desk and hauled it onto their truck I stood in the garden, Artist-King of Spiddal House for a few last golden minutes while the sounds and shouts of working men filled the air and a morning breeze blew in from the sea. That night we had a wrap-up party which began in Hughes's bar, moved to someone's back garden and finally wound up at Steve and Anto's bungalow. The last scene I remember before I went to bed was a chorus line of Waterboys and Spiddalfolk kicking their legs in the air in a kind of west of Ireland can-can, all of them shouting, smoking reefers and looking like they were in severe danger of being happy.

We returned to Dublin the next afternoon and it was like being flung out of Eden back into a crazy land. Within days I could feel the city's frantic energy scouring the wildness off me and undoing the west's enchantments. A more serious cultural decompression followed a week later when Dunford, Pat McCarthy and I flew into Britain to mix the album at Rockfield Studios on the Welsh/English border. By God, rural Britain was dull: all high hedgerows, straight-laced towns and sensible fun-free pubs. Rockfield at least was a decent studio, one I knew from earlier Waterboys records. It occupied the courtyard and outbuildings of a farm and I liked the owner, an eccentric Welsh chatterbox called Kingsley who made his rounds each evening, looking in on the bands as if he was checking the cows in the stalls. But faced anew with the job of sifting through the maze of music we'd recorded since 1986 my vacillation returned and the perennial curses of the residential studio – isolation, boredom, absence of stimuli and inspiration, set in. Slowly, crawlingly, the song selections and mixes were done until, at last in late August 1988, thirty-two months after breaking ground in Windmill Lane, I finalised the album and called it *Fisherman's Blues*.

Chrysalis released it that October with a cover picture of band and crew outside Spiddal House. But the twelve songs, six from Spiddal and six from Windmill Lane, told only a fraction of the story not just of the music we'd made but of all that had happened since I'd come to Ireland three years earlier. We'd recorded nearly a hundred tracks and twice as many outtakes, probably the largest body of work ever for one album; and the stylistic and personal changes the music documented were as deep and manifold as some bands go through in whole careers. *Fisherman's Blues* could and should have been a double or triple album but most of the Dublin recordings, including many of our best moments, would remain unfinished for another decade.

Three hundred and seventy four master reels, piled floor to ceiling and wall to wall in a room at Windmill Lane, waited for the day twelve years hence when I'd return to complete the work.

We didn't even understand the story ourselves yet. Time and the west of Ireland had changed us. Steve's marriage disintegrated on his return to Dublin; Anto would come back later to raise a family in Galway; and Trevor would leave The Waterboys in a couple of years and became a full time trad musician, never to play in a rock'n'roll band again. Meanwhile, in the months we'd been riding the winds of the old world, rock had discovered raves, ecstasy and sampling. *Fisherman's Blues* would become the biggest selling Waterboys album but at the moment of its publication our trajectory couldn't have veered further from the rock mainstream.

As for me, I figured music wasn't worth the air it occupied if it didn't change both its makers and its listeners, but I was altered by my adventures to a degree beyond my comprehension. I stood looking back over the three years, wondering what the hell had happened. Unable to articulate the contents of my mind I decided to give no interviews, and did the one sensible thing I could and took The Waterboys back on the road. We called up Jay Dee Daugherty, Vinnie Kilduff, Colin Blakey, Roddy Lorimer and Tomás Mac Eoin and went out mob-handed on a sell-out forty-five date tour of Britain and Ireland. It was a storming comeback, almost my 'colourful travelling musical explosion' band-vision made real. But not quite. The last missing elements, whatever they were, would soon appear.

CHAPTER 11

SHARON HAS A TUNE FOR EVERY BEAT OF HER HEART

Dawn in Kinvara. In the grey light a soft rain is falling, pattering gently on an iron roof somewhere nearby. I stand in a doorway looking out on a deserted street, drinking in the soul of the May morning while an achingly perfect melody, sad yet bright, gentle yet strident, comes from the front parlour of the house behind me. Through its open window, Sharon Shannon's accordion is spilling out luminous peals of melody, a cascading chain of sound that steals my heart utterly. The tune is a Celtic march that reminds me of Scotland and yet, as it rises and swoops through the morning air, Sharon's accordion evokes centuries of Ireland; its plaintive tone connects to the past that lingers like a drift of smoke over the towns and hills of the west of Ireland.

An acoustic guitar, played by an Australian hippie called Steve Cooney, backs the accordion with a ragged rootsy strut. The two musicians deal out the tune over and over, now advancing towards a triumphant climax, now dropping to a muted refrain, always in absolute sympathy and taking my stricken heart with them on every turn and twist of the journey, though neither knows I'm still here listening. As I stand at the door with my senses wide open, all the elements that make up the moment – the morning, the rain, the crying gulls, the sleeping village, the enchanted tune, the passion of the musicians, and the myriad thoughts and emotions that run like a river through my mind and soul – blend into one exquisite feeling and a thrill of joy runs through me like a white fire. And though I will spend the rest of my life yearning for what

I felt in this moment, I don't care, for I have heard the sweetest music a man can hear, in the most perfect circumstances, and my heart has been cleansed, uplifted and redeemed.

It was The Fellow Who Fiddles who met her first. Around the time I discovered Spiddal, Steve went to Doolin on the Clare coast. Every night for several weeks he stuck his fiddle under his arm and walked from his rented harbour-side cottage to the village and joined the sessions that roared perpetually in its three pubs. As well as getting a crash course in trad music he befriended the musicians who lived and played there, and among them was a nineteen-year-old kid called Sharon Shannon. She came from the nearby town of Corofin, and according to the Fellow she was something special, 'a mighty, mighty musician.' I was intrigued by this description, which conjured an image of a Herculean demi-god rather than a young girl, but it would be a year before I met her myself.

A friend introduced us on a November day outside Neachtain's pub in Galway. All I remember is an elfin face in the rain poking out of the hood of a blue cagoule, though even in that brief glimpse there was a hint of confidence and mastery. When we played Galway on our *Fisherman's Blues* tour that Christmas, Sharon came backstage. She was five feet tall with a little girl fringe and a pair of dungarees and in the broadest, most lilting Irish country accent she said, 'That was the very best concert I *ever* was at!'

I was hanging out a lot in Galway between tours, renting my favourite Spiddal cottage, and in the early months of 1989 I bumped into Sharon a few more times. She was always in a hurry, carrying her accordion – the 'box' – on her way to some session or other. We hadn't yet played together when, that May, shortly after the British leg of the *Fisherman's Blues* tour, I got a call from John Dunford inviting me to come and record with her. She was holed up in the village of Kinvara, south of Galway. Dunford, the canny operator, had had his eye on

Sharon for a while and recognised she was a player of the ages, a special talent bound for whatever form of greatness trad music could bestow. He'd offered to record an album for her, she'd accepted, and with his mate, a moustached mover and shaker called Philip King, Dunford had set up a portable recording studio in the bar of Winkles Hotel. All kinds of trad luminaries had been invited, including Donal Lunny. Lunny was The Greatest Living Irish Musician, the bouzouki-playing mastermind behind Planxty, The Bothy Band and Moving Hearts, three bands whose music ran like a bright flame through the story of modern Irish music. I'd played with Donal when he guested on a few *Fisherman's Blues* sessions, but we weren't quite at ease with each other.

This was because of how we'd met. In 1986, when I was new to Dublin, I needed information on local recording engineers. My girlfriend Irene, who managed Windmill Lane, suggested I ask Donal. She phoned and asked him if he'd meet up with Mike Scott to give some friendly advice about the Irish studio scene. Donal agreed and even remarked, 'Mike Scott? Oh, he's a fine man!' I was delighted. The great Donal Lunny thought I was a *fine man*!

The meeting was at five o'clock next day in the Palace Bar, one of those stained-glass and wood-panelled pubs for which Dublin is renowned. The place was crowded, full of Dubliners having an after-work drink, and I was standing at the bar when Donal walked in. I recognised him from album covers: a dark-eyed, good-looking man with a distinctive bushy moustache. He approached, craning his neck this way and that as he pushed through the scrum, but walked right past me to the back of the pub. Then he pushed his way forwards again, still peering all around, not noticing me despite my standing on tiptoes and trying to catch his eye. Obviously he didn't know what I looked like. As he squeezed past me for the third time, I leaned over and said, 'You're looking for someone.' At last he registered me.

'Yes,' he said curtly as if I'd interrupted him in some very important business, 'I'm looking for Robin Scott.'

Oh shit. He'd got me mixed up with another British musician. Robin Scott had written and sung a hit called 'Pop Muzik' in the late seventies, and had recorded in Ireland some years before. Clearly Donal had meant *Robin* Scott when he'd said 'he's a fine man.' He didn't have a clue who I was.

As I stood mutely assimilating this dire development, Donal forgot about me and continued scouring the bar. I wondered what to do. It was humiliating enough to be mistaken for someone else but I didn't fancy compounding the matter by revealing Donal's mistake to him and enduring the embarrassment that would follow. So I watched him give up his search and leave the bar and after a few minutes, when I figured he'd be a safe distance away, I walked out too. To my horror he was standing on the pavement a few yards away, quizzically stroking his moustache as he scanned the street looking in vain for Robin Scott. He saw me watching him and must have thought, 'There's that guy again.' Now doubly embarrassed I slunk away in the opposite direction, imagining Donal's mystified eyes burning into my back.

A few streets away I found a phone box and called Irene. 'He thought he was meeting *Robin* Scott!' I cried. Irene said she'd call and find out what happened. Several hours later she rang me at my flat. 'Donal's mortified,' she said, 'he got the names mixed up, and he's happy to meet you whenever you want.' As it happened The Waterboys were recording at Windmill Lane the next day, so I left a message on Donal's phone inviting him to come and play with us.

Donal turned up a couple of hours into the session, and when he saw me he pointed stagily and said '*There* you are!' as if it had been me he'd been looking for all the time. This was well intended, and a measure of the kind fellow Donal was, but I was too young and raw to meet this gesture halfway. The older man, it seemed to me, had papered over the misunderstanding with pretence and left the truth of the incident unacknowledged. I was stiff and uneasy with him during the session. Donal and I bumped into each other several times over the next few years, but I never got over the awkwardness of that first encounter. So when Wickham and I strolled up the main street of Kinvara village on our way to record with Sharon Shannon, and spied Dunford and Philip King walking towards us out of the dusk with Donal, moustache and all, my heart sank.

I was wearing a pale green suit I'd bought a few weeks earlier for a wedding, and when Donal saw us approaching he called out across the street, 'You'll fill that suit yet!' This genial crack, the older man's affectionate witnessing of the younger, acted like a tonic and we were friends thereafter, if never quite bosom buddies, and allowed us to relax in each other's company as we got on with the job of midwifing Sharon Shannon's birth as a recording artist.

Winkles was on a lane off Kinvara's main street, a plain white building that gave no hint of its status as a hotel or of the delicious scene that awaited inside. Steve and I entered to find a long dark bar with threadbare but cheerful décor from the fifties. At the near end a space had been cleared and a circle of chairs assembled. Road-worn acoustic instruments lay on or against the chairs, and the floor was strewn with wires, instrument cases and empty glasses. The musicians were on a break and sat at the long bar, half of them grandees like Lunny farmed in by Dunford, the rest local playmates of Sharon's such as teenage tin-whistler Brida Smyth and scowling, soft-hearted Eoin O'Neill, a giant who cradled a spindly bouzouki in policeman-sized arms. The owner, a gregarious music lover called Tony Moylan, held court behind the bar and poured everyone free drinks. A bunch of music had been recorded and the word was that Sharon was on a roll. And indeed within minutes of our arrival the twenty-year-old box-squeezer was back in position, hurtling through set after set of high-energy tunes, notes scattering from her fingers like machine gun fire in a shiny, impossibly fast but beautifully articulated stream of pure music.

I'd never considered the idea that an accordion player could be a star, but here was the reality. Sharon sat on a low chair, a small yet powerfully charismatic figure, bobbing her head cheerfully side to side with a magnetic smile as if to say 'Hello! Isn't this fun!' while functioning as the dynamo in the centre of a perpetually changing rota of accompanists. First Lunny strumming away on his bouzouki, as always like a happy clockwork toy, then Eoin O'Neill on his, then a rootsy guitar picker called Gerry, while the melody line players – whistlers, fiddlers and flute johnnies – revolved as well, each taking their turn as Sharon's partner. Even U2's Adam Clayton, entering the scene with an air of genial bemusement, having been shoehorned into the event by the cross-cultural diplomatic ministrations of Philip King, gamely added some rudimentary bass to a tune or two. Dunford orchestrated proceedings, scratching his bristling jaw at a portable mixing desk in an alcove at the far end of the bar.

Close to midnight Wickham and I were called. We worked up a bluegrass version of Dylan's 'Forever Young', which Sharon executed with a mix of sensitivity and naivety, for her forte was instrumental tunes and she was unaccustomed to playing songs. But her box and the Fellow's fiddle sounded strikingly beautiful together – a fateful, luminous sound like the reunion of two lovers. Sitting between them I heard the marriage of rock'n'roll and trad, and I was smitten. Immediately I wanted to hear it in a Waterboys context. With a sudden vision of an an all-time classic Waterboys line-up in my head I sidled over to Dunford when we finished, only to find he'd followed exactly the same train of thought. We resolved to invite Sharon to join the band for our next series of shows, a run of six, climaxing in a set at the Glastonbury Festival.

Many of the players stayed up all night, forming a once-ever ensemble called The Winkles Orchestra that made wild celebratory music till dawn, and when Donal Lunny and Adam Clayton got up at nine the next morning, fresh for the drive back to Dublin, they found us still there. I hitched a ride and drowsed in the back seat while Clayton gunned his car eastwards like a bullet and compared doleful notes with Lunny on the state of the Irish roads. Adam dropped us off on a dusty Dublin street in the noonday sun, and as Donal strode away indefatigably to another recording session I walked home, head in the clouds, whistling a tune I'd learned the night before and wondering whether Sharon Shannon would come and play with The Waterboys.

I needn't have doubted it. A week later she presented herself at the empty shop in Temple Bar where we rehearsed, tumbling through the door with several 'boxes', a couple of fiddles, and a bag of cassettes. And she wasn't the only new recruit. Seeking a gentler sound than the Jay Dee Daugherty thunder of the *Fisherman's Blues* tour, I'd brought in a subtle Dublin drummer called Noel Bridgeman, a veteran of our Windmill Lane recordings. Sharon's accordion slotted sweetly between Steve's fiddle, Anto's sax and Colin Blakey's flute, and lent the band not just an Irish feel but an unexpected cajun twist. The number of different instrumental combinations available to me as bandleader suddenly multiplied exponentially. I was like a happy Tom Thumb inside an exquisite musical box.

As we worked I took the measure of Sharon. She was a model band member, eager to fit in and a quick learner. And she knew hundreds upon hundreds of tunes, endless streams of them flowing from her box and fiddle between songs, creating a contagious musical aura. 'Sharon has a tune for every beat of her heart,' one of her friends told me, and it was true. Sharon played tunes like other people breathed. She was fun too, up for whatever mischief was going, whether donning carnival masks with the rest of us for a joke performance in the shop window, or trying to shoot a video of Jimmy Hickey's willy while the World's Greatest Roadie took a surreptitious pee in a back alley. Yet there was a powerful will behind Sharon's cheerful exterior, and no readiness to suffer fools. She was equal parts friendly fun-person and the most driven musician I'd ever met.

Our first concerts were in the South of Ireland. Before the opening show in Wexford, Sharon peeked through the curtains and ran back into the dressing room exclaiming with surprise, 'The audience is standing up!' But if this was her introduction to rock'n'roll gigging, she took it in her stride. By the second night in Mallow she was a veteran, sitting between Wickham and me on a high stool, feet off the ground, smiling and laughing at the jumping front row of the crowd as she squeezed the magic out of her box.

We were supported on these shows by a trad duo called Cooney & Begley. Begley was from an old Irish musical family, a box-playing cattle farmer with a back like a wardrobe and the most beautiful singing voice. Cooney was a dreadlocked Aussie warrior who smoked reefers, wore sandals, spoke in a hippie patois and played a battered old nylon string guitar like he was driving a tank. They made brilliant, fiery music: breakneck polkas as tough as punk rock and hypnotic hornpipes punctuated by Cooney's Spanish guitar rallies and sudden dizzy runs of Broadway jazz chords. Then they would shift gear in a nanosecond for Begley to sing a song as elegant as an Elizabethan madrigal.

We loved them so much we brought them on our next three shows, all in England, and magic followed. For with Cooney, Begley and Sharon on board we achieved a critical mass of musicality and madness, exploding into a full-tilt never-ending session. We played anywhere and everywhere: on the tour bus, on boats, on planes, in hotel lobbies, bars and bedrooms, on the way to and from gigs, and backstage; breaking just long enough to play the Waterboys' show, then jumping right back into the session. On the morning we set off for Glastonbury we played wild merry jigs and reels with the sliding door of our van wide open as the tunes floated out over the roads and fields. We continued as the van negotiated the torturously slow approach to the Festival itself, through checkpoints and streams of revellers, until finally we trundled to a halt in the artists' area behind the Pyramid Stage. There was a bonfire ablaze with people sitting round it, but we just stayed where we were in the van, unwilling to break the spell, and kept playing for several more hours.

It was three years since we'd played Glastonbury. In 1986 we'd been a rock group. Now we were a band of friends and troubadours playing a golden, flowing tumbleweed of sound, with a complement of trad alchemists who made the sweet, wild music of the ages. When we eventually alighted from the van and joined the people round the fire, keeping right on playing and sweeping the cloak of our music, our brotherhood and our bonhomie around them, I felt like I was returning with the Key.

Our set had changed too, and when we played our festival slot the next evening some people were dismayed by the absence of rock ballast and by how few early Waterboys songs were played. But we had an appointment with our evolution and were stopping for nobody. Standing on stage between Sharon Shannon and The Fellow Who Fiddles, learning to fill my suit, I was abdicating from the roles that had been mapped out for me, both by others and by my younger self. I was a singer and musician, not a rock star. Our music still expressed wonder, but now it expressed community too. We still had power, but the power had gentleness in it, and I wasn't a ladder-climbing boy anymore. I was a man. After the show we left for Bristol Airport and on the way stopped to climb Glastonbury Tor. Standing on its high crest gazing over the panorama of the West Country, all that strange ancient tract of England with its church spires, water-cuts and queer-shaped hills, I realised this line-up of The Waterboys was the fulfilment of the 'colourful travelling musical explosion' vision I'd had on the plane from Edinburgh to Dublin two years before, and I resolved to ask Sharon, Colin and Noel to join the band full time.

Back in Dublin I sounded out the three permanent members. Steve and Trevor were in agreement but the Human Saxophone had misgivings. It might work for a while, was his viewpoint, but the musical winds will change. Anto knew me well, but he said he'd swing with it if it was what I really wanted to do. So the week after Glastonbury, during a four-night run of shows at Dublin's Olympia Theatre, I made my approach to first Noel, then Colin, then Sharon, and each said yes.

The shows at the Olympia marked a peak. A spirit of camaraderie reigned over the newly constituted band, guests and friends played onstage with us, and after each show there were long sessions in the artists' bar. The country, trad and roots influences were now fully integrated into our sound and we'd blurred the boundaries – no longer rock or folk, it was all just music. The Dublin rock and trad communities turned up in force as well as R.E.M., in town for their own shows, and halfway through the week our single 'And A Bang On The Ear', itself a blending of musical worlds, hit number one in Ireland. It felt like the pagan wedding of rock'n'roll and traditional music, with Wickham as best man, Sharon Shannon the bridesmaid, and me the handfaster.

This was the high summer of the Celtic Waterboys. In July we headed out on a swing through Europe with Cooney and Begley. Sharon, Blakey and Begley each brought huge repertoires of tunes with them, while Wickham, Cooney and I were composing our own. Writing music was as natural as breathing in rock'n'roll but less common in Irish trad, where most musicians didn't write, but the bug spread through the entourage with Sharon contributing to several tunes and even the conservative Begley inventing a reel in honour of his new-born daughter. I was carrying around books of Irish poetry, American folk music and long-forgotten Victorian novels, trawling them for lyrics to set to music, putting words to melodies from Sharon's repertoire and turning them into songs. And as we progressed through Copenhagen, Helsinki, Lisbon, Madrid and Valencia, each of us growing wilder, madder and more drunk on pure music, The Waterboys morphed into a travelling school of tune writers, collectors and folklorists.

And there was mischief. After the Turku Festival in Finland a gang of us drunkenly boarded a bus parked outside our hotel, not knowing where it was going. John Dunford and I engaged the occupants, two or three dozen broad-faced beaming Finns, all men, in a sing-song of the Dublin roadies' sin-phrase, 'How's your gee?' (the third word being the old Irish word for vagina) to the tune of 'Here we go, Here we go'. Off we sped into the Finnish night, destination unknown, thirty lusty Nordic voices roaring 'Howsagee! Howsagee!' without a clue what it meant.

It was the season of the midnight sun, a flickering hallucinatory daylight even in the small hours of the morning, and as the Finnish voices echoed round my head and the scenery whizzed by I felt like I was in a surreal dream. This impression was heightened when the bus stopped half an hour later in a wooded clearing close to a broad peaceful river. As the engines cut I heard the funky silken sounds of distant soul music floating through the trees. Was this heaven? Everyone got out and we followed the Finns down a winding path, the music growing louder, till finally we came to a long wooden clubhouse. We went inside and everyone started taking off their clothes, so we did the same. Then, still following our fellow passengers, we went through a thick wooden door into a long, low-ceilinged room, which was scorching hot and packed with men and women all buck naked except for the five of us – Dunford, Anto, Trevor, Noel Bridgeman and me – in our underpants.

We'd landed in some kind of secret Finnish super-sauna, and sat down, delighted with ourselves at having penetrated the esoteric nightlife of the natives. We were a little self-conscious but no one paid any attention to us. They were all too busy getting up and running outside, jumping into the river to cool off, running back into the sauna to get hot then doing it all over again. So that's what we did too. And when we got into the water for the first time (it was deliciously, skin-poppingly cold) we discovered it wasn't a river at all but a long inlet of the sea, with the line of the ocean visible between distant woodlands. We were chest deep in the Baltic! Delighted with this discovery, John Dunford announced 'I'm taking off my keks!' And following his solemn example we each took off our underpants and left them in the water, an offering to the beneficent gods of the north.

On our return to Ireland we decamped to my old haunting ground, the Aran Islands, to play a benefit for the local Lifeboat. We landed off the ferry the evening before the show and wound up in a hillside pub called Joe Watty's. The island was abuzz with the coming concert and the atmosphere in Watty's was electric, with a session centred around a leprechaun-like islander called Mattie Mullen. Mattie was built like Popeye, with the same muscular arms and sailor's cap, and played a bodhrán with his elbows sticking out while making eyes at the girls and winking at the boys.

We fell in with Mattie and when the pub closed he brought us to a birthday party for a lady called Nanny Quinn. Nanny, newly seventy-six and grand as a queen in lace blouse and beads, invited us into her cottage and boxed Mattie's ears as if he was a naughty nephew. But this was like no old lady's birthday party I'd ever imagined. Nanny's son, a fisherman, was removing the claws from huge lobsters on the brine-wet kitchen table; fiddles were skirling in the parlour and bodhráns went *thooom puckathoom* while three girls danced wildly on the wood floor, laughing and yelling at each other in English and Gaelic. Proverbs flowed from the tongues of rough-faced neighbours who stood round the edges of the room scoffing slices of birthday cake. And Mattie Mullen had a bottle of potcheen, a fierce piss-coloured Irish moonshine. We threw down shots of this throat-burning, liquid in Nanny Quinn's backyard under the western stars in the mad night of Aran and I felt the island sway beneath me like a giant surfboard. Mattie Mullen, his face a few inches from mine, looking like a goblin in the moonlight, cackled into my eyes and said, 'You're just like me!'

We played two shows the next night in the old village hall, feeling like pioneers as we gave the first-ever rock concerts on the island for a rowdy audience blighted by neither cynicism nor sophistication, their sense of wonder absolutely intact. Almost anything we did or played, we felt, would go straight into Aran island folklore, and this knowledge added extra layers of meaning to the performance.

Next morning we sailed to Galway City, where with and without the band I played nine times in a weekend: two Waterboys shows (sports hall and circus tent), Sharon Shannon's solo gig, a guest slot with The Saw Doctors, impromptu sessions in several pubs with assorted friends and strangers, a couple of Hank Williams numbers in a rebel bar with a middle-aged country and western duo, and even a stint on the main street, blasting through 'Back In The USSR' with a band of pimply teenage buskers.

Sharon's concert was a lunchtime show in a tiny packed theatre. All of the Waterboys guested, as well as Cooney and Begley plus several of Sharon's pals and her younger sister, a freckled banjo-playing sprite called Mary. When Sharon got paid she insisted on sharing the money with us all and, despite our protests, divvied it up equally to the last penny. Each of the fifteen musicians came away with twenty-seven Irish punts and forty-eight pence. We played one more show that summer at the Interceltique Festival in Lorient, Brittany, a bustling French seaside town where massed bands of bagpipers and bombardists paraded the streets making a noise as loud as war. And then we had six weeks off to draw breath.

Perhaps because I'd done something wicked in a previous life I spent most of this break producing an album for Cooney & Begley. The owners of the English label Cooking Vinyl had clocked the duo's set at Glastonbury and talked them into making an album. I was thrilled. I figured a record of Cooney & Begley's incendiary music would be a sensation in both the trad and rock worlds, a real boundary buster, so I quickly offered to produce. Cooking Vinyl agreed, happy to have a Waterboy's name on the package. And so on a mid-August day, only dimly aware of the travails that awaited me, I took the train from Dublin to Tralee in the County Kerry, to be collected at the station by Begley in his mud-splattered farmer's car.

Cooney and Begley were two of the greatest musicians I ever knew but they were men too, subject to the foibles and idiosyncrasies of the species. Cooney was a fascinating cocktail of fierce emotion, esoteric knowledge and imagined grievances. Begley, solid as the land he grew up on, was nevertheless shy and cautious, with a countryman's mistrust of the modern media and the music business. The prospect of making a record that would actually be heard around the world turned them both slightly crazy.

They lived under a mountain on the Dingle peninsula: Seamus and family in a farmhouse, Cooney in their basement. The name Dingle sounds cutesy, but the place is anything but – it is a vast domain of sea-torn cliffs and wild promontories, cloud-capped mountains, and strange ragged islands that lay scattered like buckshot in the western ocean. The mountains were the ones I'd spied curling like smoke on the horizon from the cliff-top fort on the Aran Islands a year before, the 'lair of poetry and wizards', which was all very inspiring but not a lot of help when we got to the house and I discovered Cooney and Begley weren't talking to each other, plus Begley had a head cold and couldn't sing. Worst of all, Cooney, terrified and conflicted about whether to make the album or not, was lying in wait for me with a thousand obstructions and reasons why the record couldn't be made.

During those waning days of summer beneath the misty flanks of Mount Brandon I discovered wells of diplomacy I didn't know I had in me. I negotiated to patch up the real and imagined differences between my two charges, made Lemsip for Begley's cold, patiently fielded Cooney's infinitely creative obstructions, and finally started working with them on the selection of songs and tunes – polkas, Kerry slides and a battery of jigs, reels and hornpipes – that would comprise the album.

Guessing that if we worked on multi-track Cooney would use the subsequent mixing sessions as an opportunity for perpetual delaying tactics, I decided to record the music direct to stereo, which meant it went down on tape exactly as the punter would hear it. The recordings were to be made in the largest room of Cooney's basement, so I set out to dispose of the thousands of horseflies that inhabited his feral bachelor pad. I got a dozen old copies of *The Kerryman* newspaper from Begley's wife Mary, which I rolled into swatting shapes, and spent a morning and afternoon killing them one by one.

That night John Dunford arrived from Dublin with the recording gear, and Begley, his cold shaken off and voice restored, now rallied to the project. But Cooney continued to erect obstructions, complaining bitterly about the choice of recording space, challenging the selection of equipment and questioning my and Dunford's qualifications. And once even these assaults had been parried and it was clear he could no longer delay the onset of actual recordings, the villain cunningly shifted mode. Instead of an attitude of *I don't want this to happen and I'm going to do all I can to obstruct it*, he switched to *OK, you want to produce me? I'm going to make you work harder than you've ever worked in your fucking life*.

And he did. I had to wake Cooney each morning, tenderly easing him out of the deep funk of his sleep, roll him a reefer while he lay in bed muttering and fussing over himself and the trials that were visited upon him, light the reefer and hand it to him (not, mercifully, having to place it between his lips). When he eventually picked up his guitar and pointed it towards a microphone, he would demand I tell him whether it was in tune, though he could tell full well himself. Variations on these processes, all along the lines of producer-as-servant, continued throughout the day as Dunford and I torturously, painfully, produced the bugger's album for him, despite his every sabotaging effort.

Why was it like this? Perhaps Cooney was afraid of being tested in the world, of standing up and saying 'this is me, this is my music.' I could understand that one. Making *Fisherman's Blues* I'd been confounded by which 'me' or which Waterboys to represent in the form of the finished product. I'd bought into the illusion that the record would define us. Cooney seemed to have a similar difficulty. Deep down he wanted his music to be heard and loved, which was why he'd agreed to make the album in the first place, but now it seemed he was frozen in the headlights lest it actually come out and sum him up with all its, and his, imperfections.

But we persevered, and day by day the tally of completed songs and sets of tunes grew until we had almost enough for an album. Then, because Kerry music is dance music, Cooney & Begley requested we record the last tracks with live dancers, so for the final night Dunford and I recorded them in the local pub. It was like a re-run of Sharon's Winkles Hotel scene, but with punters who came out in numbers to support the two local heroes. Restored to their natural habitat and spurred by the crowd, the duo played to the height of their brilliance, firing out explosive polkas while four rustic couples step-danced on the floor, their stamping adding organic percussion to the music.

The guys from Cooking Vinyl arrived with a journalist from the *NME* called Stuart Bailie. Wickham and Blakey, holidaying nearby, also turned up, and when the pub closed we had the inevitable after-hours session. Cooking Vinyl boss Pete Lawrence was eager for Stuart to get an interview with Cooney but hadn't reckoned on Cooney's resistance. There followed a wonderfully farcical game of hide and seek throughout the bar as Cooney strove to escape Pete's clutches, slipping out this door or that, ducking into the men's room or secreting himself in the kitchen. Pete, at the limits of his endurance, finally caught up with his prey at the bar and hastily pleaded with a distraught Cooney, now doing his best persecuted genius impression, to do the interview. 'John,' Cooney cried petulantly to the ever-patient Dunford, 'can you get this guy *off my back*?' Underneath his tortured artist hippie act, what Cooney really wanted more than anything was to be interviewed, as the gifted artist he was, by the man from the *NME*. And shortly afterwards I noticed him sitting happily in rapt discussion with a tape recorder-toting Stuart, all persecutions forgotten.

But the villain had the last laugh – he didn't let the album come out. Though we'd got it finished against all the odds, Cooney never signed the contract, and the music he and Begley recorded that September – as raw, majestic and magnificent as the landscape in which it was made, remains unheard.

CHAPTER 12

LIKE A HOUSE OF CARDS COLLAPSING

San Diego, the last night of our American tour, and we're performing an odd new song called 'Room To Roam'. Wickham plays slithering fairground arpeggios while the band lays down a Bavarian waltz groove with baritone sax parps and a militaristic drum beat. We're midway through the first verse when I notice three of our crew members at the side of the stage bending their knees in time to the music, going comedically up and down like pantomime policemen. Well, these things happen on the last nights of tours. I'm chuckling to myself between vocal lines when I see a few people in the middle of the front row of the audience pointing at the crew members and laughing. Then they start copying the dance, bobbing up and down themselves. As the second verse starts the people on either side of them start doing it too, and soon the move is spreading along the whole front row. I'm still singing and trying with diminishing success to keep a straight face when the second row starts copying them, and then the third, until soon, as the dance spreads organically, the whole audience from front row to back of the hall is doing an up and down knee-bendy dance like a silly policemen's convention in a Monty Python sketch. And some of the audience are bending on the beat while the rest are off the beat, so that when half the crowd are going down the other half are going up. They're all laughing at themselves too, and as the realisation spreads from the rear of the audience forwards that everyone's doing the same thing, a giddy delight fills the hall. We're all one, band and crowd united in a gorgeous, golden silliness.

Semi-traumatised by my 'holiday' in Kerry, and with Seamus Begley's box melodies hurtling like wild horses around my head, I returned to Dublin for Waterboys rehearsals and a week later we embarked on a tour of the USA and Canada.

We hadn't played North America for four years and our music and the group had changed so utterly since our last visit that it was like a different band. But *Fisherman's Blues* had preceded us so the punters knew something of what to expect, and our twenty-two shows in thirteen cities had sold out fast. I felt confident as I boarded the flight to Toronto. I was queasy though that Kate Lovecraft might still be sitting in a Manhattan loft with a crystal ball, eavesdropping on the contents of my mind or planning a dramatic entrance. But when we rolled into New York a week later Kate didn't show, and several very welcome old friends did. Jay Dee Daugherty brought his kit and for our encore at the Beacon Theatre we executed the old 'Keltner and Ringo at the Concert For Bangladesh' manoeuvre with two drummers kicking up a storm. Marco Sin, who'd survived his near-death experience in 1985 and was now straight as an arrow and healthy as a redwood tree, stepped up to strum guitar, and Donal Lunny and Philip King, in town on their own musical business, added bouzouki, mouth organ and moustaches to an all-hands-on-deck finale of 'This Land Is Your Land'. The set was drawn mostly from *Fisherman's Blues*, with the addition of folk stompers like 'The Raggle Taggle Gypsy' and new numbers slated for the next album. But we also played several from *This Is The Sea*. Some, like 'The Whole Of The Moon' and 'Old England', were rearranged to include Sharon's box, while for rockers like 'Be My Enemy' we morphed into an electric blues band while Sharon took a break.

I got to know Sharon a lot better during our month in America. She may have been the most driven musician in Ireland, but she was still a young girl on her first long tour, and the only girl in a band with six men at that. As bandleader I felt a responsibility to pal up with her and make sure she was OK. Every morning I'd arrange to meet her for breakfast and in a nearby diner we'd chat over bacon and home fries while she told me about her life: the farm she grew up on in County Clare, her horses, the local school where she'd been affectionately nicknamed 'the dreaded S.S.' and how as a child she practised in the kitchen with her two musician sisters and brother all at the same time, each playing a different tune oblivious to the others in a mad cacophony. Sharon was great company and sharp as a whip, and with her natural authority I could tell she'd make a good bandleader one day. Late one night I came upon her, John Dunford and Jimmy Hickey in a hotel corridor. They hadn't noticed me and I watched amused as Sharon, five foot tall in her dungarees, clapped her hands like a bossy playmate to summon John and Jimmy to attention, while the two grizzled road warriors rallied to her like a pair of big soft dogs. The instant she saw me she dropped her hands and reverted to the unassuming Sharon I knew, without missing a beat.

We continued to play anywhere at anytime, unerringly locating in each city the best Irish or Scottish music bar for an after-hours stramash: the Plough & Stars in San Francisco, the Cat & Fiddle in Hollywood, Glocca Morra in New York. And musical pals, sometimes met for the first time the night before, guested with us on stages across the continent. This practice reached its climax in L.A. where we were joined by The Scottish Fiddlers Of Los Angeles, a wonderfully rag-tag collection of exiled Scots and assorted misfits in a riot of tartan outfits. I'd learned the slow air 'Carolan's Welcome', which we'd recorded in Spiddal, from one of their albums and I invited them to perform it with us at the Wiltern Theatre as our opening number.

I took the stage on my own, sat down at the piano, and played the first line of the courtly melody. Colin Blakey emerged from the shadows to accompany me with whistle for the next two lines. Then as we played the fourth and final line of the round, Steve and Sharon walked on holding their fiddles followed by Anto with his sax. But if the audience thought this was the band they had a surprise coming,

178

for another fiddler appeared, then another, then another in a long procession until twenty costumed fiddlers had taken their places in a line along the front of the stage. Bang on cue they struck bow for the second round of the melody, sounding like a ragged Celtic orchestra from the seventeenth century.

Our guests spent the rest of the concert lurking colourfully round the wings before rejoining us for another bash in the encore, during which I noticed one of their number, a dapper little man called Hank who wasn't Scottish at all, playing along with a set of bones, making a loud *clackerty-clack* that stuck out over the music. Spurred by some mysterious instinct I laid down my guitar, picked up a bodhrán and started beating out a Bo Diddley beat. All the instruments dropped out leaving Hank and me centre stage duelling on bodhrán and bones. Hank started soft-shoe shuffling in his white shirt and baggy black pants, turning little pirouettes and mugging furiously in the spotlight as the crowd roared him on. I knew I was beaten and took a few steps back, ceding the stage to him as he spun in triumph, a pint-sized toreador, bones held high, snapping and clackerty-clacking in the air. If anyone in the theatre was still waiting for Waterboys rock numbers like 'The Pan Within' or 'Red Army Blues', they must have thought they'd stumbled into a different space/time continuum.

On New Year's Eve we played the best venue in the world: Barrowland Ballroom in Glasgow. Barrowlands, as everyone called it, had one of those old sprung floors which made the audience bounce up and down, and its ceiling was so low that the crowd's energy was reflected back at them, setting up a perpetual flow of power till the place was almost exploding. And on Hogmanay of all nights the atmosphere was *mental*. The band and crew wore kilts, with Sharon Shannon cute in a feathered toorie hat, and as midnight approached, Wickham and I stood in the eye of the inferno and played Robert Burns's immortal 'A Man's A Man For A' That'. When 1990 struck it was as if a bomb of joy went off; we strummed the opening chords to 'Auld Lang Syne' and the broad-shouldered bouncers in the safety pit below burst into life, reaching across the barriers to grab audience members and link arms in a spontaneous and urgent expression of brotherhood. Every voice in Barrowlands rose in song, all those mad ecstatic Glaswegians *gieing it laldy*. Then as the last chord of 'Auld Lang Syne' rang out a platoon of the Glasgow Police Pipe Band marched onstage in full costume, seven feet tall in their busbies, playing a massive skirling reel as the place went mental all over again.

We flew back to Ireland on New Year's Day and began preparations for our new album. I had high dreams for this one – nothing less than the merging of pop and trad, the reunion of British and Irish rock music with its own indigenous culture: a roots *Sgt Pepper*. The blending had already taken place in the band; all we had to do now, I figured, was capture it on a magical record. And if the ethnic music of Scotland and Ireland got shoehorned back into the popular mainstream as a side effect, that would be the icing on the cake. I wasn't asking for much. And to make the record that would effect this musical revolution we needed the right setting. The Spiddal House recordings had taken place in Connacht, the western of Ireland's four provinces, and I'd got it into my head that this time I wanted to record in the southern province of Munster, Sharon and Begley's land, the ancient seat of Irish poetry and music. So Irene and I spent a week visiting castles and stately homes across the region, and even a house on the West Cork coast in a place with the tantalising name of Seven Heads, one for each member of the band. But nothing we saw beat Spiddal House, so Munster was forgotten and John Dunford did another deal with Mavis.

Returning to Spiddal after two years was a different experience. We weren't explorers heading into the unknown anymore: we were part of the scenery ourselves. And it was a bigger operation this time, with a security team, carpenters, maintenance men and assistant engineers. The effect was like returning to the frontier after settlers have moved in and civilised it; the scenery was the same but the excitement and edge were gone.

We had a new producer too. After *Fisherman's Blues* I didn't want the responsibility again, so we hired Barry Beckett, an American who'd made his name with the Muscle Shoals studio band of the late sixties and co-produced Dylan's *Slow Train Coming* ten years later. I loved the sound of that album and figured Barry was simply a guy who understood music and musicians, and that would do for us. He flew into Ireland, a thickset man, genial and slow, with a walrus moustache, a cool Southern air and about as little idea of what he was getting into as I'd had on my way to produce Cooney & Begley. After rehearsing our new songs under Barry's watchful eye in Dublin we headed westward, but the West was another world, one without the creature comforts Nashville record producers were used to, and poor Barry, like Jay Dee Daugherty before him, found himself in a phone-less bungalow up a rustic country lane overlooking sea, fields and bog-land.

Barry took this stoically though his patience was strained by the time it took our crew to install the studio, which had to be done from scratch. While hammers banged and saws whistled Barry wandered the house and gardens for several days muttering, 'When are we gonna start cutting?' Finally the great day came and we began 'cutting', but to the band's alarm we discovered Barry had very different ideas from us. We expected to play all together, live and easy, like we always did, a raggle-taggle orchestra, but after listening to our rehearsals Barry declared he wanted us to lay down bass, drums and my rhythm guitar first, then overdub the other instruments afterwards.

This spoilt our fun because part of the magic was what happened when we played all together, but as he was the producer we swung with it. But soon there was another pill to swallow. Barry had an electronic metronome, a palm-sized box that emitted a nasty high-pitched 'beep'. He'd tap it as we played and it would log the song's speed or *tempo*. Before each subsequent performance he'd switch on the beeper, playing back a 'beep-beep-beep' at the logged tempo to which we'd then start playing, so ensuring we'd always start the song at an identical speed. The problem with this was twofold: we hated the unmusical sound of the beeper; and we didn't always *want* to play a song at the same speed. Barry's distant predecessor Bob Johnston had encouraged me to set the groove and tempo of a song according to my mood in the moment, start playing, and have the band take the feel from me. That was still the model we used, and conforming to the rigid tempo of Barry's 'beeper' took some more of the fun out of playing.

After several days Noel Bridgeman and I took action. We snuck into Spiddal House in the middle of the night and found the beeper where Barry had left it on the mixing desk. There it lay, the little bastard, gleaming satanically in the moonlight ready for the next day's persecution of the band. Noel pocketed it and we buried it deep in the Spiddal House grounds where for all I know it beeps to this day, heard by no human ear.

Next morning Barry was perplexed not to find the beeper and went hunting room to room till at last he realised foul play had been employed. He sat us down in a big circle and said in his slow Alabama accent, 'Now I know someone has hidden my beeper. I'm not angry but I want to know who it was.' Seven faces held seven deadpan expressions. No confession was made. Barry accepted the inevitable and from then on we played the songs at our own chosen speeds.

Each night after work we went down to the village for a late drink and often after the pub closed we'd go back to one of the band's houses for a session. One night we were joined by Charlie Lennon and some friends. They started playing in the kitchen, always the best-sounding room in a house, and knowing Barry would appreciate the music I ran and fetched him from his bungalow. Barry loved it all right but mistakenly thought the presence of the big-time record producer would intimidate the musicians. Even if they'd known Barry's history, the boys wouldn't have been perturbed. Their view was that the Yank was welcome to listen, whoever he was. But Barry,

182

deliciously misreading the situation, made the classic trad music faux pas of clapping loudly at the end of each tune then saying things like, 'Don't you worry about the ol' record producer sittin' here. Haw-haw! Just you keep right on playing and don't mind a thing. You're doin' great, haw haw!' A silent mirth was transmitted eye to eye around the room.

Barry may have blown the protocol in the after-hours session but he knocked spots off us in the studio. His insistence that we record using overdubs, and the light this process shone on what each musician played, had an unexpected effect: it exposed fault lines in our sound. When I heard the music stripped down I realised that beneath the orchestral impact of the full ensemble, so persuasive in concert, there was a lot of odd stuff going on. People were playing wrong melodies, harmonies were off and there were tuning issues between instruments. More worryingly, the grand experiment of merging rock and trad wasn't working. Stretched between two cultures, the music was being compromised; songs that needed a tough, ballsy treatment, like 'A Life Of Sundays', were being played too soft. Others, like 'Something That Is Gone', which needed a spare minimalist setting, had too many elements; sometimes accordion, fiddle or flute, or all three, simply didn't suit a composition. In my zeal to blend the worlds, I'd neglected the needs of the songs. This necessitated a hasty reorganising of the music, with the result that several songs featured smaller groups of players. Often it was Sharon, the most traditional musician, who had to sit out, but sometimes it was Blakey, Anto, or even The Fellow Who Fiddles, my fellow walker between musical worlds, the sonic glue around whom the whole cross-cultural experiment revolved.

Matters were compounded several weeks into the sessions when Anto, Trevor and John Dunford asked me to take over the production from Barry. The band felt Barry didn't understand the Irish/Celtic side of the music and they wanted a more familiar hand at the tiller. So I spoke to Barry and he agreed to let me deal with the musicians one-on-one while he stepped back into the role of overseer. Roles duly shuffled we got on with the job and there were moments of inspiration, like when Blakey played a psychedelic fuzz flute solo at the climax of 'A Life Of Sundays'. Or when we turned Anto's sax solo on 'Something That Is Gone' backwards to discover a gorgeously weird sonic ballet that perfectly suited the mood of the song. But these were rear-guard victories in a lost war. As the album neared completion it was clear that my dream of merging trad and pop in a rootsy *Sgt Pepper* was busted. *Room To Roam*, as it was titled, was a mixed-up curio of a record: a musical kaleidoscope that had its charms but wasn't quite in focus. And my beautiful seven-piece band was doomed. Whatever the long-term future of Waterboys music was, I knew it wasn't this. Anto had been right: the winds had changed.

And more was broken. Steve Wickham had gone through a painful divorce and by the time we finished *Room To Roam* he'd gradually withdrawn into himself, becoming a shadow presence in the band. All his joy and mischief, his very *fellow-who-fiddles-ness* vanished. Even his trademark holey hat was gone, taken by the ex-wife. At first I tried to give Steve space to work out his emotions, then when he just grew more distant I tried to find out what was going on, but he was unresponsive and closed to me in a way he hadn't been before. My friend, it seemed, was lost, and I couldn't reach him.

We lost Doug D'Arcy too, our champion, when he was fired from Chrysalis. Then, towards the end of the recordings, former Waterboy Karl Wallinger, giving a series of press interviews for his new album, slagged me off for 'hiding in Ireland for three years' and cajoled me to 'stop being an Irish git'. Perhaps he meant it lightly, or maybe there were deeper emotions at work, but his statements coincided with a wider perception in the music media that The Waterboys had taken a blind alley. Coming from someone who'd been in the band, Karl's comments provided a focal point around which these perceptions coalesced and like the first shot of the hunting season, they proclaimed open fire on The Waterboys. *Room To Roam* was going to meet with a tough critical response, I knew, for it was all the things people were ready to pan us for: mellow, made in Ireland, Celtic and otherworldly. The aura of promise and momentum that had surrounded The Waterboys for five or six years was about to be shattered.

But fuck 'em all, we still had a tour to do, an album to serve up, and fifty sold-out concert halls waiting in the cities of Europe and North America. And I had other things on my mind: I was getting married to Irene. We'd set the date for 14 June and were spliced in a registrar's office on Molesworth Street in Dublin, she in white beaded dress, me in a dark blue double-breasted suit, just purchased. Steve and Anto were the best men and as we left the building they raised their fiddle and mandolin at the door, making an arch for bride and groom to walk under as confetti rained down.

The reception was in a country house hotel in the foothills of the Wicklow Mountains and everyone made their way there in a convoy. The first thing Irene said to me as we got into our chauffeur-driven car was, 'I think I'll keep my maiden name,' which wasn't the best start. Anto compounded matters by slipping me a reefer through the window before we drove off, which I casually smoked all the way to Wicklow. Deliberately or not, Anto had made it about three times as strong as any reefer I'd ever had, and by the time we drove up to the grand hotel forty minutes later, I was as smoked as a kipper. The first person I met when we disembarked was my new brother-in-law Vinnie Flynn, a cheerful, no-nonsense County Dublin farmer who'd married Irene's sister Mouse a year before. When I told him how stoned I felt he said, 'Ah, don't worry. It doesn't matter how much you drink or smoke on your wedding day, you won't be able to get out of it. You'll be fine.' This sage advice worked like a trick and my equilibrium returned. And it was true: no matter how much I drank on my wedding day I didn't get drunk.

Late that night I was lying in the bridal bed, head crooked on my arm, Irene sleeping gently beside me, my mind ranging over the day's colourful scenes, when I heard a creak. I looked up and saw the door handle turning. Slowly, silently, the door opened and a silhouette entered. Someone was in the bridal suite with us! The figure walked unsteadily across the room, looked about in the darkness, then turned, and I recognised the familiar silhouette of a gnomic man with suit jacket and Brylcreemed pompadour: Vinnie Kilduff, not as sober as he'd ever been. Having missed his lift back to Dublin, Vinnie was looking for an empty room to crash in. But when he saw me looking up at him from the bed, instead of mouthing an embarrassed apology and swiftly scarpering, he leaned towards me, smiled cheerily, said, 'Ah, howaya Mike?', as if we'd just met on a country lane. Then ignoring the sleeping bride entirely he sat down on the side of the bed expecting a chat.

Irene and I went to Greece for our honeymoon, spending two weeks in Arcadia, a land of high mountains, ancient villages, warbling clarinet music and vast hazy views; a suitable place to ponder the imminent crucifixion of *Room To Roam*. Even if the album tanked, I figured, leaning on our balcony with the sound of goat bells floating across the hills, at least the band would be as good as ever in concert. And for the first time ever, I mused with some satisfaction, I had a settled line-up and the whole touring cycle booked well in advance. But if you want to give God a laugh, the saying goes, tell her your plans, and as soon as we returned to Dublin and began rehearsing, the process of disintegration that had begun in Spiddal recommenced. With alarming inevitability The Waterboys began to crumble from the inside. After two days of running through the set it was clear the band didn't sound or feel right and Anto and I met privately to discuss the situation. We agreed we needed to replace Noel Bridgeman with a tougher drummer who could hold everything together.

Then I made a big mistake. Because of the cloud hanging over him I left Steve Wickham out of the decision, figuring, benignly but patronisingly, that it would be kinder to spare him participation in a ruthless action. Noel Bridgeman took the news well. But when I told Steve the next day, in a bar appropriately called the Waterloo, he didn't. I watched him seem to fold in on himself, a storm passing over his brow. That night he turned up at my flat and told me he was leaving the band. He offered to stay for six weeks to help me out but as that only took us a short way through our tour, and I knew he needed to leave for the good of his soul, I said no thanks. I told him he could rejoin the band at any time but I wasn't holding my breath. I got on with the task of reconfiguring The Waterboys and readying my nose for the critical bloodying it was about to receive.

We brought in a drummer from Louisiana called Ken Blevins who'd been spotted by Anto and Trevor playing with the songwriter John Hiatt. Blevins was a robust player and when we rehearsed with him it was immediately clear that without Wickham's glue holding the rock and trad players together, Sharon and Colin's instruments no longer fit. Having done the deed myself with Noel, I asked Anto and Trevor to tell the other two. Trevor told a relieved Sharon, who couldn't see how were going to play the *Room To Roam* music live without Steve's fiddle anyway. But the softhearted Human Saxophone couldn't bring himself to tell Blakey, so I did, once again in the fateful Waterloo bar, and when the words were spoken I watched Colin finish his drink in haste, nod glumly and leave. I wouldn't see him or hear his Pannish flute again for thirteen years. And so we hit the road as a four-piece rock band, me on electric guitar for the first time in an aeon and Anto scurrying across the stage changing instruments with every song, guitar to sax to mandolin to organ, plugging the gaps in our sound like the Dutch boy keeping back the sea with his fingers in the dyke.

To soften the transition Sharon guested with us for three warm-up shows on the eve of our European tour, all in the west of Ireland. At the last one, in the Connemara mountain town of Clifden, an English rock journalist turned up to interview us and after soundcheck his photographer asked if he could take a shot of the band on top of a nearby hill. Sharon was beside me and, still holding onto the last tatters of my old dream of the band, I asked her if she'd come and be in the picture. But if I wasn't ready to let go, Sharon was; she shook her head and waved us on our way as the four of us bent our backs to the ascent and started walking out of the Celtic dreamtime back to the world.

CHAPTER 13

A WALK IN THE LAKE SHRINE

Los Angeles, April 1991. I'm walking down a sunlit path in the Lake Shrine, a meditation garden close to the Pacific Ocean end of Sunset Boulevard. I've just been for a meeting with a record label that wants to sign me, and my new manager Dick Lackaday and the label's A&R man Benny Breeze, an odd-looking chap with a distressing resemblance to one of the psychiatric patients in One Flew Over the Cuckoo's Nest, *are strolling a little way behind me, heads close in conversation. The Lake Shrine was founded by an Indian guru called Paramahansa Yogananda, one of several Eastern mystics whose images George Harrison snuck onto the cover montage of* Sgt Pepper. *Lush gardens and swaying tropical trees surround the lake, and a tall white arch stands regally on the bank, crowned with a golden lotus that glints in the sun. The busy highway is close by and its roar is audible yet within the grounds of the Shrine a tangible calm prevails.*

I stop to watch some swans glide by as Dick and Benny catch me up. Benny puts his hand on my shoulder and says, 'Aw man, the Lake Shrine! Did you know my old man used to give money to this place? He told me once if I ever had a problem to go and think it over at the Lake Shrine and I'd be sure to feel better about it, and you know, I often did.' I'm impressed. A&R men aren't usually hip to spiritual places like this and I think to myself what a good guy Benny is, and what a sympathetic person he might be to work with.

We walk on round the circumference of the lake, finally returning to Benny's car. He drives us back along Sunset to our hotel and drops us off. We'll see him again tomorrow for more discussion about whether The Waterboys will choose to sign to his label, and after what he said back in the Lake Shrine I'm feeling pretty good about it. But in the hotel lobby Dick

Lackaday turns to me with a perplexed look on his face and says, 'Just before Benny spoke to you about his old man, he asked me, "What the fuck is this place, Dick?" He made the whole thing up!'

Everything changed that autumn of 1990. The Celtic adventure was over, I was married, and with the release of *Room To Roam* my old Ensign/Chrysalis deal expired, leaving me free to sign to a new label and make a fresh start. Meanwhile the actors were leaving the drama one by one and the next to go was Jimmy Hickey, fired after a Swedish rock festival for turning into Captain Muck and terrorising the local record company man. Even John Dunford was bailing out, announcing his departure in the grim waiting room of a Scottish ferry terminal en route to the first show of our British tour. I persuaded John to stay till we found a replacement soundman but the knowledge that I was losing one of my closest collaborators, the wily counsellor who'd been an inestimable part of the whole Celtic trip, was a bitter blow indeed.

The tour started with seven shows in a circus tent round the Highlands and Islands of Scotland. This had been a dream of mine, an extension of the 'colourful travelling explosion' band vision. The shows were booked before the line-up imploded and I'd imagined our merry cavalcade rolling into towns, the big top going up on the town square and a country fair atmosphere, perfect for the performance of the pop-folk *Room To Roam* music. But without The Fellow Who Fiddles and Sharon Shannon to share it with, suddenly it didn't seem like so much fun anymore. And it wasn't. The weather was brutal, the tent was invariably erected on lonesome car parks or hilly fields on the outskirts of town (once even on a building site) and the atmosphere was more drunken school disco than country fair. The experience was poetically summed up by our onstage soundman, an abrasive New Yorker called Keith who'd just joined us from a Madonna tour. Standing side-stage on the Isle Of Skye, while large globs of Hebridean rainwater seeped through holes in the tent and dripped down his neck, Keith slammed his fist on the mixing desk and howled, 'This is a *suck-fest!*'

Worst of all, the rump four-piece band could play hardly any of the new album. Without fiddle, box and flute, songs like 'A Man Is In Love' and 'The Raggle Taggle Gypsy' were impossible to do. So we came out of the traps playing a weird repertoire halfway between the past and the future; guitar-driven numbers from the first three Waterboys albums and barely finished new songs written since the split, plus a few covers like Dylan's appropriate 'Everything Is Broken'. All of which left the Scottish punters just about as bemused as the rock audiences had been when we'd first gone rootsy five years earlier. Only this time, instead of evolving, our sound and charisma had shrunk.

I kept telling myself things would get better, but the tour was like a game of snakes and ladders. From Aberdeen onwards we blessedly found ourselves in indoor venues: a ladder. A few days later the reviews for *Room To Roam* came out and were as damning as I'd expected: a snake. Roddy Lorimer's brass section, The Kick Horns, joined the tour in Cardiff and suddenly we had a fuller sound: a ladder. But they could only do four shows: a snake. And so on. The final UK show was in another tent, a whopping great one holding 8,000 punters in a North London park. We'd had over 50,000 ticket applications for this show alone and if I hadn't nixed the idea when it was put to me, we could have done multiple nights at Wembley Arena. But no, I had to do things the hard way, in another bloody tent, on a stage that, because the park wasn't flat, sloped from one side to the other. As I looked over at the Human Saxophone mid-song, he was *downhill*.

The tour was scheduled to roll on through Europe and North America for another fifty shows without a break, but our reinforcements The Kick Horns had other commitments and couldn't rejoin us till New York, thirty shows away. This was a killer. I'd made it through the British Isles but when I faced the prospect of the band shrinking back to a four-piece and looked at the endless list of cities, including those in several countries like Spain and Portugal where the audiences were wild for the Celtic music we could no longer play, I felt weariness paralyse my bones and brain. I couldn't do it. I cancelled a dozen shows and gave everyone three weeks off.

I needed some serious chill-out time, and not in Dublin, so I rented a cottage a mile from Glastonbury. I rose every morning at dawn and walked through the orchards and fields to climb the mighty Tor. High above the world I drew the sweet West Country air into my lungs and took stock. Everything was broken all right, but I still had music in my head and words to sing, and each morning I came back down from the Tor a little stronger. I spent the rest of my days sleeping and reading, and when we hit the road, though the European and American tours were tough, my mantra of 'it'll never be as hard as this again' kept coming true. By the time we came home to play Ireland at Christmas, Kick Horns and all, we were a powerful, lean machine.

Nevertheless, I missed The Fellow Who Fiddles on stage like an amputee misses an arm, and when the tour ended and I found myself back in Dublin again I missed him personally too. He was still in town, living in a little house near the Phoenix Park, but when I visited him he was distant and distracted. He was in some dark night of the soul, and until he came out the other side I couldn't communicate with him. Without my co-conspirator, Dublin was a ghost town. Everywhere I looked were reminders of times that were over; theatres and ballrooms where we'd played famous shows, streets we'd walked down when the aura of magic was upon us and the pearl was ours for the taking; the scenes and empty stage sets of a golden era that was gone, baby, gone.

The Waterboys' position in the topography of rock had changed too. It was six years since the sense of breakthrough that had surrounded *This Is The Sea*, when we'd had that most powerful of showbiz attributes, *newness*, and everyone had wanted in on the discovery. Now The Waterboys was a familiar name, if not yet an old one, and *Room To Roam* had cost us our hip quotient. If I was to bring the public on my next adventures I needed to recast the band, take the measure of the times, and make peace with the music business. And I was certain of two things: I wanted to play rock'n'roll again and I needed to do it somewhere other than Dublin.

Galway was out – too many memories there as well, and if I wanted to sharpen my rock chops my beloved west wasn't exactly boogie central. I had to get out of Ireland, and I had non-musical reasons for leaving too. One hazy morning, when my first thought on waking was 'where will I have my first pint of Guinness today?', I knew I had to escape the drinking culture. Plus I had ideological problems with the Catholic Church and the sense of guilt that seemed to be strangling Steve. After five years of being immune I'd begun to feel the Catholic pressure in the very air and atmosphere of the nation. It seemed two powers had Ireland's manhood by the throat, and each was black with a white collar.

When our tour had rolled through America the previous November I'd felt New York calling me, and so I decided the world's greatest rock'n'roll city, with all its musical, philosophical and social freedoms, would be The Waterboys' next home. But there were a few things to sort out first. Since I'd split with Gary Kurfirst five years earlier, I'd effectively managed the band myself and I was burned out carrying its affairs on my shoulders. With new labels queuing up to sign me despite the disappointment of *Room To Roam*, I was in the ideal position to attract a manager. And right on cue one arrived.

Dick Lackaday was an Englishman living in New York, a charming if insipid-looking fellow who always wore a crew-neck jumper with the top of his shirt collar poking up underneath, as if his mum had dressed him. But there was a hint of steel under Dick's Clark Kent exterior and when he pursued and wooed me towards the end of the *Room To Roam* tour, I took note of him as a real contender. When he followed me to Dublin in early 1991, full of persuasion and plans, I was won over and he was hired. As record companies usually do when contracts end, Chrysalis planned a *Best Of The Waterboys* album, and Dick's first job was to negotiate with them to ensure I got to pick the track list myself. He succeeded, and I compiled the album: side one from the first three rockier albums, side two from the Irish years. A single was scheduled too, a re-release of 'The Whole Of The Moon'.

While I'd been in the West of Ireland, 'Moon' had become a hit at Balearic clubs and English raves, where apparently it was blasted out to fields of blissed-up revellers as the sun was rising. And because the original 1985 single had been deleted for years there was huge demand for the reissue, which was expected to be a big hit. Its release date had just been set when I was invited to a music awards ceremony in a Dublin hotel. Towards the end of the evening an elegantly rumpled chap walked up to me and introduced himself as Rob Dickens of Warner Brothers. He told me one of his artists, the English soul singer Terry Reid, had just covered 'The Whole Of The Moon' and would be releasing it in a couple of months. 'If you'd recorded it properly,' he said, 'you'd have had the hit, but now we're going to have the success.' I could have told Rob our own version was coming out in four weeks, but he'd only have moved his release date forwards. So I said nothing, and said it well, and that April when the Waterboys' original version flew up the charts and took up residence in the top three, Rob was left chewing on his 'recorded it properly' chutzpah.

Like a character in a teen-rock fantasy, I was sitting by a swimming pool on a Caribbean island (an overdue holiday at Irene's insistence) when I received the phone call telling me 'The Whole Of The Moon' was in the charts. Two weeks later *The Best Of The Waterboys* followed and was a big hit album. This belated success was a sweet feeling and lent a providential backdrop to negotiations for the new record deal; that spring John Kennedy, Dick Lackaday and I met with a parade of almost every major label boss in the UK, and several Americans too. And what a marvellous roll call of the grandees of the music business this was: legends, sharks, conmen, sharpshooters, cynics, eccentrics, and a few spectacular hot air balloonists in love with the sound of their own voices.

One such was Bob Krasnow, the chief of Elektra New York, who flew to Dublin and lectured me in his hotel room for an hour on how to run my career while I sat wondering whether to sign to him or pour a drink over his head. The lecture continued over dinner, peppered with mentions of how Bob had discovered this or that band and jibes about how I needed to articulate a long-term plan and sell myself as an artist. When he started to tell me I needed professional discipline I snapped and ranted back at him that I had plenty of professional discipline and a shit-load of unfinished business with rock'n'roll, and couldn't describe my long-term plan because the music told me what to do and only gave me a little bit of the picture in advance at any one time. When I went to the men's room Krasnow remarked to Dick Lackaday, 'The cunt has seduced me.' But Bob hadn't seduced the cunt.

Then there was an English label manager called David Munns, who slouched on a hotel sofa and said, 'It's all a game, innit? Sign to me and as long as you don't cost me money you can do what you want.' I was too earnest to see the sense in this sagacious, practical philosophy, thinking it at the time absurdly cynical, and didn't give Mr Munns another thought.

We met Clive Davis of Arista Records in a private airport lounge when he was flying one way across the Atlantic and we were going the other. I admired Clive, an old-school music man who'd signed Patti Smith at the dawn of her career and knew how to treat artists: part impresario, part talent-spotter, part CEO and part street-fighter. Though he was courteous, almost avuncular, there was a bare-knuckle boxer in every cell of Clive's body. You wouldn't want to be his enemy. Irene, sitting in on the meeting, didn't get this. Bamboozled by the genial exterior, she came away cooing, 'What a lovely old man!'

A few days later Dick and I dined in Los Angeles with a legendary promo-man-turned-company-executive called Charlie Minor. As we approached the restaurant I saw Charlie, who I'd never met before, standing in the window mugging and gesticulating urgently to me with his arm in the air, doing a 'Get in here, Buddy' act like I was a member of his gang. He continued this pally performance through lunch, talking as if we were paisanos from a mafia movie and furiously mollycoddling me with his arm around my shoulder so I'd be charmed and sign to his label. That arm worked hard. A few years later Dick asked me, 'Did you hear what happened to Charlie Minor?' I hadn't, but I guessed right – he'd been shot dead.

The procession of meetings was a good opportunity to observe Dick in action, but though he talked a good game, some things made me wonder if I'd picked a stinker. When we received record deal offers with sums ending in a certain amount of 0s, Dick would become fantastically animated. There was something out of control, almost vulgar, about the display, as if the prospect of earning big bucks was jerking Dick's puppet strings, and this suggested where his fundamental interests lay. More worryingly he was oddly passive in the meetings, caught, I realised, between sticking up for me and ensuring he never offended anyone who might be useful to him further down the road. He always let me ask the tough questions, and if the executives we met stepped over the boundaries of good manners, like when Krasnow lectured me, Dick remained sheepishly silent and let them go right along. Irene might not have had Clive Davis's number, but she had Dick's. 'He's got no balls,' was her pithy prognosis. But it was too late now. I'd signed to Dick for three years and making the best of the relationship was more attractive than a legal bust-up in the middle of choosing a record company, and a return to having no manager at all. I accepted Dick's frailties, focussed on his attributes and got on with the beauty parade.

Our next appointment was lunch with David Geffen in his Malibu beach house. A casually dressed butler greeted us at the door and showed us into an elegant lounge where Edward Hopper paintings hung on the walls and vintage Sinatra (Capitol years of course) wafted airily from a stereo in the next room. Through the huge windows lay the living vista of the Pacific Ocean, its blue-grey surface torn by the dark sleek shapes of dolphins. Geffen received us like a Zen emperor, sitting on a sofa wearing jeans and shirt in that loose style favoured by ultra-rich people who know their wealth and status are so magnetic they don't even need to dress sharply. He shook my hand, smiled and said, 'I tried to buy Enigma.' This arcane utterance had me confused for a few seconds, before I realised he'd got Ensign's name wrong and was letting me know he'd tried to sign, or buy, me in the past. We sat down to lunch at a round table, waited on by the butler. Geffen pulled up his chair and sat an inch from the side of my face, scrutinising me. But it felt funny rather than intrusive, and when I turned to meet his eyes Geffen was grinning.

I liked him. I liked the atmosphere of his record company too, with its storefront offices on Sunset Strip and the friendly staff members who didn't gush or bullshit me. But I didn't take to the first Geffen A&R man I was introduced to and when I told David this, he suggested I meet with some others and see who I liked. There were two to pick from and they unwittingly played a sting on me that couldn't have worked better if they'd planned it. First John Kalodner, a cheerless chap dressed as John Lennon circa 1969, long hair, granny glasses, white suit and all, sat magisterially at his desk and told me in a weird high-pitched voice how rubbish he thought *Room To Roam* was – 'you should charge people half-price if you're gonna make an album like that' – and made it clear that if we signed to him his junior assistant, a docile, cross-eyed fellow, would A&R The Waterboys. 'And I won't be available,' he added snarkily, in case Lackaday and I were in any doubt. Half an hour later in another office in the same building, Kalodner's rival, a rotund, soft-voiced mover and shaker called Tom Zutaut, told me I was 'one of the great emotional rock singers and performers of all time'. Relieved, I almost fell into Tom's arms.

197

Zutaut was riding high on the success of having signed Guns N' Roses and clearly thought of himself as the guy with the Midas touch. Though Guns N' Roses were everything I thought rock should have evolved beyond by about 1970, I respected Zutaut's nuanced opinion of my new song demos (his favourites were 'The New Life' and 'The Return Of Pan') and I fancied a bit of the Midas touch myself. I signed to Geffen.

With an L.A. record company and a New York manager I was ready for the move to America. I gave Anto six months' paid leave, made a farewell trip to the West of Ireland, and in August of 1991 Irene and I moved into a brownstone apartment on Hudson Street in Greenwich Village.

I hit the ground running, embracing the city like a lover, going to concerts every night and bringing myself back up to speed with rock'n'roll. I prowled the great Avenues and felt New York's crackling energy seep into me, recharging my sense of wonder. The city was like a huge roaring engine and in those first months it swept me up in its momentum and put wings on my heels. Then, as now, Manhattan was the world centre of live music; you could catch Ray Charles in a jazz club, see Prince at Radio City or score front-row seats for a Ravi Shankar concert. There were new bands to check out, bluesmen in from Chicago, jazzbos and folkies in the clubs, old-style gospel groups come over the bridges from Brooklyn and the Bronx holding jubilees in downtown church halls, and even American Indian music if you knew where to look – and I did. Soon my head was buzzing with new information and inspiration. I even plucked random shows from the listings in the *Village Voice* and bought tickets on the basis of a band name or concert theme.

This musical roulette led to wonderful discoveries like The Anonymous Four, an *a cappella* group singing medieval rounds and chants in the perfect environment of a masonic chapel somewhere uptown one winter afternoon; four crystalline female voices as pure as the glacial New York day outside. Or it threw up weird eccentricities like The Stellar Singers, an ensemble performing something called 'Anthem For The Earth' at the prestigious Lincoln Center. I went to the concert accompanied by my trusty roadie Ken, a lanky Dubliner and the last survivor of The Waterboys' Irish road crew, who'd moved to New York with me. We found our seats, the lights went down and five men and five women came on stage and stood in a semi-circle. Then a little guy walked on with a bald head, white mutton-chop sideburns and a shiny dress jacket. He acknowledged the audience with a pained expression as if either embarrassed or suffering from a great burden, then turned to face the singers. He clasped his hands in front of his solar plexus – a curious gesture, which the singers all copied – and after a long, significant moment of silence began to conduct them with great intensity, as if drawing the music from their very souls.

I glanced at my concert programme to read that this chap was called Gareth B. Woods and that he 'spontaneously composed' the music and had 'received' the composition we were now hearing while driving through the Mojave Desert. I began to develop distinct feelings of scepticism. The singing was semi-operatic with high soprano flourishes and low basso drones, but though gymnastically impressive it wasn't actually very good. The high 'tra-la-las' were slightly curdled and the low manly voices unintentionally comedic. It was as if some critical self-awareness on the part of conductor and performers had been suspended and replaced by devotion to the significance and indeed wondrousness of what they were doing. I sat listening, my curiosity fully engaged, and began to realise I was witnessing a marvellous example of the Emperor's New Clothes, made all the more remarkable by the rapt commitment of the Singers, now in transports of artistic ecstasy and held in thrall by the arm-waving of the dubious maestro, Mr Woods, who they clearly idolised.

I was so engrossed by this tableau that I'd forgotten roadie Ken sitting next to me. I turned to look at him and he glanced shyly back at me with a deeply conflicted expression. The poor man's face was a picture. Suddenly I needed to laugh. Very loudly. But before a sound could come out I wedged my knuckles in my mouth and dissolved into an explosion of silent mirth, joined seconds later by a relieved and liberated Ken, which of course made it funnier still. Somehow we kept our laughter under control until the merciful release of the intermission whereupon we ran out of the hall and howled like daft wolves in the New York night.

Meanwhile on Hudson Street I turned one of the rooms into a music den, with all my usual instruments and a selection of oddities I found at my new favourite shop. Music Inn was a tiny store on West Fourth Street, run by two grumpy sixties survivors who charged a one-dollar entrance fee and tried to scare away non-serious customers at the door. Like a musical ark it stocked every acoustic instrument in the world, from Afghan zithers to Zambian finger pianos, which hung from the ceiling, lined every millimetre of the walls, overspilled from ancient shelving and occupied almost every particle of floor space, save for two narrow channels via which the customer could just about negotiate his way from one end of the shop to the other, a feat impossible without banging one's head at least six times. From my various expeditions to this archaic grotto I emerged the possessor of Indian harmoniums, Navajo rattles, Chinese cymbals and rattling clusters of Bolivian goats' hooves, all of which found their way onto the next Waterboys album.

I returned to another rarefied establishment, the witchcraft shop I'd visited in 1985, to buy a new Black Book to put my songs in. During my travels in the West of Ireland I'd written on anything I could scratch a pen on, a method which had suited that free-flowing adventure. Now I wanted to feel again the sense of my writing flowing in one focussed stream of energy, and gathering it in a Black Book was the way to foster this.

And there was another revival: auditions. Envisioning a new Waterboys that would tour and play for the next ten years, I rented a Midtown rehearsal room and welcomed a stream of bass, drum and keyboard hopefuls and even, for the first time, a couple of lead guitarists. As always the process doubled as a way to try out songs, and I used new numbers like 'Preparing To Fly' and 'The Return Of Jimi Hendrix' as musical workouts. But while some good jams were had, none of the musicians felt like Waterboys to me, and after a couple of months I decided to look beyond New York.

Dick Lackaday had a friend in Chicago called Jim Powers who offered to show me round the city's blues clubs so I could check out the players, and in late October I flew out to meet him. Jim was a handsome young white guy with a big heart and an ultra-positive business-like manner as if he'd just attended a motivation seminar. We spent a weekend taking in the clubs together and though I didn't find any new band members the experience was fantastic. At Kingston Mines we watched the harmonica devil Sugar Blue make his entrance from the back of the hall, blowing blues hunched over his harp like a shadowy spirit of the night as he bobbed and ducked through the crowd to the stage. Across the road in B.L.U.E.S we soaked up the workingman's grooves of Magic Slim, a great avuncular bruiser of a man rendered a foot taller by the massive Stetson that balanced like a lampshade on his rock-like head. And in a stone-floored cave the size of a tuck shop we breathed the energy of the voice-crackling banshee Junior Wells.

Late on the Saturday night we were sitting in a club on the Southside called the Checkerboard Lounge, when I mentioned to Jim that I loved gospel music and had always wanted to see a real gospel church service with a choir. 'I've always wanted to do that too!' he replied. He called over the barmaid, a middle-aged black lady, and asked if she could suggest a church we might visit in the morning. 'Y'all oughta come 'long to mine,' she said and promptly wrote the address on a piece of paper: The Paradise Baptist Church, 1163 East Forty-Third Street.

Next morning, smartly dressed, we set off in Jim's car. Forty-Third Street was an endless straight road through the most forsaken urban landscape I'd ever seen. Louis Armstrong had lived there in the twenties when the place was hopping, but it wasn't hopping now. We drove past block after block of burned-out lots, overgrown waste ground and functional grey buildings until at the very end of the road, where Forty-Third Street fizzled out at a railway line, there was a low, flat-roofed hall.

Even as we got out of the car I heard the music; a women's choir rising like balm over the doomed streets. We went through the entrance door into a dark hallway where a black lady in a Sunday hat greeted us as if she knew we were coming. Jim and I had decided we'd sit in the back row, so that if the service got too emotional for our white-boy sensibilities we could slip quietly away. But the lady in the hat ushered us into the church in full view of the congregation and showed us instead to two empty seats in the centre of the second row, next to which sat our barmaid from the night before, radiant in her best clothes. She glanced up at us discreetly and nodded. I looked around.

Along every pew sat black people, dignified in their hats and smart coats. We were the only white faces. In the centre of the floor, facing the congregation, stood a youngish man wearing a suit, Bible in his hands and tears streaming down his cheeks as he cried, 'Thank you Jesus for gittin' my children safe to school every day. Thank you Jesus for gittin' my kids through school safe every day. Thank you Jesus for bringin' my kids back home to me safe every day.' Members of the congregation encouraged him with interjections of, 'That's right' or 'Hallelujah'. On a raised podium behind the young man two rows of women in immaculate pale blue robes were laying down a sympathetic moaning chant. On the floor to the right was a teenager playing an organ, and on the far left were a young drummer and bass player waiting for their cue. Then a tall, distinguished man in robes swept in from a side room and took his place behind a lectern. He welcomed us all, 'including guests', and then simply threw back his head and sang:

'Jeee-eee-suu-uh-ussss is myyy guiii-iii-iii-iiide!'

What a voice! It soared through the air of the church, glad and rich, the long warm syllables rolling across the room like an unfurled banner. He sounded like Marvin Gaye's brother or the honey-toned son of Sam Cooke and clearly, unquestionably, if he hadn't chosen the ministry could have been a great soul singer. And then he began his sermon.

I don't remember a word the pastor said, but I'll never forget what happened. He spoke in a humble yet powerful voice and warmed to his theme gradually, using repetition and rhythm to build emotional intensity the way black preachers do, and every time he said something that moved them, which was every few seconds, the members of the congregation responded with, 'Ain't that the truth!' or 'Ain't God a good God!' About ten minutes in, the three musicians began to punctuate the pastor's words with short soulful riffs, and sudden drum flourishes or cymbal crashes like exclamation marks. Then the choir started interjecting *Hallelujahs* as the clamour of sung and spoken responses grew. For thirty minutes the pastor threw forth his voice and the church responded, and all the time the sermon gathered power and intensity until it filled the room with a sense of raw, unpredictable emotion, of something urgent about to happen: exactly the kind of 'hot' event Jim and I had been worried about.

Suddenly the atmosphere changed and the pressure crackled like the moment before a storm breaks. I looked at the pastor and it was as if an invisible hand took him by the scruff of the neck and lifted him in the air. He started bouncing haphazardly up and down, alarmingly out of control, shouting 'whooo … whooo … whooo' in a wild ecstasy, arms waving and gown flapping like great black wings. Several men moved towards him and took his arms, holding him close enough that he wouldn't fall but lightly enough to allow his rapture to continue. The congregation was electrified: people were on their feet in the pews, shouting, dancing, some 'falling out' like the pastor and being held by those next to them. For a long wild moment – a minute that felt like an hour – the preacher rocked, eyes rolling, in the grip of something bigger than himself, and it was as if an energy descended through him and bathed the church and everyone in it with power. I could feel it affecting me, making my chest hot, raising goose bumps on my neck and arms, drawing from me a response of profound but inarticulate emotion that made me want to cry, jump, hide and fall on my knees all at the same time.

Then gently the power changed and the climax subsided like a musical note falling in pitch. The pastor gradually came back to himself, the men let him go, and the music dropped to a soulful slow groove like an afterglow, the women of the choir waving their arms and singing long, deep *Hallelujahs* like I've heard they used to sing on the banks of Southern rivers. His face glowing, the pastor smoothed the sleeves of his robe and said: 'Praise the Lord! It doesn't happen every week, but it happened today!'

When Jim and I tumbled out into the Chicago daylight and got back in the car we were dazed and thrilled. Christianity wasn't for me but Spirit was Spirit, by whatever name, and we'd just met It. I flew back to New York without any new Waterboys, but with a deeper sense of inner wellbeing than I'd felt in a long time.

CHAPTER 14

LOCKDOWN IN THE BIG APPLE

I stand on a cliff above the Hudson River, legs slightly apart, holding a gold Telecaster chest-high, awaiting orders. Several goats are nuzzling my legs and making plaintive little bleating sounds. They smell funky. A spring breeze ruffles my shirt and dashes strands of hair across my face. A boat chugs by on the river below, a round-Manhattan day-tripper, the amplified tour guide's voice echoing tinnily across the landscape. A hubbub of conversation emanates from behind me. Some of the voices are casual and conversational, but two or three are super-intense, not at all happy, fixated on some urgent process close to action point.

Suddenly what I've been waiting for – dreading, even – comes from behind and to my left. 'NOW! DO IT NOW!' Jeff screams. His voice is manic, like an unhinged sergeant major or a startled lunatic. A man, from the sound of it, at the end of his tether. In response I slowly raise the gold guitar above my head, hoping to my timing is right, and angling the guitar, as best I can without looking, so its surface will catch the sun's rays and create an aureole of light.

Suddenly Jeff barks: 'THE GOATS! PUSH THE GOATS CLOSER TO HIS LEGS!' I hear scrambling sounds mingled with bleating. Then a short blissful calm before he redirects his attentions at me with the inevitable frantic repeat of, 'NOW! DO IT NOW!' Doesn't he know I can hear him? I raise the guitar again, hold it in place above my head, and see another boat passing on the river below. I'd like to be on that boat, I muse, arms aching, Please let there be only a few more seconds of this. And if only he'd stop screaming at me.

I drop my arms and dare to sneak a glance behind. There's Jeff crouching in a ditch, baseball-capped and sweat-soaked, like a homicidal mole dramatically focussed on a tiny metal box in front of him, his video monitor. He raises his arm to alert the crew. Showtime again. I face forward, brace for the onslaught and remind myself it's all in the name of rock'n'roll.

Not finding Waterboys was becoming a hallmark of my sojourn in America, and as time came to make a record and the first highs of being in New York wore off I began to notice a new feeling: I was musically lonesome. I loved the city and its twenty-four hour parade of human life, but I missed the old world and above all the company of musicians who inhabited the same imaginal space as me. The players I met in New York had no idea what I'd experienced in Ireland and I didn't know how to convey it to them. And as a conspirator Dick Lackaday was no substitute for Dunford or Wickham. Anto, on sabbatical fronting his own band round the London clubs, knew and understood, but he wasn't here. And in his absence a shocking thing had happened: running my new songs on the tape loop of my mind I didn't hear the Human Saxophone at all. There was no place in the music for my oldest colleague.

Anto had played many roles in the band – soloist, sideman, foil, partner, wildcard – and our telepathic radar was so sharp I knew what he was going to play before he played it. But that was the problem: Anto and I had exhausted every combination I could imagine and however much his presence would have eased what was beginning to feel like exile, the music said no. After wrestling with this conclusion for several months I returned to Dublin at Christmas 1991 and told him it was over. He didn't believe me, just kept looking at me as if I'd grown an extra head. But once he realised I meant it, he was shocked. And when he didn't turn up to a meeting that evening I figured he needed time to adjust. It would be years before we spoke or played together again.

I flew back to New York and dived straight into making the new Waterboys album, already titled *Dream Harder*. I'd been postponing the sessions while I looked for musicians, but with Zutaut and Dick Lackaday breathing down my neck, and dates booked round the availability of co-producer Bill Price, I couldn't put it off any longer. In the nick of time I found a girl drummer, Carla Azar, and a New York bassist called Charley Drayton, and we gathered for rehearsals with Bill.

Bill Price was a veteran English recording engineer who'd been around for years. I'd bought singles he'd made in the sixties, like Marmalade's Reflections 'Of My Life', a hazy pop hit that sounded to my ten-year-old ears like tears alchemised into music, and he'd mixed all the best punk classics, crunching blasts of energy such as the Sex Pistols' *God Save The Queen* and The Clash's *London Calling*. Thirty years of rock had been processed through the discerning filter of Bill's ears, and by late 1991 he was enjoying a run of autumnal success having mixed Guns N' Roses' *Use Your Illusion I* and *II* for Tom Zutaut. Whatever I thought about G N' R's neanderthal efforts, the albums sat like a pair of fat crows on top of the American album charts crapping on all competitors, fabulously mixed in Bill's ballsy yet luminous trademark sound. And when Zutaut introduced us in a swanky hotel overlooking Central Park I liked Bill straight away. The mark of the wizard was in his face and he had piercing dark eyes, wore pressed jeans and a hooped rugby shirt (I forgave him these) and walked with a soft padding lope as if perpetually tiptoeing round dangerous or volatile people, which for much of his career in music he probably had been. He was no fool either. When Charley Drayton started arriving late for rehearsals and neglecting to learn the songs, Bill fired him without a qualm.

Charley made one brilliant musical suggestion before he was axed: a key change in the intro of 'Glastonbury Song'. And the dude who replaced him was no less creative. Scott Thunes was Frank Zappa's bassist, a bug-eyed, pony-tailed West Coast genius, suggested by Bill, who invented killer hooks, learned songs in a nanosecond and did the *New York Times* crossword between takes. Drummer Carla was

207

a sassy tomboy from Alabama via L.A. who spent most of her time on the phone dissing her previous employers, Wendy & Lisa. When Bill coaxed her from the hospitality lounge to sit behind her low-slung kit she played lopsided, jittery grooves punctuated by fabulous drum fills that sounded like sudden bursts of machine gun fire. The music the three of us made together was a kind of faux rock'n'roll, not exactly powerful (Carla wasn't that kind of drummer) and nothing like what I'd had in mind when I wrote the songs. But it had a quirkiness I liked and, with the clock ticking, for the first time in my life I sacrificed the sound in my head.

The work progressed swiftly enough, but there was a difficulty with one musician. Scott and Carla had a bickering, juvenile attitude to each other and spent all day squabbling comically like brother and sister. Despite this, or perhaps because of it, they gelled musically. The band member I had a problem with was myself. I couldn't find my demon inside, the iron musical will that had propelled me through the eighties. Maybe the act of giving up my musical vision in the haste to start recording had self-sabotaged me, or my confidence was shot because I was following-up an unsuccessful album. Or maybe the act of co-producing, deferring to other people's opinions instead of taking sole responsibility for the record, blunted my edges. Whatever, I wasn't on fire. I wasn't even smouldering. Nor could the presence of this era's Black Book, laid open like a talisman on the mixing desk with all its hieroglyphic notes and instructions, rouse my musical demon. It was proof that money isn't everything. I had a $2.8 million record deal and studio time in the poshest recording parlours of Manhattan, but no mojo.

And though I dug Bill and savoured his wizardry, our imaginations didn't crackle on the same wavelength. A groove that sounded stiff to me sounded fine to Bill. Or he'd say I could sing a song better when I felt I'd already nailed it. We worked to accommodate each other but a shared understanding didn't develop. Zutaut and Dick Lackaday were happy with the work, so I relied on their opinions and by May the album was complete, but when I played it at home the music sounded too generic, with not enough Waterboys spirit. Stung, I shook some semblance of my old willpower into action and spent half the summer hunkered down in Electric Lady, Jimi Hendrix's funky old studio in Greenwich Village, overdubbing new parts, re-doing vocals and bringing the record closer in line with my own taste.

In the autumn of '92 the amended work was mixed by a young L.A. producer called Brendan O'Brien. I liked the results: fashionably dry, with no reverb, and a tight modern edge. But Zutaut didn't dig it and insisted Bill Price remix the tapes again in his more traditional rock sound. I wasn't sure enough of my opinion to fight the corner and Tom got his way, finishing the album himself with Bill in early 1993. When *Dream Harder* came out that May it debuted high in the British charts, getting sufficiently good reviews to restore some of The Waterboys' critical status. But I knew the record had captured me at half power and was leagues short of the restatement of purpose I'd hoped for. I would put this right by doing a killer concert tour.

I needed a properly powerful band, and Carla and Scott, for all their charms, weren't the players I needed. So I held further auditions in New York, a grand parade of hot session drummers and beetle-browed keyboard players so hip that Dick Lackaday's hands shook when he whispered their names. But no combination of these players made a band. The closest I got was a trio of guys I played with on a musician-seeking trip to Texas: Bukka, Joey and Brad. After a monumental jam in an Austin practice room I brought them to New York where we were joined by a brilliant lead guitarist called Chris Bruce. But the music still wasn't right: our styles were too different and didn't add up to a coherent musical identity. Nothing I put together had the flavour that said *Waterboys*. I was beginning to feel like I was banging on a closed door, and as the prospect of a tour evaporated it seemed clear I needed to try something different, like ditch the Waterboys name or leave America. But first I had to make videos to promote the album.

I considered video a bastard mongrel medium that shouldn't even exist, for it violated the prime directive of song writing: *thou shalt cause images to arise in the listener's imagination*. There were as many interpretations of a song as there were minds and hearts that heard it, and video crapped all over this subtle miracle, branding the same set of images onto the brain of every punter. That the images in videos were often shallow and moronic fuelled my conviction, and as soon as I had sufficient authority over my own career I stopped doing them. By 1993 I hadn't made a video for eight years.

This had cost The Waterboys in sales, as record company staff always liked to remind me. I knew our late eighties singles like 'Fisherman's Blues' would have been bigger hits if they'd been promoted with videos, and by the nineties I was questioning my attitude. Might it be worth sacrificing the listener's imaginal relationship with the singles in order to make an album a hit and have its ten other tracks reach more people? But what if the spread of video was neutering the power of song, diminishing its capacity to move people? Perhaps the times had changed and swimming against the tide wasn't doing me or anybody else any good. It was written into my Geffen contract that I didn't have to make videos, but uncertain of my rightness I decided to join the parade and give it a try.

First I needed help learning how to project to camera and not get put off by film crews so I went to an acting teacher, a theatre director called Stephen Jobes. Stephen was the first person I'd met in New York who'd have looked at home in Spiddal; he had Pan eyes and a bushy white beard, and when he looked at me I could feel him looking into my soul. At our first session he taught me to keep my focus and close out distractions by imagining the rest of the world held at bay behind an invisible boundary that I controlled. The second week he had two young actors crouch close to me and make faces while I sang 'The Return Of Pan' with my guitar and ignored them. The third week six actors ran in and out of rooms. The fourth week they started fighting. The fifth week a tall hostile man stood above me and insulted my song while a pretty woman sat at my knees and spoke words of seduction. Through it all I kept playing and singing, shutting them all out, an education which, quite apart from its application on video sets, taught me a lot about maintaining focus on stage.

Meanwhile Geffen had video directors drawing up plots, called 'treatments', for the videos. To my dismay these were mostly filled with clichés and misinterpretations of the songs. Or they missed the point completely: one noted video auteur submitted a script for 'The Return Of Pan' that included an orgy on top of a Mexican pyramid, melting faces and an 'atmosphere of black magic'. The lurid description climaxed, like *Apocalypse Now*, with the words, 'The horror! The horror!'

I turned them all down, which made me unpopular at Geffen, where artists were expected to be 'reasonable'. And because no one shared my view that video was a debased medium, or agreed with me that the treatments were rubbish – and let's be frank, all my handlers really wanted was a glossy three-minute ad to fit MTV's programming style – the focus of the search became 'finding someone that difficult Mike can work with.' I knew this was how the Geffen video department felt because they started suggesting random maverick directors they thought I might take to.

One of these was a cackling misanthrope called Jeff Stein to whom I was introduced in a Sixth Avenue coffee shop. Because Jeff was wearing a t-shirt with the same psychedelic design as a magnet on the fridge in my kitchen I decided to take a chance on him. I was determined to ensure the video conformed to my sense of the song and that it shouldn't contain an irrelevant storyline, so I tried to control the choice of ideas. I showed Jeff a photo from the *Dream Harder* sleeve in which I sat on an amp playing a gold guitar and insisted we recreate it on film with me performing sitting down. Jeff, gleefully and with a touch of sadism, indulged this foolish request, which of course resulted in a passive performance. When I suggested we have some goats in the video Jeff obligingly shipped in a truckload of the little blighters from a farm. But while I'd imagined the goats looking wild and Pan-like, on film they were goofy, like wacky pets at a children's zoo. The grand finale was a trip to the New Jersey Palisades, a line of gaunt cliffs across the river from Manhattan. There we filmed a clip of me standing knee-deep in goats, raising the gold guitar over my head to catch the sun's rays as the camera tracked back to reveal the city skyline. Inevitably the goats broke free and ran amok over the cliffs. A luckless camera assistant broke his leg trying to catch them and had to be airlifted out by helicopter.

When I saw the final edited film I realised the folly of controlling the content myself; though the video was well shot by Jeff it was stiff and kooky, a thousand miles from the intent of the song. Chastened by this experience I veered the other way for the second single, resolving to let whichever director got the job do whatever he wanted. Surely it couldn't turn out any worse! So tapes of 'Glastonbury Song' were sent to a dozen top video-makers in America and Britain, and soon the treatments were jumping out of the fax machine.

Most were the same old procession of clichés and I didn't feel good about offering myself up as a sacrifice for any of them. In desperation the Geffen video staff sent me boxes of directors' showreels to look through and I dutifully knuckled down to the mind-numbing homework of watching hundreds of rock videos. The horror! The horror! But among them was one I admired. Peter Gabriel's 'Digging In The Dirt' was directed by a wildlife video-maker called John Downer, and Gabriel was brilliant and persuasive in it. His lyric, about scrutinising his pain to learn how to heal it, was well served by the visual imagery. So I told a relieved Dick Lackaday, who told a relieved Geffen Records, that I'd do a video with John Downer. The treatment when it arrived was, alas, yet another set of clichés – time-lapse photography of clouds speeding across the sky, freeze-frame drops of water exploding – mixed with Downer's wildlife microfilming techniques and a smattering of misinterpretations of the

'Glastonbury Song' lyric. But I'd said I'd do it and, hoping that because the Gabriel video had been so good somehow this one would be too, I flew to Britain.

The first scene was shot in a field in the West Country. As a smoke machine pumped out billows of mist I was filmed lying on a fallen megalith in the midst of a stone circle. I wasn't just watching a clichéd rock video now; I was in it! And I wasn't Peter Gabriel. Without a musical performance to focus on, my attempts to be natural on camera were awkward. Realising I was ill at ease, John decided to closely direct my every movement.

Over the years so many rock videos have been made starring musicians who aren't actors that directors have developed ways of working around them with the minimum disruption to egos, filming schedules and budgets. An emphasis falls on scenery and context, rather than the individual's performance, 'acting' shots are filmed in a minimum of takes, and a tacit understanding spreads among the crew that, like a ship obliged to carry a landlubber on a voyage, we have a dud amongst us. I was now experiencing this and felt tightly controlled, a prisoner in my own promo: a kind of animated, patronised prop. I was filmed climbing up and down Glastonbury Tor, running across fields, being hosed with water and lying in a pool of dry ice smoke, the film of which, John explained, would be turned upside down so it would look as if I was flying through the clouds. 'It'll be brilliant,' he assured me.

With the video filmed, but not yet seen, I returned to New York and on my first day back encountered an unexpected figure from the past. Karl Wallinger was in town with his group World Party, opening a show for one of Dick Lackaday's other artists. I'd forgiven Karl for slagging me off in the press a few years earlier, and was interested to see him play live. It was an evening concert in Central Park. Irene and I were sitting in guest seats, awaiting the start of the show, when a woman stepped out from the wings onto the stage. She had red hair, wore a black dress and carried something metallic. And she was looking roughly in our direction. I watched her crouch on the lip of the stage and slowly, deliberately point what appeared to be a video camera right at me, as if she knew who I was and where I'd be. Suddenly I realised who it was. Kate Lovecraft was filming us!

She continued for a few seconds then abruptly stood up and went backstage, and almost immediately Karl and his band came on and struck up their first number. They sounded good but I couldn't focus on the show. I was totally unnerved by Kate's little performance, and I felt violated too. I'd lived in New York for two years without running into Kate and I'd almost but not quite forgotten about her. She clearly hadn't forgotten about me. What I'd just witnessed was almost an exact replay of when she came to the South of France, sat in a conspicuous position for the whole Waterboys show, then came backstage to bogusly tell me she was dying of tuberculosis.

I was expected to say hello to Karl afterwards and this meant I'd have to meet Kate. I thought about leaving but I was damned if I was going to give her power over me again by running. I could and would face her – and face her down if I had to. So when the set ended I walked to the backstage entrance and showed my pass to the security guard. Karl seemed unaware of the drama that had played out before the start of his show, and stood with his band outside the dressing room tents, cheerful after their successful concert. And there behind them, watching for me, was Kate. Fear ran through me as I approached. The power she'd once wielded over me still had a grip. I decided to try to defuse this power by being bland, revealing nothing of myself and letting her attitude, whatever it was going to be, wash off me; an improvised form of self-protection. I walked up to her, proffered my hand in customary fashion and said, 'Kate. How nice to see you again,' in a colourless voice.

She looked me up and down deliberately, as if summing me up, with an air that suggested I was lower than the worms in the ground.

'You haven't changed,' she said witheringly, and I felt her painting me back into the dynamics of our old relationship. Then she added,

'People keep telling me I shouldn't turn up for this or that event around town. Why is that?'

There was truth in this. When The Waterboys had played in New York in 1989 and 1990 I'd given strict instructions to my agents not to give Kate guest access, should she come asking.

'I haven't the faintest idea what you're talking about,' I lied, bland-voiced, looking her in the eye. 'Good,' she said, trying to score the point. But my boundary had held and there was nowhere else for her to take the matter, or the interaction. Not yet powerful enough in myself to call her out, or to meet fire with fire, at least I could deal with her while keeping my cool. I left, heart beating like an army of drummers, but as I returned home the emotion turned from fear into a delayed rage. How dare she look me up and down and judge me! How dare she walk out on someone's fucking stage and point a camera at me and my wife! Rage can be the most useful and healthy of emotions. A cathartic transforming fire burned in my guts for a week. If I ever met Kate Lovecraft again she'd have no more power over me.

Then, when I'd just about cooled down, the edit of the 'Glastonbury Song' video dropped through the mailbox at Hudson Street. I unpacked it, stuck the tape in the player and sat back to watch. A clock appeared on screen ticking down the seconds to zero. The song began. As the intro guitars played I lay on a standing stone in the mist, looking like a sixties pop star who'd stumbled on the set of a low-budget remake of *Wuthering Heights* and fallen asleep on the scenery. And it didn't get better. The video was a load of cleverly filmed nonsensical tosh. Worst of all, every time the chorus came round the dry ice footage showed me portentously sticking my head, Jehovah-like, from a cloud high above Glastonbury Tor. And because viewers assume artists to be complicit in their videos, it made me look like an egotist with a messiah complex who thought I was god. The horror! There was only one thing to do: I pulled the fucker.

When I told Dick Lackaday and Geffen's video people that on no account was the promo to be shown, they accepted it in a resigned sort of way. It was just the latest example of 'difficult Mike'. But when John Downer heard he blew his nut, phoned me at home, and ranted bitterly at me for cancelling his film and destroying all his work 'on a whim.' I was unmoved; it wasn't his public image that was on the line, nor his song buried neck-deep in baloney. The top brass at Geffen were understandably perplexed, though, and when the company boss, an old-school American gentleman called Ed Rosenblatt, called to persuade me to let the video be shown, I could sense the frustration behind his measured tones. The implied choice was clear: release the video and save my relationship with the company, or pull it and suffer that most dreaded of music business shutdowns, record company demotivation.

But whichever way I weighed it, the video was unacceptable. I stood my ground and put my hopes in 'Glastonbury Song' being a hit in Britain; if that happened Geffen would be motivated again soon enough. And for a moment it looked like the gamble would pay off. The single entered the top thirty and I flew to London to perform on BBC's *Top Of The Pops* with a one-off Waterboys featuring Carla, Scott and Chris Bruce. But the following week 'Glastonbury Song' stalled in the lower twenties, just as 'The Return of Pan' had done three months before. The gamble had failed.

The only way to promote *Dream Harder* now was a tour. But I still had no band; further auditions had drawn another blank and I'd begun to accept I was flogging a dead horse. The Waterboys had stood for a shared vision, a band of musical friends and soulmates, and no combination I'd found in America had come close to living up to this. I didn't want to sully my band's reputation by heading out on the road now with an ill-matched set of hired hands. I was caught between a colourful past and a dysfunctional present and could find no way forwards. The game was up and this campaign was over.

So was Dick Lackaday. After two years his charm had expired. He'd made an art form of gilding his image as the man people liked to do business with, even when it meant isolating his artist as the bad guy. When disagreements with Geffen arose, instead of saying, '*We* don't want such-and-such to happen,' Dick would say, '*Mike* doesn't want to do this. I've tried to persuade him but it's no use.' I could be wrong as often as anyone, and I'd probably made more daft decisions in the last two years of my career than in the first ten combined, but for his twenty per cent I required a manager who'd call me out in private and present a united front in public. After one backslide too many I visited Dick on a hot August day in his Upper West Side office and uttered the overdue words: you're fired.

I had one more album to make for Geffen but with no band and no manager there wasn't a whole lot of anything keeping me in New York. Nor could anything have kept me now, for a new and profoundly different adventure was already calling.

CHAPTER 15

THE PHILOSOPHY ROOM

On a spring day in 1983 a taxi speeds along Oxford Street, hangs a right at Centrepoint and drops a twenty-four-year-old me on Charing Cross Road. I slip through the hordes of shoppers and enter Foyles, the largest bookshop in London. Looking round for an assistant, I spot a guy placing books on the shelves. 'Excuse me,' I say to him, 'where will I find The History Of Magic *by Eliphas Levi?' He thinks for a moment then replies, 'Anything like that would be in the Philosophy Room on the top floor. Take the lift over there.'*

The lift is ancient, looks like it hasn't been upgraded since Albert was the Prince Consort, and it takes forever, wheezing and rattling all the way up. Finally it shudders to a stop. I pull the heavy iron grille open and emerge onto a quiet floor with an air of academia and shelves full of music books, manuscripts of Broadway shows, and sheafs of folk songs and jazz standards. I ask another assistant where the Philosophy Room is and she points to a small archway in the far corner.

I cross the room, go through the arch and down some steps which lead into a small antechamber. Here the atmosphere is different, less fusty than the music department I've just left, more rarefied. As I scan the category signs on the shelves my eye takes in Buddhism, Tao, Zen, Hinduism, Christianity and Judaism and I realise the Philosophy Room is really the religion or spirituality room. There are philosophers here too, though, from Socrates on the lowest shelf to Bertrand Russell at the top. And some weirder subjects: Paganism, Witchcraft, Rosicrucianism, Western Mysteries. I didn't know there were books about things like Paganism, and as for the Western Mysteries, I haven't the faintest idea what those are. But the titles are intriguing: The Esoteric Orders and Their Work, The Training and Work of an Initiate. *What's all that about?*

Magic is next to them. And yes, here's Eliphas Levi's History Of Magic, *a thick black paperback with a strange diagram on the cover. I scan through the pages. My God, there's a whole world in here. The chapters include Hermetic Magic, The Mathematical Magic Of Pythagoras, Mystics, The Occult Sciences, Rosicrucians … that word again. It's all wonderfully archaic and fascinating and I want to read every page at once. I stick the book under my arm but I'm not quite ready for the checkout desk. I'm going to root through all the other mysterious wonders on these shelves, for I've the queerest feeling that in this tiny room at the top of Foyles I'll find something I didn't know I was even looking for, but which I've been seeking my whole life.*

When I lived near the Portobello Road in the eighties I used to frequent Elgin Books, a quiet cerebral bookstore of the kind that stops time and casts a spell. One day, browsing in its poetry section, I embarked on an unexpected journey that was to run parallel with my music, sometimes informing it, sometimes wholly separate, and which ten years later would summon me from exile in New York to the most unlikely circumstances I could have imagined.

For that day in the sweet silence of Elgin Books I came upon a scarlet-covered volume of *A Season In Hell* and *The Illuminations* by Arthur Rimbaud, the teenage French poet of the late 1800s. I knew Rimbaud's name because my old heroine Patti Smith was always raving about him in interviews and dropping him into song lyrics, but I'd never been tempted to check him out. Perhaps Patti made Rimbaud sound too ineffably hip and arty, a concept better left unexplored, its glamour and mystery intact. Or perhaps I just hadn't been ready. But here was the real thing within my grasp. I bought the book and read it that night by the light of a table lamp in my basement flat.

It was spectacular: a storm of philosophical and visionary imaginings and dramatic self-histories expressed with boldness, passion and a wickedly grotesque humour. I found it absolutely compelling and immediately saw where Patti had got a truckload of her ideas. Rimbaud's writing had a fire and edge that bypassed the tyrants of my mind and spoke directly to my imagination. My fascination was particularly gripped by a letter of his quoted in the introduction, an apparently famous item called the 'Lettre Du Voyant', in which the sixteen-year-old Arthur, writing to a friend, expresses his belief in the poet as a *voyant*, a visionary whose work will one day lead to the discovery of the 'universal language of the soul.'

I was fascinated by this idea, which suggested the existence of a state of consciousness, a wavelength, on which all human beings could be connected. If there was such a thing, and if the amazing Rimbaud had gone on to find it, I wanted to know. So next day I returned to the bookshop to buy Rimbaud's *Complete Works* and a biography of him written by an Irish scholar called Enid Starkie. *The Complete Works* yielded another motherlode of charismatic poetry, though no further clues about any universal language. But in the biography I read that Rimbaud's ideas had been influenced by a contemporary Frenchman called Eliphas Levi, author of something called *The History Of Magic*. I didn't know what this magic was, but clearly Eliphas wasn't talking conjuring tricks. Starkie summed up the core of Levi's teachings:

> If man can slough off human egoism and human personality and learn to use his faculties, he can illuminate the darkness with light and seize possession of the treasures of the universe. Nothing will be able to withstand the power of his will when he has learnt to move it in harmony with the force of divine love. He will become an illuminist, one who enjoys and possesses light. By continued effort at self-culture and the eradication of human egoism the soul becomes worthy of receiving this light, of becoming the conductor of this radiance. When he has placed his own frail will into direct communication with the eternal will, he will be able to direct that will like the point of an arrow, and to send peace or turmoil into the souls of other men.

Wow! I had to find out more about this Eliphas Levi, so I went back again to Elgin Books. The store was run by a quiet, courteous and soulful lady with short greying hair. I asked her if she stocked Levi's *History of Magic*. Playing her appointed role in the unfolding drama of a young man's life, she replied no, but told me where I'd find it. I thanked her, strode down the street, hailed a taxi on Ladbroke Grove and instructed the driver, 'Foyles bookshop, please.'

From the dozen books I purchased at Foyles that day I learned there existed infinitely more types of spirituality than those I'd heard of – that there were indeed more things in heaven and earth, Horatio, than were dreamt of in my philosophy. Hindu god-men, Persian mystic poets, techniques for expanding consciousness, nature-worshipping pagans, energy centres called *chakras* in the human body, levels of existence beyond normal perception … it was dizzying. Once I'd adjusted to the onslaught of information I began to grasp that the different spiritual systems shared a belief in a transcendent, attainable reality to which all the world's religions pointed: that all is one, that our sense of separation is an illusion and that the entity or force we call God is actually inside all things, including us.

The great religions themselves, I learned, had begun as the methods by which different cultures, races and times addressed and approached this reality, and that there was a tradition of reserved or hidden teachings behind the public faces of the religions, comprising deeper wisdom attainable only through prolonged dedication and discipline. These teachings, called *The Perennial Wisdom, The Perennial Philosophy* or simply *The Mysteries*, had been the preserve of closed religious orders and discreet groups, sometimes known as *Mystery Schools*, but in the twentieth century were increasingly being made public through books and spiritual workshops. They included now-commonplace subjects like meditation and yoga, and were gathered under fabulous names like Anthroposophy, Gnosticism, Sufism and the mysterious Rosicrucianism. I stood before this new world like an explorer in the foothills of a great mountain range. I had a long way to go before my crude mental grasping of spiritual principles turned into experiential understanding, but the discovery, while challenging, was a huge relief. I'd always found British church Christianity a depressing, soul-numbing enterprise, which spoke to me about neither the mysteries of life nor the content of my heart. That I could now explore forms of spirituality that did was thrilling.

I read and I read. My favourite book was Peter Russell's *The Awakening Earth*, a mighty treatise on the evolution of consciousness, which confirmed all my heart had ever told me about the adventure of being human; and my favourite writer was Dion Fortune, a Welsh mystic of the thirties and forties whose books, written in a sturdy, powerfully poetic voice, provided me with my preferred font of spiritual knowledge. By the end of 1983, six or seven months after my epiphany in Foyles, I knew my way pretty well around the basics of esoteric and new age literature. These included *karma* – the law of cause and effect – and the universal principle that energy follows thought, a process to which every enterprise and intrigue in history attests. I had countless opportunities to observe the action of both in my own life.

I tried using 'energy follows thought' as a home-made spiritual practice, and developed over a period of several years a daily discipline of visualising trouble spots in the world (Iran and Iraq, then at war with each other, for example) surrounded by energies of peace and lovingness, and holding this image in my mind. There was no way of knowing the effectiveness of this, and for all I knew I was wasting my time, but I kept doing it, hoping my efforts would merge with similar intentions on the part of others, whoever and wherever they might be. I used the same principle with my music: like any ambitious rock'n'roller worth the leather trousers he walked around in, I deliberately envisioned my songwriting exploding into greatness and my band being successful.

I learned discernment, too: how to identify and avoid dubious information, charlatans, self-glorifiers and fools, for there were plenty of those in the spirituality business. And by trial and error I learned my way through the maze of ideas, which meant not simply cramming my head with information but recognising which books were dodgy, which were too impossibly advanced, and which were just right for me at that moment. Once I came across *The Perennial Wisdom* my ambitions began to shift. I still wanted to be the best songwriter and rock'n'roller in the world, but overruling that was the growing desire to increase my awareness. I lost all interest in the lyrics of rock musicians unless they addressed or contained something of *The Mysteries*. Van Morrison's 'Haunts Of Ancient Peace' (a sublime *Perennial Wisdom* song), Little Richard's 'Tutti Frutti' (pure energy) and Hank Williams's 'Your Cheatin' Heart' (an elegant discourse on the law of karma, filtered through the vernacular of rural American folk-wisdom) were food for my soul, but the intellectual ruminations of most adult rock singers now held no attraction whatsoever.

My own writing was hugely affected. I'd addressed spiritual matters in my songs before but it had been like fumbling in the dark, not even knowing what I was looking for. Suddenly someone had switched the light on. 'The Big Music', with its lyric about discovering *The Mysteries*, was the first number I wrote after the expedition to Foyles, and every song on *This Is The Sea* was full of my new discoveries. Sometimes the influence was direct, like on 'The Pan Within', an occult love song, the premise and title of which came from Dion Fortune's writings; and sometimes more general, as on 'Trumpets', a kind of gnostic devotional addressed to a being who was part God, part lover. *The Perennial Wisdom* fired my imagination and emotions and without its inspiration songs like 'The Whole Of The Moon', 'Medicine Bow' and 'This Is The Sea' wouldn't have been written. One of Dion Fortune's maxims was *when the student is ready the teacher will appear*, and figuring that I must be ready (after all, I'd followed a trail and found *The Perennial Wisdom* for myself) I cocked an eye and an ear for my teacher. But no one appeared. I didn't coincidentally meet a wiser older person who took me under their wing; I didn't stumble upon a Mystery School.

There weren't many people I could talk to about these interests apart from a couple of intrigued Waterboys like Steve Wickham and Karl Wallinger, a few old friends and my mother. Others, like Nigel Grainge who spotted me reading Dion Fortune's *The Esoteric Philosophy Of Love And Marriage* in the Ensign offices one day, thought I'd lost a few screws. The only people I came across during the eighties who revealed a knowledge of *The Perennial Wisdom* happened to be three of the most intense characters I'd ever met, Steve Cooney, Kate Lovecraft and Robbie The Pict.

Cooney had been initiated by Aborigines in his native Australia and had the chest scars to prove it, and he understood those central pillars of the Aboriginal mysteries, the dreamtime and the songlines. But trying to talk to him about it through the swirl of his passions and paranoia was like trying to free a songbird from a thicket. Kate Lovecraft had knowledge of many kinds of spirituality and had been to India where she claimed to be on first-name terms with gurus like the godman Sai Baba, of whom she cooed, 'he's my friend!' She showed me yoga exercises as well as techniques to change my attitude before going into a room, and how to attract spiritual experiences to myself by repeating 'I want God' over and over again like a mantra. I'm grateful to her for those, however ill-starred our relationship was. Robbie The Pict had owned a new age bookshop in Edinburgh and this involvement ran parallel with his campaign for Scottish independence and his fondness for blowing harmonica with grungy blues bands. We discovered our mutual interest in *The Mysteries* after a Waterboys show when Robbie, holding forth in a hotel bar about the condition of the world, exclaimed, 'The problem is everyone's afraid of three little words …' and looked at me to see if I knew what he was going to say. Suddenly I did. We locked eyes and said in stereo, 'I am God.'

When I moved to Ireland *The Mysteries* continued to inspire the writing of songs, including 'Fisherman's Blues' and 'Strange Boat', until I headed west and became absorbed in the Celtic world. Here my absorption in spiritual literature receded; there was too much else to learn. But when I came out the other side of the Celtic mists at the end of 1990 I found my interest in *The Perennial Wisdom* awaiting me like an old friend. This time I was determined to go beyond learning on my own, which meant joining a group and receiving instruction in a specific system. And I figured that when I moved to New York, with all the different kinds of spirituality available in that most culturally liberated of cities, I'd at last find my teacher or school.

So between recording sessions for the *Dream Harder* album I kick-started the process by taking meditation classes. Meditation was something I'd been meaning to do for years. Being unable to meditate, despite all I'd figured out for myself, meant I felt like a spiritual virgin. If I could meditate, I imagined, I'd be able to access another mode of consciousness, and experience or perceive things that now I couldn't. So I signed up for a Raja Yoga course at a New York bookshop and spent my evenings sitting in painful folded-leg positions, while inwardly repeating a mantra with twenty other beginners under the gimlet eye of an ascetic lady instructor called Lois. Lois was an initiate of the Hindu mysteries with a sharp but distant air about her, who'd never make eye contact with anyone in the class yet appeared to always know what we were all thinking and feeling. After a few weeks I discovered my preconceptions about meditation were absolutely right; it was like opening a new wing in the house of my mind from which I could observe myself and understand with more clarity why I did things. I could watch my thoughts and emotions without *being* them; a delightful liberation. But though meditation was a great tool, and one that I continued to practise, the path of the East itself didn't appeal to me. I was still searching.

In the summer of 1992 Irene and I rented a house near Woodstock, a couple of hours north of New York, to which we'd retreat when the Manhattan heat got too crazy. My mother came over for a holiday, and one day she and I were browsing in one of Woodstock's many cute new age bookstores when she spotted a video about a community in Scotland called Findhorn, which she'd recently visited. I dimly remembered reading an article about this place in the eighties and seeing a photograph of its founders, three respectable-looking elderly people with white hair. There had been something special about them, I remembered, but at the time I wasn't drawn to explore further. My mother bought the video (its rather obscure title was *Opening Doors Within*) and that evening we watched it together, me doing so not because I was particularly interested but to keep my mother company. But as the film began, I found myself being pulled in. After five minutes I was gripped. After ten I was turning into the guy in Dylan's song 'Tangled Up In Blue', who on reading a book of poems says, 'Every one of those words ran true and glowed like burning coal, pourin' off of every page like it was written in my soul.'

The agent of my electrification was one of the elderly people I'd seen in the photograph years before, a perm-haired lady called Eileen, and what she said in her down-to-earth way about the power of gratitude and love hit me like a thunderbolt. I'd come across such teachings before – the importance of loving oneself, the nature of unconditional love, and how a sense of gratitude is what keeps love flowing – but something about Eileen's delivery made me hear these things as if for the first time. For in her voice was a profound yet gentle power, a mix of compassion, experience and grace, I came to realise later, that spoke directly to my heart. And a crucial thing: she wasn't trying to make the viewer follow or believe her. She was showing them the way to their own wisdom, and because of this I instinctively felt right about her. Without knowing it I was responding to the hallmark of the true spiritual teacher, one who shows you how to access your power rather than taking it from you.

Yet Eileen was the most unlikely teacher I could imagine – a thousand miles from my 'spiritual master' preconceptions of beetle-browed men with cloaks and hats, or sylph-like women carrying old books down city streets on their way to secret meetings. No, my teacher had manifested after all these years as a cosy white-haired granny, and coming from her was everything I most needed to hear. When the film finished fifty-five minutes later I knew I would visit this Findhorn place. I'd found my school.

For several months I read everything on the Findhorn community I could find. It had begun in 1962 with a few mystics living in a caravan on some waste ground, then grew into a community based on *The Perennial Wisdom* premise that 'God' – or whatever name you want to give to the organising principle of the universe – is inside everything and everyone. The Findhorn people claimed to have found ways of contacting this inner spiritual source, and Eileen apparently could hear its guidance as a 'still, small voice' inside her. But what sealed it for me was that there was no pomp or fanfare. If these people were fakes they'd be hyping it to high heaven. Findhorn seemed to be a combination of the deeply spiritual and the deeply normal, and that felt authentic. But reserving judgment, I decided to go and see for myself.

The community was in Northeast Scotland and I flew from New York to Glasgow and thence, on a dark October night, to Inverness. From there a taxi drove me through a windblown landscape past dark pine forests and through small depressed towns with boarded-up churches and bright fish and chip shops. The driver chatted to me, 'So you're going to the community, eh? Oh aye, they're very impressive people there, very impressive people,' without giving more details. Nor did I ask for any; I was deep in my thoughts, wondering what this place I'd read and thought so much about would be really like. And who would I find myself to be when I was there? After half an hour we veered onto a narrow road and drove several miles along the side of a moonlit bay. We took a sharp left down a switchback lane and a grand house hove into view. I recognised it from photographs: Minton House, a decaying stately pile run as a B&B by community members. We pulled up, I paid the driver, walked up a flight of stone steps to the door and rang the bell. I heard a creaking of floorboards and the approach of heavy footsteps, then a tall bearded man opened the door and scrutinised me, registering in one sweep of his eyes my long hair, leather jacket and guitar case. I told him my name and said I'd booked a room. 'Oh?' he replied, surprised, '*You're* not what we expected.'

This was an unnerving start and it didn't get any better when he brought me into the lounge and introduced me to the inmates, a ragtag crew sitting around with dodgy jumpers and sharp eyes. My host, whose name was Ian, seemed just as spooked by me as I was by him. He gave me an awkward tour of the tea-making facilities then showed me to my room. I unpacked, strummed a few chords on my guitar and went back downstairs where an elderly English fellow called Reg, one of the lurkers in the lounge, offered to take me across the road to the community for 'Sacred Dance', whatever that was. It sounded awful but figuring I should enter into the spirit of things I agreed.

Reg threw on a jerkin and we walked out of the house back into the wild night, across the main road then down a dark country lane lined by high trees that roared in the wind. Suddenly on our left a fantastical structure appeared through a gap in the trees like a hallucination. Forty feet high with a roof like a giant, cocked wizard's hat, its front a stained-glass riot of psychedelic patterns, the thing looked like an Atlantean fire temple or something out of a futuristic episode of *The Flintstones*. It was absolutely, loopily, magnificent.

'This is our Universal Hall,' said Reg, as deadpan as if he was pointing out the British Legion, and led me up a crunchy gravel path through the building's huge wooden doors and into an odd, shabby interior. There was a beautiful smell of timber but the carpet was worn and the walls were peeling. From somewhere came the muffled sound of burbling folk music. I was thinking that Universal Hall wasn't much to look at on the inside when Reg tapped me lightly on the shoulder and indicated I should follow him up a curved wooden staircase. At the top was a felt-covered door. Reg led me through and I realised what I'd seen downstairs had been only the lobby. For below us was an august five-sided performance space like a Greek forum, with high vaulted ceiling and rows of purple and gold seats on three sides, descending to a polished wooden floor. On this, dwarfed by their surroundings, a dozen people were dancing in a circle, hands linked, to Balkan music coming from a slightly distorted boom box. Reg and I sat down in a back row and watched them, a motley bunch: several middle-aged ladies, some shy-looking men, a gangly chap in a fair isle sweater who stood a foot taller than anyone else, and three or four cheerful girls. When the tune ended Reg nudged me and to my terror indicated we should join them.

Holding hands with strangers while performing Eastern European folk dances in a new age theatre-temple was a novel experience. A lady instructor with a German accent showed us the steps and we whirled round and round to the warbling of clarinets and balalaikas. It was good fun in a gusty kind of way, though I had no idea where the *sacred* part came in. When we finished, four or five dances later, the instructor told us to hug at least three other people before saying goodnight. Another terrifying prospect. I managed two. That night I rested well in my little room, the wind in the trees lulling me to deep sleep, and next day, after breakfast with the other inmates, I explored Findhorn. The community turned out to be a rambling settlement of old caravans, fantastical trees (someone had done a lot of planting twenty years earlier) and pristine Scandinavian-style wooden houses, several of them round, like something out of a nursery rhyme or a Dr Seuss book. There was a Royal Air Force base immediately south of the site, with shockingly loud jets taking off and landing, while to the north stood a deep forest of pine trees. The place confounded all my ideas about what a spiritual community should be: there was no monkish music drifting out of the buildings, nobody wore robes. The people I saw on the paths or through windows were absorbed in their own business and no one paid any attention to me. Nor did anyone recognise me as Mike Scott of The Waterboys, or if they did they weren't letting on.

I hung around all that day and some of the next and even once caught sight of Eileen, the lady in the video, distinctive at a distance with her white permed hair. But though I liked the place I didn't experience anything like the spiritual charge I'd felt watching the film. Then shortly before I left for the airport on my third day I went to a lunchtime meditation at one of the community's sanctuaries, a plain wooden building unassumingly placed between some sheds and a garden. I walked in and twenty or thirty people, most with eyes closed, were sitting on a circle of chairs centred round a candle on a low wooden plinth. I sat down in an empty seat, closed my eyes too and waited for whatever was to happen. A woman began to speak in a clear English voice and asked us to imagine a golden light, like a pillar of energy, in the centre of the sanctuary. I did this, enjoying the novelty of knowing that everyone else in the room was doing it too. Then she asked us to visualise this light filling the whole sanctuary. I did this too, finding it easy enough, with an extra little thrill at the knowledge that all our mental images had just expanded together. Next she instructed us to see the light radiating out into the local area, blessing and loving all it came into contact with. And as I did this there came a change. I felt my emotions engage, and as I pictured the light 'blessing and loving' whatever it touched, a jet of compassion begin to flow in me. Then her voice continued, asking us to imagine the light spreading to Scotland's holy isle of Iona and to England's sacred centre, Glastonbury, then expanding to cover all of the British Isles. After each place name she allowed a short space of silence, and in one of these something very powerful happened. My sense of this 'light' shifted from being something imagined to something *experienced*. By some alchemy, by the working of some process or law beyond my ken, the light became real. I could feel it buzzing like a pressure, flowing through me as if I was some kind of battery. It was like taking a potent drug, except with a feeling of immense natural wellbeing.

The woman's voice broke in on my awareness again as she directed us to imagine the light spreading beyond Britain, across Europe, then America and Africa and finally round the whole world. And as I consciously directed the light to do this (for it was a question of directing now, rather than imagining) I felt waves of inspiration flow through me as if I was part of a mighty system. I was awed in the presence of something far bigger than myself. And as I sat in silence for the last ten minutes of the meditation, the power radiating around and through me, I felt like I'd come home after wandering all the days of my life, and realised I was living the vision in the Eliphas Levi passage that had begun my journey all those years before. I'd found it! And when a small gong sounded to signal the meditation's end and everyone silently stood up, I walked out of the sanctuary, stunned, into the cold Northern Scottish air, ready to proclaim to the skies that love was alive and everything was going to be all right forever. Though I could tell that wasn't the done thing here; I didn't know what the other meditators had experienced but when I looked at them emerging from the building they were quiet and relaxed, already strolling off to their afternoon duties. They inhabited a culture where this kind of work was simply part of daily life.

In transports of inspiration I went back to my B&B to collect my bags and bumped into Reg. 'Come into the office with me, Mike, would you?' he asked. Figuring it must be obvious to an old hand like Reg that I'd just had a serious spiritual experience I followed him, ready for something very meaningful to happen in the office. Perhaps Reg was going to welcome me to the inner group of super meditators or impart to me some final key of wisdom, a seal on the experience I'd just had. He lifted a slip of paper from the top of a cluttered desk and silently handed it to me. I looked. It was my bill for two nights' bed and breakfast. This was a good reminder to keep my feet on the ground after spiritual experiences. Nevertheless, what had happened was immense. As I flew back to New York I felt I was returning from another civilisation. It was like when I'd gone to the West of Ireland, only that was an older world, and this was a new one. I wanted to explore this culture, to absorb it, become it, and receive whatever lessons and experiences it had to offer. And something else: what would happen if I could connect the machinery of my songs, lyrics and band to the flow of inspiration I'd felt in the Findhorn sanctuary?

CHAPTER 16

SOME KIND OF POP STAR LIVING UP AT CLUNY

January 1994. Evening in the Northeast of Scotland. The waters of the Moray Firth are dark and restless. A harsh wind barrels down from the Arctic. A few lights glow in little hamlets and isolated cottages. Occasionally a car whizzes down a coastal road, its headlights making elliptical patterns in the night.

But from a long wooden building by the edge of a bay comes cheerful music. The Findhorn community is celebrating Burns Night with a ceilidh, and inside the community centre a veritable league of nations is gathered: boisterous German women, fine-boned Spanish men, visitors from Capetown, Rome and Buenos Aires, a troop of teenage American students, a muster of Antipodeans and even a few native Scots in kilts. Around the sides of the hall sit mothers with babies, middle-aged men out of puff, and a gaggle of wise-eyed old ladies. Supper was served an hour ago, the address to the haggis has been given, and a ragged eightsome reel is in full flow, ninety-six feet clumping on the wooden floor.

I'm watching this merry scene from my vantage point as guitarist in the ceilidh band. And man, we're the weirdest ceilidh band ever: a bagpiper, a classical violinist, a bongo-playing Dutch girl … and me. Our music hurtles along with a kind of one-legged lope as the multitude parades in front of us. When the dance ends I strum a loud rally on the guitar, Margo's bongos slip slightly out of time, and Rory's pipes wrap up the tune with an ear-blistering squeal The next number is announced, 'The Gay Gordons', a Scottish country jig with a ho-ho rhythm. I turn to Rory and ask what the accompanying music will be. He replies, 'The March'. Ah yes, 'The March', properly named 'The Liberty Bell', but most famous (though my three exotic bandmates don't seem to be aware of this) as the theme music to Monty Python's Flying Circus.

Rory squeezes his pipes, emitting another bloodcurdling wail, and launches haphazardly into the tune. And as I strum along, watching the dance, it strikes me that this has got to be the most surreal moment of my life. Three years after my last show I'm somewhere in rural Scotland playing the Monty Python theme with bongos and bagpipes, while forty or fifty cheery foreigners frolic back and forth doing The Gay Gordons.

When things collapsed with Geffen, Dick Lackaday and New York, my next move was clear. Set up camp in the powerful atmosphere of the Findhorn community. This was a leap into the unknown, not just for me but also for rock'n'roll: basing a band's centre of operations in a spiritual mystery school had never been done before, as far as I knew. And in the late summer of 1993 I dragged my poor wife Irene to Scotland with the intention of convincing her to live in Findhorn.

When I'd returned from my first visit a year before, spectacularly inspired and excited, and having made a U-turn from my usual diet of chicken and chips to nothing but vegetarian food, Irene thought I'd been brainwashed, and decried the community's philosophy as 'codswaddle'. And she wasn't much happier now. We drove up through Scotland, checked into a local hotel and made daily excursions into the community, Irene reluctantly tagging along. I couldn't get her near a meal in the community centre, though I managed to persuade her to take tea with a few friendly members in their wooden eco-houses. And after a week it was official – she wasn't having any of it.

I accepted that Findhorn wasn't for everyone, least of all my wife, and so we focussed instead on relocating to Dublin, which was close enough to Findhorn for me to visit regularly. We rented a house called Campanella, an ivy-draped gaff with a walled garden, a gate lodge and a 'Napoleon room' full of grim-looking busts of the Emperor, a few hundred yards down the hill from Bono in the posh 'rockbroker'-belt suburb of Killiney. But it was a dark, cheerless time. People we knew kept dying and we seemed to be forever attending funerals, while the house, set deep in the shadow of a hill and facing eastwards over the Irish Sea, got about an hour of sunlight a day and was cold and frayed. And all the while Irene and I grew further apart, the gulf between us expanding as our desires and ambitions diverged. As for Dublin, it was still a city full of ghosts, even more than when I'd left for New York two years earlier. The Fellow Who Fiddles and Anto were long gone, Vinnie Kilduff and other pals had decamped west. I still heard the odd busker doing a Waterboys song in the city centre, but the old magic was gone, and in my heart so was I. My physical form may have been wandering Grafton Street but my imagination was roaming in the clear northern air of Findhorn. It was only a matter of time before I cut loose and in the first week of 1994, promising Irene I'd be back in spring, I flew to Findhorn to begin a three-month stay as a guest, living and working in the community.

The North of Scotland was spectacular the day I arrived: serene and inscrutable under a pristine carpet of snow, with endless sailor-blue skies and barely a wisp of wind. I was billeted in the community's main guest enclave, Cluny Hill College, a massive Victorian mansion, once a spa hotel, that nestled on the flanks of a pine-forested hill a few miles from the main campus at Findhorn. The taxi rattled up a curling driveway past cliff-side gardens covered in snow, then swung right. The College stood before us, gothic and sprawling like a great grey dragon, bright and stone-glistening in the winter sun.

'Cluny' was the very embodiment of the mystery school, a secret place set apart from the bustle of the world. It brooded in its hillside location like a fortress, cloistered by the deep woods. Its public spaces – long pale green corridors, quiet lounges and a majestic dining room – vibrated with a tangible meditative presence, a kind of buzzing stillness. Guests arrived every Saturday, some staying a week, some like me for longer, and around forty full-time Findhorn members lived there. A flotilla of cheerful white minibuses ferried people between Cluny and the main community site several times a day.

I'd stayed in Cluny once before, on a weeklong stay at the end of 1992, six weeks after my first visit, and I was beginning to find my place in the Findhorn universe. The community may have been a conglomeration of a few hundred souls gathered in a caravan park and a converted hotel, yet its imaginal space seemed limitless. Dozens of spiritual disciplines from East and West were practised here, and layers of knowledge and experience seemed to hang in the very air. It was like the bookshelves of Foyle's Philosophy Room turned into a living village. Or a spiritual Spiddal, with the deeper wisdom crackling in the atmosphere around me just as the rarefied wavelength of the Gaelic language did in the west of Ireland.

I'd also begun to get the range of the Findhornian 'contacting God inside' philosophy, at least as it applied to me. Two things had happened. During my 1992 visit I'd experienced what that hackneyed phrase 'an open heart' really means. I'd done a lot on deep meditation work that year, and after three days in the spiritual hothouse atmosphere of Cluny I felt my heart begin to 'come on', as if I'd taken some kind of drug. The feeling was of a fire in the centre of my chest, emotional, physical and metaphysical all at once; tender yet at the same time incredibly powerful, like all the loves of my life rolled into one. And then some. I was enfolded in a wave of intense lovingness and awareness that lasted a week, a kind of transfiguration that left me changed and seeing the world through new eyes. For the first time I witnessed everything as it really is, part of a vast functioning system beyond the capacity of my mind to grasp but all looped and bound together with love and purpose. I recognised human society as a crazy dysfunctional thing that even with all its madness somehow played its perfect role in a far bigger picture. I could feel compassion for everyone and knew beyond doubt that under the surface, beneath the contrivance of all personas and disguises, we all had the same needs: to love and be loved, to feel useful and valued. What I was experiencing, I now know, was a classic spiritual heart-opening, an initiation undergone by countless seekers of all disciplines and hues both before and after me. I had found the central secret of *The Mysteries* in my own heart, and its name was Love.

When I returned in January 1994 there wasn't a repeat of this heart-fire experience, but there was something else. After a couple of weeks I noticed a subtle inner will constantly directing me. I knew this reflex from my songwriting, the itch in my soul that impelled me to choose a particular line of lyric or twist of melody. Now I recognised that this inner prompting, my intuition, had been active at crux moments of my life: when I felt the impulse to befriend Z, when I walked away from Kate Lovecraft, when I first heard Steve or Anto. It had been present too when I'd made some of my worst decisions, and those, I realised, were the times I'd ignored it. Now, in the mystery school of Findhorn, I learnt that this guiding impulse was always available. If I bypassed the bustle of my mind and the clamour of my emotions I could feel it quietly directing me. Then all I had to do was trust it. There was nothing exotically mystical about this, and it pretty much equated to "if it feels right, do it, and if it doesn't, don't", but the realisation that I was free to act when something felt right inside was deeply liberating after decades of basing decisions on mental calculations, fears or blind hope. And though it would take me years to integrate it into my daily life as a functioning modus operandi, and there would be slip-ups and fuck-ups along the way, I'd found my inner groove.

Such a process of getting real with myself meant a lot of changes, and a big one was accepting that I wanted to split with Irene. This had been a long time coming. I still cared for Irene but the marriage was going nowhere. I needed to forge my own trail and in early February I returned to Dublin to tell her. For two afternoons we sat in the gloomy lounge at Campanella and like negotiators on a knife-edge worked through the terms of the split, emotional and financial. Then I got in a taxi to Dublin Airport and flew back to Scotland.

All that winter I lived on the top floor of Cluny in a room overlooking woodlands and green hills. My days began around 7am. I'd meditate sitting on a chair by my bed, then go downstairs to the sanctuary, a sparklingly silent room with tall windows, once the billiards parlour in Cluny's previous incarnation as a hotel. 'Morning sanctuary' was optional and every day between ten and thirty people gathered for a group meditation lasting twenty minutes, sometimes silent, sometimes with instructions like the 'sending light' meditation I'd already experienced. Then I'd have breakfast in the cathedral-like dining room, sitting at a table with friends or strangers, the sounds of cutlery and conversation in our ears, early morning sunlight blazing through the bay windows.

Twice a week I took the ten-minute bus ride to Findhorn and spent all morning with the community garden team, donning gumboots, digging, gritting icy footpaths or collecting seaweed on nearby beaches. The rest of the time I worked in the Cluny kitchen, at first humbly chopping carrots and spuds, gradually progressing to accomplished soup-smith and pizza maker. I was part of an eclectic crew that included a passionate Dane called Neils who played loud opera music on the kitchen hi-fi first thing in the morning and said admirable things like, 'May we never have another boring moment in our lives!', a good-looking Swiss lady named Anita, and Wolfgang, a gentle German fellow who was curious about my life in music and asked me if I really knew U2.

For the truth about my day job had begun to slip out. I knew this for sure when I was in the community centre one lunchtime and fell into conversation with an Irish lady who remarked, 'Have you heard there's some kind of pop star living up at Cluny?' After a second of confusion (I hadn't noticed anyone like that) I realised the pop star was *me*. I wasn't the first interloper from the world of show business to descend on Findhorn. Several people more famous than me had already showed up, but Shirley MacLaine and Van Morrison, who visited separately in the eighties, had come as their celebrated selves for day trips and only got a tourist's eye view of the community. I asked Van about his visit some years later and all he remembered was 'a bunch of old hippies'. It must have been the spectacles he was wearing. Burt Lancaster on the other hand, passing through in the late seventies, enrolled in a Findhorn programme and worked in the community. I suspect he also found, like me, that star status in the outside world didn't automatically translate into opportunity and admiration in the parallel universe of Findhorn.

The community members took visitors as they found them. I learned this when I offered to perform at one of the regular Friday night concerts known as 'sharings'. The organiser, a fearsome American lesbian called Patsy, told me I could have three minutes of performance time and no more. Relishing the prospect of surprising Patsy and her fellow organisers by being unexpectedly good, I chose a song which fit the prescribed length and let it rip on stage. But if I was expecting to win instant acclaim from the Findhorn audience, I was wrong. The applause was fair to middling and I was roundly upstaged by a comedy fashion-show given by the builders' group, a motley parade of men in drag, G-strings and feather-strewn crash helmets, which drew from the scattered crowd all the enthusiasm my slot hadn't. But I'd been noticed. Next day there was a little folded-up message for me on the Cluny noticeboard from one Rory O., inviting me to play guitar with the community ceilidh band. A swift rehearsal later I found myself pressed into service playing reels, strathspeys and the whole surreal glory of the *Monty Python* theme at the Findhorn Burns Night.

Being a community musician hadn't been on my list of ambitions, but it was an unexpected consequence of my Findhorn odyssey. After the ceilidh I was asked to back all kinds of community singers, usually women. These included Nikki (willowy English rose with earnest songs), Diana (classy American singer with a penchant for showbiz numbers) and Julia (intense German lady who delivered, with great gusto, a Sarajevo women's anthem she'd learned during a visit to the war-torn Bosnian city). It was a novelty being on stage without the pressure of being the star and I took to my new role with relish. For the first time I learned repertoires of other people's songs and played the supportive sideman, and because I was backing amateurs, I had to learn how to sheath my onstage energy – my job was to let each singer shine, not overshadow them.

These concerts, like the 'sharing' I first guested at, were all in Universal Hall, the five-sided edifice I'd been stunned by on my first night in Findhorn. The Hall had a peculiar aura: used for performances, conferences, and community meetings, its atmosphere fell somewhere between a hallowed temple of the arts and a futuristic new age congress. And it was a highly exposed environment in which to work. Performers were on floor level surrounded by banked seating, and the community atmosphere dispelled the usual mystique and distance between artist and audience. Performing at Universal Hall was like stepping out on a high wire and the only way to keep balance was to be authentic. Any artifice or pretension was fatal.

This intensity blended comically with the inept. Despite its neo-Atlantean grandeur, Universal Hall was a local theatre deep in the provinces run by amateurs on a shoestring. Microphones failed, the sound system flipped on and off mid-performance, cats or children would wander on stage and once I even experienced that most cruel of onstage mishaps: the slack-jointed microphone stand that progressively tilts downwards through the duration of a song, rendering the luckless performer, by number's end, a knee-buckled, shoulder-arched hunchback, desperately trying to make the enforced posture look deliberate. I also had to be my own roadie: there was no Jimmy Hickey now to string my guitar or scurry on stage if something went wrong. But all this was good for my rock star ego. Any lingering tendencies I had towards performers' afflictions, such as self-aggrandisement or a yen to take myself too seriously, were roundly punctured in the crucible of the Hall.

At Friday night concerts I'd sing my own compositions, serious new songs like 'What Do You Want Me To Do?' or comedic numbers poking fun at community life. I was in good company. There was a tradition of lampooning at Findhorn and a talented troupe of comedians – Americans Rolf and Marietta, Jordi from Spain and a dry-witted Aussie called Peter Z – would roast the community for its idiosyncrasies every Friday. Targets included the tendency of members to wear purple, the perennial presence of parsnips on the dinner menu and individuals who used ostentatious meditation postures to show how 'spiritual' they were. Soon my increased profile meant I could command two songs a time at sharings, a Findhornian measure of success, and in the late spring of 1994 I finally did my own solo concert where I showed the community what I did for a living.

It was strange playing as a one-man band to an audience so totally different from a rock crowd. There was nowhere to hide, no moment when I wasn't the focus of attention, and the community members weren't cognoscenti with a grounding in the rock'n'roll I'd grown up with or the roots music I'd played in Ireland. They were people from many different cultures with casual musical tastes that tended to the conservative (pop, classical and singer/songwriters) or the far out (hypnotic new-age sounds and ethnic fare from India, Africa or Tibet). From my experience of Friday night shows I knew the songs that would make most sense in this context would be the ones that carried the deepest personal and emotional charge. The man standing alone with all safety nets and boundaries removed, I figured, was most effective when he dug inside and sang from the soul. But sustaining this level of intimacy for a full show was a new trick for me, and as I played my set – a mix of new songs and numbers from Waterboys albums – the mood in the Hall was strangely restrained. I played for seventy-five minutes in a pin-drop atmosphere, the songs punctuated by polite, quickly dissipating smatterings of applause. I had no idea what the audience was thinking until, as the last chord of the last song faded away, the place erupted into a blaze of applause, whoops and stomping feet. The show was a stupendous success! In the basement dressing room post-encore, with the Findhornians still stomping upstairs as wildly as any rock audience, I knew I'd struck on a new way of performing and that soon I'd take it out into the world.

After this my star shone brightly in the Findhorn firmament and I found myself called on to sing at holidays, funerals, weddings and, most of all, charity shows. For as soon as it became clear I could pull an audience, I got asked to do every benefit gig going. Everyone at Findhorn seemed to have a pet project. I played for the Nepal Trust (providing health care for families in the Himalayas), Ecologia (housing orphans in the former USSR), the local Steiner School (educating the community kids, perpetually short of funds), and even for the restoration of the Hall's grand piano. But my one-man show had another quite unexpected side effect: a local paper got wind of the performance and before you could say 'codswaddle' a national tabloid sent a muck-raking journalist and sidekick snapper-stooge to dig up the dirt on the rock star who'd given it all up and joined a commune. I'd just moved into a little fisherman's cottage by Findhorn Bay, my three-month residency in Cluny having come to its end, when these two characters knocked on the door and asked me all kinds of questions with a dubious relationship to reality.

The story appeared as a double-page spread in the following week's Scottish *Sunday Mail* (with a spin-off feature making it to the front page of the now-defunct *News Of The World*), and was an imaginative work of fiction wonderfully titled 'Cult Saves Rock Star From Drinks Hell'. The writer had read an old interview in which I'd talked about giving up drink some years earlier and wove this into the article, making it look like I'd come to Findhorn to dry out, as if the community were some kind of new-age rehab centre. To support this premise, the article carried a decade-old photo that showed me sitting with a glass of water, mischievously captioned to suggest I'd been putting away multiple neat vodkas. The only thing the tabloid journos got right was the mention of a 'mysterious barefoot lady' who opened the door of my cottage. For there was a new love in my life.

Janette was a Findhorn member, originally from Glasgow, who facilitated workshops and led dance classes. At first I'd admired her from afar across the Cluny dining room or caught my breath as I passed her in the corridors. In stolen glimpses during the daily life of the community, Janette impinged on my consciousness little by little and, without ever knowing it, took over my heart. I was convinced Janette was the one, my future ally, collaborator, lover and best friend, the partner-woman of my life. I'd been wrong about such things before, but this time I was deeply certain. I could feel it in my guts as sure as breathing. I asked my kitchen colleague Anita what the community protocol was when a man wanted to meet a woman. She told me to leave Janette a message on the noticeboard asking for a chat, then simply tell her how I felt. This was a few million degrees more upfront than I was used to being, but I did it, gingerly sticking my little folded-up scrap of paper on the 'J' space of the Cluny noticeboard late one Friday night.

Next morning I was making lentil soup in the kitchen when Janette walked in holding the note and asked if it was from me. I said yes and, though mystified, she agreed to go for a drink with me that evening. We met in the Cluny lobby and walked through the woods to the bar of a nearby hotel. As soon as we sat down I declared myself. She was amazed. Far from expecting a suitor, she'd imagined she must have done something to offend this man she hardly knew, and that I wanted to tell her so; a logical supposition in the community culture, where 'giving feedback' was a common occurrence. She told me she felt flattered but that she 'hadn't thought of me that way'. It was a courteous refusal and after a pleasant conversation we walked back to Cluny, said goodbye in the lobby, and each headed off to our different parts of the building. I was deeply embarrassed to realise that all my romantic certainties must have been mistaken. How could I have been so sure and yet so wrong? In order to avoid Janette I didn't go to the dining room for several days. Then one morning I bumped into her on the stairs. She stopped me and said she'd like to meet up again.

Reluctantly, and thinking she was just being sorry for me, I agreed to meet her that night.

When the hour came it was my turn to be amazed. She was dressed for a date, glamorous and elegant in flowing clothes, a symphony in brown, green and gold. As we strolled down the Cluny Hill driveway she took my arm and this time when we got to the pub *she* declared herself to me, saying that since our previous outing she'd found my face constantly appearing in her mind's eye and that she wanted to give us a try. My declaration had worked! We conducted a magical courtship in Cluny, holding hands under the table at breakfast and lunch, kissing discreetly in the corridors, spending nights in Janette's room, and bumping into each other with delight several times each day. In March we flew off for a dreamlike week in that most romantic of all cities, Venice, where we stayed in a sea-green room overlooking the lagoon, loved ardently, went for endless walks, first began to call each other 'Darling', and told each other our life stories in waterfront cafes.

In April we moved into a cottage on Findhorn Bay and set up home. We had a front parlour overlooking the water, a tiny kitchen, and a bedroom with a window onto a whitewashed lane leading to the centre of the old village of Findhorn. There we witnessed our new love maturing into deep partnership. I'd been right after all: Janette *was* the one.

In the cottage's attic space, too low-ceilinged for me to even stand up straight, I created my smallest-ever music room and started writing songs articulating the experiences I'd had at Findhorn: 'Bring 'Em All In', 'Long Way To The Light', 'Wonderful Disguise'. Soon I was ready to record an album that would tell the story of what I'd found.

The previous year I'd met a recording engineer in New York called Niko Bolas, a handsome Greek-American with a skinful of attitude whose name I'd seen on a couple of Neil Young album covers. I hired Niko to record my B-sides for the singles off *Dream Harder* and it turned out to be a momentous session. He was a terrific catalyst: a no-nonsense bullshit-busting cheerleader. In a couple of days, with a raunchy pick-up band and Niko at the controls, I laid down ten cracking tracks, which had all the power and passion *Dream Harder* itself lacked. I wanted more of the same. But in keeping with the nature of my new songs I decided to play every instrument myself and record not in a big city studio but in the charged air of Findhorn. And amazingly the community had its own studio, a magical grotto in the basement of Universal Hall, built in the seventies. It was rarely used and its gear was prehistoric so we brought our own. Niko flew in from Los Angeles, having just fired himself from a Rod Stewart session ('he asked me to do everything I hated').

Niko and Findhorn shouldn't have gone well together but they did. Extroverted and stupendously tactless, Niko's native repartee included bon mots such as, 'It ain't knockin' my dick in the dirt' (when something didn't sufficiently impress him) and his customary greeting to, say, a fellow recording engineer was along the lines of, 'Yo, man! That your mix playing? Sounds like a piece of shit!' But he took to his new circumstances like a champ, cycling to Universal Hall each morning, attending meditations in the sanctuary, mucking in behind the bar at the hotel where he was berthed, and even going to a community lecture by a visiting Tibetan lama.

Niko also made friends with the most unlikely people, including a local RAF crew who flew him illicitly across Scotland in a transport plane, making him spectacularly sick by doing loops and rolls over the Cairngorms. And a Swedish community member, a bearded intellectual called Stefan who noticed Niko's fidgeting, antsy demeanour one morning and said to him, 'So. Who *was* it?'

'Who was *what*?' retorted a bemused Niko.

'Who drove you relentlessly as a boy', replied Stefan, 'to always excel, and turned you into the self-criticising, nervous lunatic I see before me now?'

Niko stood stunned for a second, all the colour draining from his cheeks, then a smile cracked open his face and he broke out laughing.

'Shit! That was my dad!'

Niko was outrageously direct in the studio. He could tell me when a song didn't quite make it ('OK, now play me something with a chorus') or indicate when I wasn't nailing a performance ('You suck today, man'). There was none of the let's-mollycoddle-the-artist's-feelings crap so many people in the music business deploy because they're afraid of causing offence. And he had a cute, understated way of letting me know when I'd got it right. 'You're in the wrong room!' he'd call cheerfully through the intercom while waving me through to the control booth. Best of all Niko recorded me as simply and directly as he communicated and the result was a clear, natural sound which absolutely suited the music.

The experiment of recording in the community worked too. I was happy singing the songs in the atmosphere that had begot them, and something of the Findhornian aura found its way onto tape. There were drawbacks, however. The studio was sufficiently soundproofed to keep out the sounds of the planes taking off and landing at the neighbouring airbase, but not the sounds from the Hall auditorium above. These included Sacred Dance on Wednesday evenings with its familiar Balkan folksy burblings, Five Rhythms on a Monday (spacey new age dance grooves and clattering feet), and loudest of all the Dance Drama room on the other side of the studio wall, which hosted everything from aerobics to acting classes (shouts, mock-fights and very convincing screams). This was a far cry from the big city studios we were used to, where any distraction would be swiftly nuked by a phone call to the studio manager, but there was nothing we could do about it, and we accepted the mosaic of noise as the price of recording in a living, breathing community theatre.

Halfway through making the album we received a visit from Jim Powers, my friend from the Chicago gospel church trip, who'd become an A&R man at Geffen Records. Poor Jim was despatched by the Geffen bosses to come and talk some sense into their wayward star and impress upon him the importance of delivering a commercial record with 'three hit tracks that can get played on American FM radio'. This meant modern rock drums, lead guitar hooks and all the sonic paraphernalia of the grunge-centric mid nineties. Niko and I listened to Jim dutifully deliver his script in a café overlooking Findhorn Bay on a gorgeous Indian summer's day, while clouds sailed regally across the blue northern skies and the mystery school of Cluny Hill brooded in the distance, and it was like hearing a bulletin from some old, half-forgotten nonsensical world.

Though I received Jim's entreaties with some sympathy for his position, I ignored them completely and kept right on making the music that was in my heart. When I delivered the finished album to Geffen in late 1994, it didn't feature a single drumbeat. It was an almost wholly acoustic record: a despatch from my soul, yes, but a concoction with which the lumbering promotional machine of an American record company could seemingly do nothing. And to compound matters, I insisted on going solo in name. As there was only one person on the album, and all my current concert ambitions were based on the one-man show I'd tested at Universal Hall, I wanted to put out the record as Mike Scott. My Geffen contract stipulated I had to release all my work as The Waterboys, so I conferred with John Kennedy, still my trusty solicitor, and he suggested that if we spoke to Geffen in a language they understood they might let me have my way.

Geffen were due to pay me a huge advance so Kennedy contacted them and offered to take a million-dollar cut if they'd let me release the album as Mike Scott. This was the right language indeed, for the change was promptly agreed and papers authorising it soon dropped through my cottage letterbox. The album was added to Geffen's release schedule (they were bound by my water-tight deal to release whatever I gave them) but it was clear from the absence of communication coming across the time zones that they'd rather be rid of the whole thing. And me. I could understand this – my actions hadn't made any sense to them for a couple of years now, if indeed they ever had. Kennedy's canny advice was to wait till I received the balance of my recording advance and then negotiate to buy my way out of the contract: another million dollars. Once my freedom was secured we'd find a new record company who understood the acoustic Findhorn album and were willing to properly support it.

With a record in the bag and Kennedy engaged in the delicate process of finessing my Geffen exit, I was ready to explore the prospect of touring from my base in Findhorn. In November 1994 I embarked on several short concert trips round Britain, my first anywhere in four years. I travelled bandless, accompanied only by Janette and a road crew from Glasgow, and on bare stages in small theatres I replicated the sound and atmosphere of my Universal Hall show, rediscovering my performance mojo along the way. Playing live night after night again was like breathing the fire of life. How could I have functioned without this for so long? Yes, I still wanted the life of the performer. Yes, I still wanted greatness. And I loved the freedom of being solo; I could take the music in any direction and throw in songs spontaneously without having to wonder if the band could play them. Perhaps best of all was the rekindling of my connection with the audience. The last time I'd met them, in the dimly remembered warzone of the *Room To Roam* tour, my back had been against the wall and the wind again me. Now, in calmer circumstances, we shared an intimate musical conversation.

As the concerts progressed I noticed another desire rumbling inside, one I thought I'd lost somewhere back along the line – the yen for commercial success, as if now that I'd fulfilled a spiritual quest it was time to return and claim the things of the world. Soon I knew I'd want to make a band album, compete again with my peers and re-engage with the circus of publicity and stardom, but this time on my own terms and from my new perspective. And because in Findhorn there was none of the apparatus of my trade – managers, musicians, rehearsal studios, record companies – I'd have to move back to the city. After eighteen months the time in the mystery school was over and London beckoned. But London, rock'n'roll and Mike Scott had all changed in the ten years since I'd lived on Ladbroke Grove and made *This Is The Sea*. I would need my sense of humour, as well as all I'd learned in Findhorn, for I was about to embark on a mad rollercoaster ride through a depraved new world.

CHAPTER 17

MY WANDERINGS IN THE WEARY LAND

I walk up the ramp of the Pyramid Stage as Ian McNabb calls out my name over the P.A. and the Glastonbury Festival crowd cheers. Ian's backing band, unbelievably, is Neil Young's Crazy Horse, with whom I shake hands with for the first time as I take the stage. Ralph Molina and Billy Talbot are grizzled Americans with the mark of the sixties on their faces, and there's a younger dude too, Mikey, whose impossibly low-slung spare guitar I'm borrowing. I plug in, glance at the sea of faces, register the presence of the TV cameras, and await the count for the first number.

Because I've just flown down from Scotland and couldn't get to rehearsals I asked Ian to prepare 'Glastonbury Song' at a stately, slow-burning tempo, and to rock up the second number, 'Preparing To Fly'. But as Ralph Molina counts in 'Glastonbury' I realise to my horror that Ian must have got the message mixed up and flipped the tempos. The groove is seriously fast. The intro melody sounds like The Pogues playing a jolly Irish reel and, fucking hell, I'm having to sing so speedily I can't get all the words out. Somehow I make it to the end and catch my breath as Ian orchestrates one of those endless Crazy Horse outros, everyone gathered in a centre-stage huddle playing crash chords for what seems like forever.

Then Molina leads us into 'Preparing To Fly', which, miraculously, is the right tempo. And with the full ragged power of the Crazy Horse rhythm machine we sounds immense; a steamrolling golden tumbleweed churning into infinity underpinned by the earth-shuddering thoom *of Billy Talbot's bass. In the midst of the sonic mayhem I look around me. The West Country hills are green, the punters are grooving, there's an electric guitar in my hands and I'm back!*

Or so I think.

I'd handled my own affairs since the demise of Dick Lackaday, and while I was in Findhorn there hadn't been much for a manager to do, but with the move to London there soon would be. John Kennedy faxed me a list of possible candidates and I met several of them at the end of 1994. One was a chap called Dave Jaymes. His name stood out on the list because he spelt 'Jaymes' the same way as David Jaymes, bassist in the early eighties pop band Modern Romance. Back then, my punk rock prejudices had been severely challenged by this geezer, a preening, cheek-sucking, blonde-bobbed poseur at whom, every time he appeared on *Top Of The Pops*, my mate Joe Kingman and I would gleefully yell 'BASTARD!'. But Kennedy didn't think it wasn't the same guy. And sure enough, when I met Dave and his business partner Diane in their office in Notting Hill he was nothing like the Modern Romance bassist. He was a dapper, dark-haired chap, sincere and enthusiastic, with a golly-gosh cockney accent and a firm, winning handshake. Janette accompanied me, Yoko-like, to all my meetings, and at this one something magical happened: we fell in love with Dave and Diane. As we talked, some alchemy, a kind of shared empathy, filled the room. Dave and Diane were a relatively inexperienced team but, moved by the encounter, I asked them to manage me.

Kennedy meanwhile had extricated me from my Geffen contract, so Dave and Diane started touting my Findhorn album, titled *Bring 'Em All In*, to British record companies. In the spring of 1995 the field narrowed to Alan McGee's Creation and my old label Chrysalis, now part of EMI. McGee told Dave and Diane the album was a work of 'beautiful genius' and they arranged for him to fly up to Glasgow, where Niko Bolas and I were doing final mixes. But McGee pulled out

251

of the trip at the last minute, which my managers read as a portent of future flakiness. I'd only met McGee once, at a party seven years earlier where the sum total of our conversation consisted of him leaning into my ear and yelling above the sound system, 'One day ah'm goan tae sign yew tae mah label, man! Fuckin' brilliant!', so I didn't have an opinion about the guy other than a dim recall of Caledonian enthusiasm. But I was as perplexed as Dave and Diane when, a few days after cancelling his trip, McGee submitted a modest financial offer for *Bring 'Em All In*, which indicated that he expected sales to be low. Chrysalis on the other hand made a handsome offer, turned up for their meetings, and convinced Dave, at least, that they were the right home for me.

I wasn't so sure. When I walked into their offices the first thing I saw was a huge framed photo of Karl Wallinger, whose band World Party had been assigned to Chrysalis along with the rest of the Ensign acts in 1986 when Chris Blackwell had given me power of veto over Ensign's sale. 'Uh-oh,' said my guts, 'this is your old life. Steer clear.' But I hadn't yet learned to fully trust these inner promptings and I was swayed by the enthusiasm of the Chrysalis bosses, a convivial old music biz cove named Roy Eldridge and his intense label manager, Mike Andrews, who loved *Bring 'Em All In* and expected it to sell by the truckload. So I re-signed to Chrysalis in July 1995, and that month Janette and I left our Findhorn cottage and rented a pale pink four-storey house on Lansdowne Road in my old Notting Hill stomping ground. These were happy, optimistic days – new record company, new management, and a powerful sense of purpose. But forty tons of karmic rain were about to come crashing down on my parade.

For if it was one thing finding my inner groove in Findhorn's conducive, meditative atmosphere, it was quite another doing it in the belly of the metropolis. Swept up in London's juggernaut momentum I could hardly hear myself think, let alone discern the still small voice of my intuition. And it wasn't just that I was beaming down from a pastoral mystery school; it was that London itself had changed. Everything seemed several degrees cruder, brasher and more ... what would be the word? ... *loveless* than I remembered. To my 1995 eyes London looked insane. In the ten years since I'd left the city had morphed into a playground of beer-bellied men with shirts hanging out and dyed blonde cropped hair in the style of troubled footballer Gazza, drinking in the open air and spilling across the streets like tribes of boorish overgrown babies. The cultural wars of the fifties and sixties were lost and the youth of the nation strode forth as identikit-clad, money-hungry business bastards. When I took my first look at British TV in a decade I saw a new generation of comedians who farted, swore and wove cruelty into their acts, using humiliation and vindictiveness to get their laughs and kicks like bullies I remembered from school. A plague of gossip and celebrity rags befouled the shelves of newsagents, the bastard spawn of *Hello!* magazine, all face-lifts, private hells and diet freaks packaged as superficial entertainment. And everywhere I looked huge billboards had materialised, bright-lit and cliché-ridden, dominating skylines and street views, for London had sold its soul and its civic spaces to the marketing industry. Living in the heart of the metropolis was like walking through a giant promo display.

To escape from horror, the saying goes, bury yourself in it, and there was nothing to do but dig in and get on with the job of promoting my record. But how to explain where I'd been and what I'd done to a sceptical media to whom the esoterics of somewhere like Findhorn were beyond any comprehension? I accepted the challenge gamely, struggling for the language that would express my experiences in a manner intelligible to hard-boiled *NME* journalists or speed-talking DJs without my sounding like a lunatic. And sometimes I even managed it. Running parallel was the realisation that my status was diminished without the charisma of the Waterboys name. *Mike Scott* meant little by comparison, and I recognised how successful I'd been throughout my career in camouflaging myself behind the Waterboys brand. I was in a position the opposite of the 'star gravity' I remembered from the days of *This Is The Sea*, when I was a music business supernova about to burst into flame and my entrance to a room would change its atmosphere; or the era of *Fisherman's Blues* when my arrival on any Dublin scene would magnetise all attention in my direction. Now I was just some dimly remembered guy, an impression confirmed by the number of entry-level interviews I found myself doing with obscure cable TV channels, and from the shrunken coverage I got in newspapers and music magazines.

Rock'n'roll was a changed landscape too. I was deposited as if from a spacecraft into a world I hardly recognised. Most of our contemporary bands of the eighties were gone, including all the best ones – The Clash, the Bunnymen, The Smiths – while Mick Hucknall and Geordie Michael were global superstars. How had *that* happened? Only the renewed success of Paul Weller seemed logical, as if the world was still spinning on its right axis. Even the music I'd picked up on during my still-recent spell in New York was looking old: grunge was passé and Kurt Cobain, as they say in Glasgow, was deid as the day is long. And a pantheon of new, dark-browed musical godlings was on the rise: the thuggish-but-melodic brothers Gallagher, intellectual barrow-boy Damon Albarn, and Richard Ashcroft, a cadaverous stick insect bringing back speed-freak chic with his band The Verve. The scene struck me as a warped twist on the mid sixties just before psychedelia hit; the days of 'Paint It Black', mods, greasers and the pomp of Tamla Motown. If I'd been twenty I'd have known where to pitch myself and my music in relation to this retro-hedonistic topography, preferably in a position to rip it down. But I was a name and face from a recent past that was itself busy being ripped down. And more than that: having parachuted in from a mystery school with a headful of songs about inner experiences and mysticism I was hopelessly out of step with the times. Cosmic drug explorers apart, there was no archetype in rock'n'roll for 'seeker returning with news from the unknown' for me to play with. I couldn't work out where to insert myself into the picture.

Nor could I figure out my sartorial style. Confounded as to whether I should look like a star or a regular person, I would overdress to compensate for my confusion, walking round London rehearsal rooms in flash clothes while everyone else was in trainers and t-shirts. It's easy to dress down when the world wants to know you. I'd spent 1987 dressing like a scarecrow while a huge audience wondered what my next move would be. Now, with diminished status and a wardrobe of Versace gear, I couldn't seem to stop dressing up. This tendency reached its apogee at a show in Edinburgh where I wore the nightmare rig-out of spotted jacket, striped trousers, hooped socks and a checked shirt. I was finally cured when I turned up at BBC radio in a pair of plush velvet trousers with a glittery spangle. DJ Mark Radcliffe, amused that I should wear such luxurious pants for a radio show where no one could see me, roasted me on air, commenting in his withering Lancashire brogue, 'I bet you don't do the gardening in those.'

Meanwhile, as if in a weird dream, I found myself invited to perform on Christian youth TV programmes. The producers of these breezy Sunday morning shows knew I was singing about spirituality from a perspective other than theirs and extended the hand of brotherhood across the metaphysical divide, which was admirable, and I agreed to appear because I liked the idea of infiltrating mainstream religious broadcasting with my heretical, gnostic songs about *The Mysteries*. But my fifth-columnist efforts had an undesired result: most people tuning in just thought I'd become some kind of Christian rocker.

Things weren't going at all as I'd envisaged when I'd left my Findhorn eyrie, and when the single of 'Bring 'Em All In' got hardly any radio play and didn't chart, a doom threatened to descend on my team. But it dropped big-time the day the album was released. I was in New York, getting ready to perform a show, when I got a phone call in my hotel room telling me Roy Eldridge and Mike Andrews had been fired. My mental picture of working with these guys for years of campaigns, tours and follow-up albums burst into smithereens as I stood with the receiver to my ear. I knew such things happened to artists: your allies at the label get the boot and you have to work for the rest of your contract with new people who may have no feeling for your music. Now it was happening to me, which was tough enough, but coming on the day of my album's release it was a catastrophe. And a *creepy* catastrophe: the EMI bosses behind the firing must have monitored the situation for a while – these guys don't just piss in the wind – and would have known the axe was set to fall when they authorised my contract eight weeks earlier.

On our return to London, Dave, Diane, Janette and I went, like a confused, bereaved family, for an audience with the EMI division chief. J.F. Cecillon was a lewd Frenchman with crafty eyes and a sharp line in the kind of frothy repartee the music business loves ('I will not zleep till I 'ave a number one'). J.F. was detailed to steer Chrysalis till a new label boss was chosen, and sat purring in his office like a great fat cat, receiving the parade of shell-shocked managers anxiously wondering what future their artists had under the new regime. He said all the right things – 'You are a priority at zee label', 'We will make your next seengle a heet' – and maybe even meant a few of them, but here was no chemistry between us and I found myself stuck for the next several years with a record company man I hadn't signed to, nor would have.

Creeping out against this unhappy backdrop, the *Bring 'Em All In* album snuck into the charts at a lowly 22 and disappeared the following week. This was confirmation of my diminished status and of Alan McGee's sober estimation of the album's hit potential. And most of all it told me I'd missed the target. I'd sought to make a record about my Findhorn experiences that would resonate with a mass audience, and I'd called it wrong. An unadorned acoustic record, it seemed, wasn't a persuasive enough medium, and I made a mental note to give my next album, which would have similar lyrical themes, a robust, commercial band sound.

Two weeks later I went on tour. The shows were good but Dave Jaymes and I had started to argue about anything and everything: which interviews to do (Dave wanted me to do them all, I wanted to be selective to keep my currency high), the length of my one-man shows (Dave's view: if I played shorter gigs I'd have more energy for interviews), touring costs, and how to deal with the new order at EMI. And when records aren't selling the scope for disagreement between artist and manager expands exponentially. A particularly fractious issue was the question of whether to release singles in multiple formats. I'd always resisted this music business ploy, designed to get fans to buy the same record several times and so give a single an inflated chart entry. The scam worked by offering different tracks on the B-sides of the various editions, all of which the diehards would feel compelled to buy. It was scuzzy of record companies and artists to take advantage of this degree of fandom, a kind of bullshit tax on the devoted. But after the single of 'Bring 'Em All In' sank I came under intense pressure from J.F. Cecillon and his minions to issue the follow-up, 'Building The City Of Light', in two CDs and a seven-inch single, each with differing bonus tracks. Dave agreed with them.

I was still holding out when one day, as Diane and I stepped into a hotel lift together, she suggested I should take Dave's opinion seriously because 'he's got lots of experience of having hit singles'. 'What do you mean?' I asked as the lift whirred upwards. 'Oh,' she replied, 'he was in Modern Romance. They had seven top-ten hits, you know.' The lift stopped, but I felt as if someone had opened my skull and the contents of my brain were still ascending into some abominable ether-land. *I was being managed by the bass player from Modern Romance!* This distressing revelation didn't help my relationship with Dave, for now whenever I looked at him I saw the spectre of the blonde-bobbed geezer preening away on *Top Of The Pops* like a mocking shade. Our days were numbered.

Nevertheless I caved in and let Chrysalis have their 'formats' for 'Building The City Of Light'. But it availed us nothing; the single bombed and I felt I'd compromised myself, the fans and the music. Nor did we have any more luck in North America, where the album was dead in the water. Having disappeared not just once, but twice (in 1986 and again in 1993) I was seen in the States as someone who'd passed up his chances, and the US rock media had no further use for me. Even worse: by sodding off to Findhorn it looked like I'd spurned success to pursue spirituality instead, thus defying the prime credo of fame at the fag-end of the twentieth century: *thou shalt have no other gods than me*.

Then John Kennedy called to tell me, almost tearfully, that he was giving up his lawyer's practice to become head of Polygram Records. I was glad for John, but gutted for me. My ally of a decade, the artful big brother who'd been my consigliore, fixer and protector, was gone. So soon were Dave and Diane. Whatever the nature of the alchemy at that first meeting, it hadn't translated into a successful working relationship, and shortly after the end of the *Bring 'Em All In* tour I let them go. Their place as my advisers was now taken by Alan McGee, who emerged as an unexpected friend and mentor. I asked Alan to listen to the demos for my next album, *Still Burning*, and after hearing them and pronouncing himself excited he offered to be A&R man for the record and oversee the recording process from start to finish. This was highly irregular considering I wasn't on his label, but working with a man like McGee, who lived and breathed rock'n'roll, was more attractive than running my songs by the new guard at Chrysalis.

Alan became a regular visitor to the house on Lansdowne Road, where I played him my songs and listened to his comments. And it was a lot of listening, because McGee was one of the world's great talkers. A gregarious Scottish skinhead invariably dressed in a checked shirt, Alan would hold forth in Glaswegian tones for twenty, thirty, forty minutes non-stop, while I sat on the edge of my chair trying to find a gap to get a word in. He had a cunning, honest-but-flattering way of giving musical criticism. 'That song's no as guid as some o' yer ithers,' he'd say tactfully when underwhelmed by a demo. And when he liked something he was spectacularly positive. 'It's a thing o' genius, man,' he'd coo. 'Beau'iful, beau'iful.' At that precise moment in rock history McGee was king of the castle, having discovered the era's totemic band, Oasis. This wasn't a big deal to me; what mattered was that he understood Mike Scott/Waterboys music. But the fact he was championing me, waxing lyrical about my new songs and old records in newspapers and on radio, was a boon. McGee's word carried weight in the music media and if anything could buy me a hip ticket and restore my commercial and critical fortunes, it was his patronage.

EMI, meanwhile, were perplexed. Here was the famous boss of a rival label advising their artist, stealing the A&R cap from under their noses. But though I'd lost leverage at EMI due to the failure of *Bring 'Em All In* and the firing of the men who signed me, I still had some layer of mystery, a cultivated fog of professional distance between me and the company. I deployed it now, staying out of range and phone contact till my creative relationship with McGee was established and the direction of the album was set. Then one morning McGee and I went to see J.F. Cecillon's new label manager at Chrysalis, a chubby boy called Mark Collen who was still getting used to the dizzy novelty of finding himself in charge of a major label. Deploying our best diplomacy we sold Mark on our song selection and reassured him I wasn't about to do a bunk to Creation Records. To my amazement he agreed to everything we asked for. As we left the EMI building, McGee, impressed by our smooth passage through what we'd expected to be hostile territory, trilled, 'Ye're wi' the right record company, man. They luvv yew in there, they luvv yew!' They wouldn't for long.

Now the wheels clicked into gear. Chrysalis booked recording time and I flew Niko Bolas over as co-producer. Niko and I put together a top-notch studio band: Jim Keltner, whose drumming on the

Waterboys San Francisco sessions in 1986 I'd never forgotten; Chris Bruce, the ace lead guitarist I'd met in New York; and Pino Palladino, a tall, gangly bassist mate of Niko's, best known, rather unjustly, for his slithery 'pyoing, yoing' fretless playing on hits by British singer Paul Young a decade earlier. I was especially thrilled to be on the cusp of working with Keltner again. In the weeks before the sessions I listened over and over to his playing on John Lennon's 'Jealous Guy', George Harrison's *Concert For Bangladesh*, and the 1986 Waterboys tapes. When the first day of recording came I couldn't quite believe he was really in London, but my crew manager Malcolm confirmed that yes, Jim had already checked into the hotel and was waiting for me at Olympic Studios. I walked in and there was the old god standing by his drum kit wearing what looked like the same shades and leather waistcoat he'd worn all those years before in Fantasy Studios. He addressed me as 'Michael', smiled like a million dollars through his scrubby buffalo beard, and held out to me a sure, steady hand with long wizard-like fingers.

When we played Keltner was as great as I remembered, driving the music with a profound combination of power and sensitivity. And I could see why Pino was known in music circles as one of the world's best bassists: every economic note was in the right place, the fabled *sweet spot*, for maximum funk and groovability. Chris Bruce was no slouch either: a fashion-conscious black dandy and switchblade-sharp guitar player who invented all his own parts, choc-full of hooks, and never needed a word of guidance. But working with a hired one-off band and a set of structured songs was very different from blowing free improvised music the way Keltner and The Waterboys did in those far-off days in San Francisco. This band didn't have the telepathic familiarity I'd enjoyed with Steve and Anto, and the sound we made devolved to the area of crossover between our various skills and styles – a kind of classic-but-conservative rock meets soul hybrid. Working Nashville style (me showing the guys a new song each morning then spending the next six or seven hours recording it), we cut ten tracks in as many days including at least one potential hit. 'Love Anyway' was a mid-paced rocker with a hustling Keltner groove and a hazy, chiming guitar figure, which both McGee and EMI, in their different ways, pronounced a winner. 'It's fuckin' beau'iful genius, man!' said McGee like the Glasgow punk rocker he was. 'It eez ze beezness.' said J.F. Cecillon, purring like the crafty fat cat he was.

The playback for Chrysalis was held in the Olympic control room. I'd always found playbacks excruciating and preferred label executives to listen to my new records without me there, so they didn't feel they had to feign enthusiasm or dance round my feelings. But the maintenance of good relations required I bite the bullet this time and invite J.F. and Mark Collen to the studio; after all, they'd played more than fair by indulging my work with McGee. To my surprise, they were remarkably well behaved. Properly house-trained, they didn't make the usual record company faux-pas of getting song titles wrong, nor did they mark the tracks out of five like Geffen's Tom Zutaut had done once (but only once). The playback was a success and the only jarring note was Niko's unwitting insistence on addressing J.F. as 'Jeff' throughout, which the Frenchman admirably contrived not to notice.

J.F. and Mark were sufficiently enthused to pay for the recording band to reassemble for a one-off show at the EMI conference, a three-day junket in a motorway hotel somewhere outside Birmingham. Keltner, Pino, Chris and I descended on this wasteland and in a garish neon-lit conference suite one lunchtime we romped through two songs for the gathered executives – possibly the strangest gig I'd ever played, right up there with the Maybole Orange Lodge and Burns Night in Findhorn. But it worked. EMI and Chrysalis were 'motivated', I was suddenly popular at my record company (a welcome if unfamiliar feeling), and 'Love Anyway' was proclaimed by one and all to be a 'smash'.

Before I could get back to the happy land of chart success, however, I had to find new management. My first choice was Alan

McGee but he refused, saying, 'Ah dinnae want tae take yer money, man.' Instead he suggested a then-successful English fellow called Osbert Prince who, Alan claimed, 'got the big picture.' Osbert was a well-tailored fellow who knew his way round a wine list and a tour schedule, but Alan undercut his recommendation by warning me, 'Dinnae trust him wi' yer money', which didn't exactly sell me on the guy. Next I beat a path to a selection of London's greatest living managers, including Dire Straits' veteran gatekeeper, a deliciously dodgy bon viveur called Ed Bicknell who I'd turned down when he'd courted The Waterboys in the late eighties and who now got his gentle revenge, keeping me dangling for several months before regretfully declining my overtures.

In fact all the managers I approached turned me down. I'd just had an album that stiffed and any bigshot with a grasp of arithmetic could see there wasn't money to be made unless *Still Burning* went seriously sky-high. Even if it did I was known to be a difficult, driven customer who didn't like making videos, argued about single formats and, for all anyone knew, would up sticks after the next tour and vanish to a commune or the rustic fringes of Ireland. After a long series of courteous refusals and unreturned phone calls – music biz refusals are almost always unreturned phone calls – I accepted defeat.

Finding a live band was easier. A combination of auditions and chance encounters produced three new confederates: a wily keyboard player called James Hallawell, a Keltneresque drummer called Jeremy Stacey, and a young Dublin guitarist, Gavin Ralston, the rock'n'rolling nephew of my old trad mucker Seamus Begley. Moonlighting on bass was Liverpudlian singer Ian McNabb. I'd met Ian in the eighties at a posh Liverpool hotel after a Waterboys show. He turned up with Mac from the Bunnymen, we had a rollicking three-way argument about politics and world peace, almost came to blows, and I never heard from either of them again till McNabb phoned me out of the blue in Findhorn in 1994. To my surprise he asked me to come and do a couple of Waterboys songs with him at the Glastonbury Festival – the appearance that turned out to be my bracing reintroduction to the British rock public.

This new ensemble was a happy band of compatible personalities and, as happens in happy bands, everyone soon had a nickname. McNabb was 'Boots'; James, who had a penchant for impersonating English movie gangsters, was 'Razors'; Gavin was 'Fingers' on account of his speedy guitar playing; and I, not unreasonably, was 'Tonsils'. Only Jeremy had a nickname he didn't much care for. McNabb, ribbing him unfairly for being a bread-head (a player motivated by money, not music) suggested Jeremy stick a credit-card machine on his bass drum and swipe my card every time he played a cymbal crash, a suggestion which lumbered the unfortunate drummer with the name 'Swipe'.

A fortnight before *Still Burning* was released we played our debut shows – my first electric band concerts in an unbelievable seven years – at a grimy London rock club called the Garage. This was the brainwave of my then-agent Paul Boswell, who figured the best way to regenerate some rock cred was to play in a khazi. But the shows coincided with a monstrous pre-millennial heat wave and for five broiling nights band and audience sweltered in a maelstrom of furnace-like temperatures.

The day before the first gig the group went to Johnstons on the King's Road to buy stage clothes. I gave each musician a budget of £500 and for an hour we plundered the shop like a bunch of kids, finally emerging with our sartorial booty. But instead of looking like a gang with a unified style, which I'd forgotten takes months or years of hanging out together to achieve, when we took the stage at the Garage the following night we were like The Five Ages Of Rock. Razors was a fifties zoot-suited thug; Fingers, with pointed sideburns and broad-shouldered pin-stripe jacket, looked like a refugee from a 1981 Ultravox video; Boots sported the maroon two-tone suit of a spivvy Berwick Street mod; Swipe was a Seattle grungemeister with goatee and camouflage jacket; and in my velvet flares and ruffled

Regency shirt I was a cross between a cabaret singer and one of The Kinks circa 1967.

By the end of the show these disparate visual identities had devolved into a single heat-smelted human mass, jackets, shirts and cool attitudes long discarded. Except for Boots McNabb. For as the last chord of our closing number, 'Building The City Of Light', ripped through the fetid air of the Garage, Boots was still inscrutably sharp in his two-tone suit, the sweat-drenched jacket of which he refused to remove despite the supernatural heat. But in the naked light of the dressing room the cost of Boots' dedication to style was revealed. 'Bloody hell!' he exclaimed in horror, pointing at his legs. We all looked. The turn-ups of his pants hovered a full inch above his exposed ankles. Surely they hadn't been like that when he bought them? Then he stuck his fists out and his jacket cuffs were a third of the way up his arm, revealing several inches of soaked skin above the wrists. Suddenly the penny dropped and everyone burst out laughing. The suit had shrunk on him while he'd been sweating in it!

Shrivelled suits apart, Boswell's ploy was a success. Tickets sold out fast, reviews were encouraging, and things were even stirring for me at radio. 'Love Anyway' was Record Of The Week on two Radio One shows on consecutive weeks, an almost unheard-of feat. And the single sounded great on air. I'd pulled off the trick of making a record about my spiritual experiences that, unlike the acoustic 'Bring 'Em All In', slotted into the contemporary landscape. 'Love Anyway' didn't sound out of place next to singles by Oasis or The Verve, with whose 'Bittersweet Symphony', then rioting up the charts, it shared a fat drum sound and a luminous string section. It looked, just *looked*, like we might actually have the hit everyone was predicting.

The reckoning that would determine our fate was the 'midweek chart' position of the week of release. It worked like this: records came out on a Monday and the final weeklong chart, the one the public cares about, was based on all the sales from then to the following Sunday. But a tally of Monday's sales alone was announced within the music business on Tuesday lunchtime and called the 'midweek chart'. And because an act's diehard fans typically bought records on the day of release, this midweek chart tended to show newly issued singles in a higher position than their eventual placing in the real chart five days later. A strong position in the midweek was deemed essential to ensure a healthy showing in the subsequent real chart, but a bad position meant failure, and in such a case the record company would give up. For 'Love Anyway' to be a hit we needed a midweek position comfortably in the top thirty, preferably high in the top twenty. I was halfway through a long day of interviews in a Brussels hotel when the call came. Our midweek position was seventy-five.

That a record's destiny could be determined by such a paltry accounting of fate as its first day's sales was crazy but true. In the chart golden age of the fifties, sixties and early seventies, records were released into a world where anything could happen. A single might meander for weeks in lowly regions of the charts before catching on with DJs or the public. Then it would creep its way upwards and, if the winds were fair and the tune was good, become a hit. Its passage might take eight, nine weeks, sometimes more, and this ascent was an authentic log of a song's conquest of the public's affections. But over the years the charts had become so manipulated, so gamed by the music industry, that they were stretched out of all shape and logic. In their time, twelve-inch singles, coloured vinyl, picture discs, hyping scams and the dreaded multiple formats had each made their contributions to the ruin of the system, progressively distorting the chart, little by little, in favour of gimmicked or aggressively-marketed product until the distortions had become the system. Now a single's fate was determined largely by the ingenuity and muscle of its marketing and by the size and dedication, or gullibility, of the act's fan-base, and its lifespan comprised the six torturous pre-release weeks of 'plugging' at radio, an insane system whereby the public could hear the record for an age but not buy it. By the time a single actually came out, its orbit was almost over – even huge selling records dropped in their second week of release. The charts, once a barometer of the listening tastes of the nation, had become a sham.

I was part of this insanity too; I'd allowed Chrysalis to game the system by surrendering to their demand for formats. And now 'Love Anyway' was kaput, despite having been issued in two matching-sleeved CDs with four different 'exclusive' B-sides, plus, God help us, a limited-edition cassette single – a manifestly useless item in the late nineties. Despite all its radio play the song hadn't caught on with the public. As soon as the damning midweek chart was announced, everyone involved accepted the record wouldn't be a hit, including me. And because Chrysalis viewed 'Love Anyway' as the sole potential hit on the album, from this point onwards they treated *Still Burning* as a lost cause. Yet the whole cycle of touring, travelling and promotion still lay ahead. Fulfilling such a schedule once the bottom has fallen out of a campaign is an experience most recording artists have gone through at some time or another: a dogged, keep-smiling-through-the-wreckage trudge, and I geared up psychologically for it now.

The saving grace was the music, which flowed as always, for my new band was playing focussed, tough shows and never giving a hoot about such things as chart positions. We played a short tour of Scandinavia during which we found both our musical muscle (best gig: a barnstormer in Stavanger) and our band *esprit* (funniest moment: McNabb's impression of a terrible Nordic Eurovision song on the tour bus without his realising the Norwegian EMI rep was sitting in front of him). The only blip was the firing of the luckless Jeremy Stacey, on the day of Princess Diana's funeral, when I got wind he was planning to defect to the reformed Echo & The Bunnymen. His replacement was a pile-driving Glaswegian skin-basher called Geoff Dugmore, and thus reconstituted we worked till the end of the year, touring Britain, Europe and Japan.

For a singer/guitarist, Ian McNabb was an unexpectedly good bass player. He and Dugmore developed a visceral swagger that drove the music like a threshing machine, and their empathy extended offstage,

Dugmore becoming the foil for McNabb's non-stop comedic horseplay. Ian's speciality was a deadpan impression of Rolf Harris singing Prince's 'Sign 'O' The Times', wobble-board sounds and all, which he'd break into at artfully chosen moments, destroying everyone within a twenty-foot radius.

Fingers was funny too, though not always intentionally. A handsome, extremely tall Irishman, possibly of giant stock, he used wonderfully meaningless Father Dougal-esque phrases such as 'in fairness, now', and his moment-to-moment consciousness bubbled from an inexhaustible store of speedy enthusiasm and boyish good nature. He also wore pomade in his hair and on stage in Wolverhampton he got it on his hands and thus onto the neck of his guitar, which made playing difficult. During 'Rare, Precious And Gone', a song with a three-second break of silence at the end of a verse, Fingers calculated he had time to grab a towel off his amp, wipe down the guitar neck, and still hit the first chord of the next verse on cue. His prognostications were correct, but he forgot to turn his volume down, and the three-second break was filled by an unholy skittering sound as Fingers frantically rubbed the towel up and down the neck.

It was a bit like being in one of my teenage bands, only with better gear. During the boogie shuffle 'Blues Is My Business', Boots and I did Chuck Berry duckwalks from opposite ends of the stage. In Japan we all bought half-size guitars with fuzzy built-in speakers that enabled us to jam loudly wherever we liked. But fun times and a good band wasn't all I'd signed up for, and between concerts I had plenty time to think about what had happened since my return to London. My commercial standing was at an all-time low and at the end of the campaign I'd be dropped by the record company for the first time in my career, of that I was sure. The last vestiges of the aura that had surrounded me and The Waterboys for ten or twelve years were gone like so much smoke and vapour. I was nowhere, man.

I'd turned my Findhorn experiences into songs and forged 'em onto records, figuring there was a world out there of people hungry for the things I'd found. But either there wasn't, or I'd failed to do it in a way that reached them. Or perhaps my timing was wrong and in this cockeyed era people only wanted entertainment, not some fucker philosophising or questing. Or maybe the tunes simply weren't good enough. Whatever, I'd offered up my wares and the buffs weren't buying. There was a kind of grief involved. I felt scoured and empty, insubstantial, as if I wasn't fully in the world anymore. After Findhorn the mainstream world didn't appear quite real to me, and I wondered now if *I* didn't seem quite real to *it*. The community and its blue northern skies hung on the horizon of my mind like a towering backdrop, a life I could step back into in a heartbeat. Should I retreat there and immerse myself again in the mystery school?

But no. In December, two days after the last show of the tour, Janette and I were married in Chelsea Registry Office, and that Christmas my heart and my wife told me to stay in the game, that there was some drama yet to play out. And I still had an eye on the glimmer of a new recording home. After a London show in October Alan McGee had said, 'It's inevi'able ye'll come tae Creation, man.' I was eager to join my benefactor there and counted down the weeks till the expiry of my Chrysalis contract.

The great day arrived in March 1998. The confirmation of my release from Chrysalis came through and I sat down to call McGee. I hadn't heard from Alan in a couple of months, which was kind of odd, but I figured he must be busy and we'd had spells of not being in touch before. I dialled his office. His secretary answered and said he wasn't available so I left a message: 'Would Alan call me please. Mike Scott. He knows the number.' After a few days I hadn't heard anything so I called again and got the same answer. I left another message. A few days later I called a third time. McGee picked up the phone. 'Alan, I'm free from Chrysalis!' I told him, and there was an awkward silence, four or five seconds which told me all I needed to know.

Not signing to Alan meant the end of our creative relationship, though not, in time, of our friendship. Meanwhile, with no more touring, the band dissolved. Boots returned to the 'Pool and Fingers to Dublin, Razors and Dugmore to the life of the London session musician. I would work with them all again, but for the moment and for as far as I could see I was on my own. Unable to afford the house on Lansdowne Road anymore, Janette and I rented a semi-detached on a suburban street in Kew, on the western edges of London, and I began to begin all over again.

CHAPTER 18

A MAN WITH A FIDDLE AND A DOG AT NUMBER 12A

The taxi drives down the main street of Sligo and I look out the window scouring the pavements for a glimpse of Steve Wickham. I haven't seen Steve since he moved here a few years ago but I've heard he's been kicked out by his second wife, might even be sleeping rough, and I've come here on something of a mercy mission. But there's no sign of my old friend on the streets, so I stop the taxi at the best place to begin a search for a fiddler: the town's music pub, a colourful hole in the wall called Shoot The Crows. The pub has just opened, and there's an intoxicating smell of beer and old wood. Shafts of sun fall through the window and the ghost of a breeze blows from an open door somewhere at the back. A young barman pops up from under the counter and I can tell by his double take that he recognises me. 'Do you know where I'll find Steve Wickham?' I ask, and he replies, 'Oh, he's staying out in Rathbraughan. He'll be glad to see you, I can tell you that.' There's an understated edge to his voice which confirms my information that Steve's in some kind of trouble. A few more questions establish that Rathbraughan is a modern housing estate at the butt-end of town but the barman doesn't have an address for my friend or even a street name. All I can do is go and knock on doors.

I get back in the taxi and five minutes later, after a slalom through the higgledy-piggledy streets of Sligo's Northside, the cabbie drops me off at the entrance to a depressed estate. I stand on the roadside and register the scene: identical terraced houses in every direction, bleak December fields in the semi-distance. I'm wondering where to start when I see a woman coming out of a house. 'Excuse me,' I say, 'do you know where Steve Wickham the fiddle player lives?' She looks back at me and in a no-nonsense country accent says, 'Well now, I've heard there's a man with a fiddle and a dog at number 12a' and points up the street. I walk in the direction indicated and after fifty yards I find number 12a, a shabby house with an unkempt garden. I stand on the pavement trying to imagine my friend in this unlikely place, then stride up the path and knock on the door. Through the frosted glass I make out the dark shape of a man approaching and the door opens to divulge a dodgy-looking bloke with a thick beard and suspicious deep-sunk eyes. I'm thinking it might be the wrong house when to my amazement I notice the bloke's wearing Steve's old stage waistcoat, a once-fabulous black, red and gold embroidered garment worn at a hundred shows from Hammersmith to Hollywood, now faded and torn, hanging dolefully from this guy's slightly hunched cadaverous frame. My mind grasps for explanations. Maybe Steve's so broke he's had to sell his old stage gear; maybe this weirdo's done some deal with Steve, giving him room and board in return for getting to wear his clothes. All this flits through my mind in one surreal slow-motion second before the scrambled picture comes suddenly, shockingly into focus and I realise the stranger is Steve.

What had happened to The Fellow Who Fiddles? When he left The Waterboys in August 1990, Steve hitched up with some old Dublin mates in a country & western band called The Texas Kellys, playing show band-type gigs up and down Ireland. This was a mystery to me and to a lot of other people too. I'd expected Steve to walk into another top band or form his own; a psychedelic folk-rave combo, perhaps, or a neo-trad ensemble pushing the boundaries of Celtic music. But no, he dropped down several divisions of the rock'n'roll league to join a semi-pro band of Dublin journeymen going nowhere. Had the black night of the soul that followed the breakup of his marriage scuppered Steve's image of himself as a musical force? Or did he just not want the pressure anymore?

Steve stuck with The Texas Kellys for a couple of years and played on their only record, an EP called *Stay All Night*. The cover showed the band wearing cowboy hats and sitting on the edge of what looked like a slagheap, with Steve spaced off a little way to the side as if he couldn't make up his mind whether he was in the band or out. The Kellys played well but their world was a far cry from the professional one Steve had inhabited with The Waterboys. Their modus operandi was to drive five or six hours to the gig, pick up a couple of girls in the audience and persuade them to let the band crash on their floor. If this gambit didn't work, their roadie would drive the band back to Dublin through the night, struggling to stay awake, a crash only a moment's slumber away.

All musicians take this risk at least once in their early careers, and the traditional way of avoiding disaster is for a band member to sit up front with the driver and keep him talking, and therefore conscious. I remember it myself, Johnny Waller dozing at the wheel on the way back from a 1979 gig in Aberdeen, the van veering alarmingly close to the barrier as we crossed the Forth Road Bridge at five in the morning. Most bands, wishing to stay alive, evolve swiftly past this state of affairs and develop the habit of booking hotels. Not so The Texas Kellys, still riding their luck after years on the road.

Steve may have given up on stardom but he still valued his skin. After one too many hair-raising drives he laid down the law: a hotel or guesthouse on the next trip or he was out. Halfway to the next show he asked the bandleader, a banjo-bothering Dublin cowboy called Jimmy Kelly, where they'd be staying that night. 'Ah, don't worry,' said Jim, 'sure, we'll sort somethin' out!' 'Stop the van!' retorted Steve, and when it wheezed to a halt on the outskirts of a midlands town he jumped out with a parting shot of 'Call yourselves cowboys? You couldn't even catch an Indian!' and hitched a lift back to Dublin. And that was the end of Mr Wickham's career as a Texas Kelly.

Next Steve moved to Sligo, an old market town eighty miles north of Galway, where he lived with his second wife Annie and their baby daughter in a Methodist church hall Annie had inherited from her grandmother. The building was under the shadow of Ben Bulben, the strange flat mountain that looms over Sligo and provides the dramatic backdrop to several weighty W.B. Yeats poems. And now Ben Bulben formed the backdrop to the unravelling drama of Steve's life. For when the marriage came unstuck in late 1993, Annie changed the locks and Steve found himself out on his ear, walking the roads of the world.

Steve and I sat at the kitchen table, his little dog scurrying and snapping at our ankles, and I got the story. He had indeed been kicked out by his wife, for reasons too arcane to untangle, but the accounts of him sleeping rough were an Irish exaggeration. Steve was in fact working mornings at a local youth club, teaching kids to play football, and just about keeping body and soul together. Well, body anyway. It was alarming to see my old friend so wounded. Looking into his once-merry face was like intruding on a private tragedy. He was like one of those characters in a comic strip with a personal black raincloud following them around. I tried to get him to open up about what had happened to him, and what he could do about it, but it was like trying to draw water from a stone. Steve was deeply troubled, close to his personal rock bottom. Only time and love might cure what ailed him.

We wandered the fringes of Sligo together, rambled by the seashore and poked around country lanes, and even played a few old Hank Williams songs together back at the house. But Steve's fiddle had a curdled sound to it, as if it had been in the fridge too long, and Steve played like what he was, a distressed man lost in a thicket he couldn't yet find a way out of. Still, I perceived something gnarly at work in him, some instinctive self-preservation under the surface that would have its say in his destiny, and I got the feeling that the next time I saw him he'd be in better shape. And he was. On an August day eight months later he turned up out of the blue, on a bicycle, at the bay-side cottage in Findhorn where I was now living with Janette.

Janette answered the door and called me. 'It's Steve, the friend you told me all about.' And as I greeted him I felt like Dean Moriarty in *On The Road*, the time Sal Paradise visits him, and Dean, gobsmacked, says, 'Sal! You've finally come to *me*!'

Steve had cycled across Ireland and up the whole length of Scotland to find me. He was still bearded, somewhat hunched at the shoulders, and the eye contact wasn't great, but otherwise he was fit and sharp, with the faintest hint of his old humour about him. We spent the day walking the shoreline of Findhorn Bay, among the pine trees and eco-houses of the community. The conversation was clear and open, our friendship intact, and I knew my friend was on the mend. I saw him a few more times over the next couple of years and every time he was a little more returned to his old self: clearer-eyed, clean-shaven, standing more upright. In the spring of 1995 he came to my one-man show in Galway and hung out backstage. Six months later his new folk trio, The Connacht Ramblers, supported me at Dublin's Olympia Theatre; and in 1997 he made a brief visit to London for a Ramblers' gig and stayed with Janette and me in the pink house on Lansdowne Road.

The Connacht Ramblers, like the Texas Kellys, played around the pubs and shebeens of Ireland. They flourished, after a fashion, from 1994 to 1998, playing a repertoire of Woody Guthrie covers, fiddly instrumentals and quirky original songs. The vocals were by Steve or his mate, an Irish poet/guitarist called Peter Brabazon. I asked Steve about their life on the road, and he regaled me with woeful but funny tales of mildewed boarding houses and crooked rustic pub-owners, the indignities of being upstaged in Killarney by a magician who puked up live fish, or being misbooked to play in a rebel bar in front of an audience of hardcore Irish republicans. The diehards, unimpressed by the Ramblers' cheery fare, requested throughout that they 'Play a fuckin' rebel song, boys!' and when Steve declined with a spirited, if inadvisable, riposte of 'Rebel songs are shite!' someone punched him in the face, knocking him out cold.

Or the time they were booked to play at Puck Fair, a semi-medieval travellers' shindig in a hilly crossroads town called Killorglin. Atop a narrow twenty-foot-high platform in the village square a wild Billy goat, captured a few days earlier in the local mountains, and with a metal crown stuck rudely on his hairy head, presides over the festivities. This is King Puck, after whom the fair is named. Steve and his mates played on a makeshift stage on the square during the afternoon, and at one point Steve thought it had started raining. He could feel the drips going down his neck, yet when he looked at the audience it didn't seem to be raining on *them*. He looked up and with horror realised he was standing under King Puck, who was majestically relieving himself.

At their London gig I saw the Ramblers for myself. The show was at the Weavers, a folk music bar with photos from ancient gigs lining the walls and a proper stage in the back room. A perfect setting, therefore, except no one turned up and the band had to play their two sets to an audience of seven. This they did with a dogged, self-deprecating resilience which suggested they were used to this kind of occurrence. Steve had invited me to join them on stage but sensing disaster, and with the moral rectitude of a rat on a doomed ship, I declined and let the Ramblers die their own death of a thousand silences. They battled gallantly and Steve was a cheerful frontman, making hopelessly bad jokes and giving charming explanations of the songs, but he was no lead singer and nor was Peter Brabazon. It was nearly amateur – not the worst gig I'd ever seen, but not by any stretch worthy of Wickham's talent.

Nor were the various summer jobs Steve told me about, which he got via the Sligo Tourist Board to make some cash when gigs were scarce. Yet there was a certain magic about the thought of him being a 'fiddling tour guide' at a local castle, or a 'ghost fiddler' hiding on an island on picturesque Lough Gill and playing tunes from the trees as tourists took their lunch in a ruined abbey, or acting the part of W.B. Yeats's 'Fiddler Of Dooney' at a fair in the town of Dooney Rock while people danced, as the poem said, 'like the wave of the sea'. And there was something noble about it too – a man doing work beneath his station in order to feed a family. For as well as providing for daughter Amy, who lived with his estranged second wife, Steve had married again and he and third wife Heidi now had a baby son.

In the summer of 1998 I played a solo show at the Galway Arts Festival. Steve and Anto Thistlethwaite were in the audience and joined me for the encore, and I heard the old magic in Steve's playing. In fact, it was as if he *wanted* me to hear it. On 'Fisherman's Blues' and Hank Williams's 'Honky Tonkin'' he reprised all my favourite Fellow Who Fiddles tricks: dizzying harmonic swirls, bright bursts of happy melody, lazy country double stops. It was as if I was being musically seduced.

By now I was living in Kew, gathering my wits after the crash and burn of my solo career, busy writing my next album. It was shaping up to be a fuzz-driven psychedelic rock record, and after the way Steve played with me in Galway I tried to imagine his fiddle in its sonic mix, but no matter how I approached it, fiddle didn't fit. Sometime in the future, I figured, perhaps when I finished the unreleased *Fisherman's Blues* music and stuck it out as an album, a project I'd been planning for years, I'd ask him to come on board.

As things turned out, Steve came to me first. In the autumn of 1999 he rang me out of the blue and said, 'How about doin' a gig in Sligo? I'll put together a band to back you.' I thought for a few seconds then replied, 'Forget the band – let's do a two-man show, just you and me together.' And so it was that in the last weeks of the twentieth century I returned to the west of Ireland to restore my creative partnership with The Fellow Who Fiddles. Steve was well recovered by now from his Rathbraughan doldrums. Time and the self-healing power of the human heart had done their work. But when I arrived in Sligo and visited him at his new house I began to see there was another reason: new wife Heidi, a bustling, no-nonsense blonde English dynamo. Heidi ran the place, boxed Steve's ears, looked after three-year-old Tom, designed stage sets for local theatrical events, and produced countless paintings of inquisitive ducks which festooned the walls of their home, Harebell House, which Steve and she had built a few years earlier.

Harebell House was a pale blue cottage on a plot of rough land under a hill four miles from Sligo. Mimicking the style of old Irish cottages it had one main room, running almost the length of the house, with a small bedchamber at each end. But there the traditional similarities ended. For stepping into Harebell House was to enter a wonderland. The walls were bright green with orange skirting, the windows were set in scarlet wooden frames, hanging from the rafters were strings of bells, bright ribbons and spider plants with heart-shaped leaves and curling tendrils. On the window ledges stood tattered piles of dictionaries, cookbooks, music folios and picture books. Cats slept on high shelves. The mantelpiece was a wooden railway sleeper Steve had found by the side of a road. A huge carved leaping hare, the totem animal of the establishment, was fixed majestically to the wall above a cheerful roaring fireplace. And at one end the room was overlooked by a minstrel's gallery stuffed with boxes, theatre costumes and Steve's musical instruments. It was a magical mad delightful place, the product of Steve's and Heidi's personalities, and the absolute opposite of the dump I'd found him in during his soul's dark night at Rathbraughan.

Our concert was booked a week later at The Hawk's Well Theatre in Sligo, and I was billeted in a guesthouse half a mile away on the shores of Lough Gill, opposite the island where Steve had been a 'ghost fiddler'. Each day he picked me up in his ancient banger of a car which shunted and chuntered (often giving up till Steve performed some unknown rustic alchemy on it) back to Harebell House where we rehearsed. Or tried to. For it was tough pinning Steve down to rehearsal. Every time we started work we'd get an hour of playing done before he would lay down his fiddle and announce he had to go into Sligo to see a man about a dog, or some other dubious business, leaving me to gaze at the bright walls of Harebell House or moulder in my B&B.

After three days of stop-start, stop-start I exploded and told Steve in exasperated tones that I was used to rehearsing professionally, that it was arrogant of him to attend to all this other business on my time when I'd come from London to work with him, and that he couldn't 'just keep walking out'. 'If you don't work a bit fucking harder,' I said furiously, 'we'll be shite on stage on Thursday night.' All of which, while pertinent to the work in hand, was also a coded way of saying *I'm still mad that you fucked off and left me in the shit with a world tour to play back in 1990!*

As if opening a floodgate, my outburst had the effect of unleashing a wild reciprocal rant from Steve containing all manner of long-buttoned-down grievances, real and fantastical, climaxing in his passionate assertions that I'd forced him out of The Waterboys ten years before and that my royal arrogance quite equalled his own, with particularly emotive reference being made to my insistence that he sing no songs at our upcoming gig and leave all the vocals to me. With a sudden jolt to my guts I realised I'd muscled back into the role of Steve's boss instead of being his colleague and partner, and that I must have done this so many times in the past that it was an old, acute wound for my friend.

I was stunned into silence. Both sets of words hung lividly in the air above our heads ... and then evaporated. For while the eruption had exposed the unspoken undertows of our past, it had another more profound effect. As we sat facing each other, scoured and unburdened of our baggage, a deep recognition passed between us. Steve's jet black eyes glittered at me and I knew who we were: two musical soulmates. And none of the other stuff – the who did what to who back when – mattered a jot. What mattered was the deep feeling of old comradeship and something that felt a lot like love. And the love was flowing both ways. Quietly and humbly we hugged each other and set about the business of rehearsing properly, with no more men to see about dogs, and a couple of Steve's vocals included in the set.

The show was on Thursday 7 October, and as we soundchecked at the Hawk's Well Steve was more nervous than I'd ever seen him, and not with excitement. The man was terrified. But when we walked out

278

on stage in front of a packed audience his old performing nature kicked in, and though it took him a couple of songs to settle into his groove soon he was playing eloquently with a restrained version of the power and flair of old. We did songs from several Waterboys albums, mostly those Steve had played on, plus a version of 'Bring 'Em All In' with a local string quartet he'd assembled. We sweated, cruised, played off each other, negotiated a few tight musical corners and broke through to some high, power-driven uplands, and ninety minutes later it was all over. Or rather, it was beginning. The Fellow Who Fiddles and I had reclaimed our musical brotherhood from the wreckage of the past, and the fire was burning again.

CHAPTER 19

HOOP DANCING

On a summer's evening in the early nineties I'm at a theatre on Seventh Avenue, watching a troupe of Native Americans perform a modern take on traditional American Indian dance. Towards the end a young man in feathered costume and headband walks onto the stage alone, carrying a set of thin white wooden hoops, which he lays at his feet.

As the music begins he flicks one of the hoops into the air with a movement of his foot. He catches it deftly and begins to dance, twirling the hoop, slipping inside it, spinning it around his hips and shoulders. Then he gathers another, then another and another, integrating each successive hoop in an increasingly complex dance, forming them into the shapes of wings, tails and perfect spheres. He adds hoops until he's dancing with thirty of them in a dizzying, blurred myriad of patterns, never falling out of graceful movement and symmetry. The performance is visually stunning, but has a deeper significance: the hoops symbolise the different parts of the dancer's life and culture, the threads of his world, and the dance is a celebration of his having learned to move between them with balance and mastery. As the Hoop Dancer spins he is demonstrating not only his power over the tools of the dance, but his mastery of himself. Watching from my balcony seat, I want this mastery too.

Finding myself in suburban Kew in the spring of 1998 felt like a banishment, as if I'd been spat out by the machinery of pop and left to fester in a snoozy hinterland. To my mind Kew was a way station, nothing more, an impression heightened by the railway line at the end of the garden and by our location directly under the Heathrow flight paths. Planes flew over the street every forty-five seconds, while

Concorde, loudest of all created beings, went by twice daily, renting the fabric of reality with an ear and earth-splitting roar.

This was not a landscape designed to hold me, and within weeks of arriving in Kew I felt the familiar wanderlust. As if on cue an old haunt soon beckoned. That May I returned to Spiddal to film a performance for Irish television, and was stirred all over again by the beauty and wild charm of the place. On the three days of my visit the Connemara coast was windless and sun-sharpened, its crazy fields and rocky slopes shining silver green in the Atlantic light, appearing to my hungry eyes like nothing less than the primordial paradise of the philosophers' golden age. What's more, though I was yesterday's man on the British rock scene, I was a folk legend in the West of Ireland. Everywhere I went people I didn't know said hello to me, nodded or said things like, 'I was at The Waterboys' show in Ennistymon in 1989, 'twas mighty!' And when the television filming was completed everyone went to Hughes's bar, where I was feted like the long-lost prodigal son and a giant music session ensued. I flew back to Kew ready to up sticks and move once and for all to County Galway, and cajoled Janette to come with me on a fortnight's exploratory trip.

We rented the same rural bungalow I'd stayed in during the making of *Room To Roam*, but while Janette liked the place for a visit and could see why I adored it she didn't want to live in Spiddal. I had to decide between two of the great loves of my life: my wife and the west of Ireland. No contest. I sacrificed the dream of moving to Spiddal and we returned to Kew. But after every sacrifice comes a gift of grace, and Kew had some unexpected gifts in store for me, starting with a revelation. For twenty years I'd moved from place to place, immersing myself in the atmosphere and character of each new location. Edinburgh, Notting Hill, Dublin, Spiddal, New York and Findhorn had all impacted on my imagination, my music, and my sense of identity. But somewhere along the line I'd fooled myself into believing that where I was defined me and my work. Now, exiled amid the strait-laced terraces of Kew in a location that said little to my soul, this illusion was unravelled. For instead of finding inspiration in my physical or cultural surroundings I had to find it inside myself. As I prowled Kew's leafy streets that first year I heard the music in my head still rolling, unfurling itself into new shapes and forms, and I became aware of an internal battery located in my guts, a kind of growling Mike-Scott-ness like the steady roar of an engine, still full of drive and ambition. Denuded of a magical environment in which to dream, I dreamed anyway and finally learned how to embody a line in one of my old songs: *Home is in me wherever I roam.*

In this state of mind I began making the music that would get me back in the game. And because my stock was so low it had be spectacularly good if I was going to get people listening to me again. I had a crop of new songs, harder numbers than I'd written for years, with cut-glass guitar grooves and titles like 'The Charlatan's Lament' and 'Dumbing Down The World', each an autobiographical snapshot exploring the ebb and flow of my emotions and how alien I felt in the crazy London I'd returned to. As I rotated them on the radio of my imagination they crackled with a psychedelic, elemental roar. This would be the sound I recorded with, but I had to bring myself up to speed with rock'n'roll first; I'd been out of sync with rock for so long I'd stopped being creatively removed from it and become simply out of touch. If I wanted to make people pay attention to me I needed to absorb, master, and subvert the sonic fashions of the day. So I spent a year filling my head with Radiohead's *OK Computer*, Mercury Rev's exquisite *Deserter's Songs*, Beck, The Wu-Tang Clan, Death In Vegas, Cornershop and a hundred other late-nineties luminaries.

In the process I rediscovered the thrill of following the creative edge of rock. I decided to approach every instrument, voice and sound on my new record in a spirit of invention; to use the recording process itself as a form of creativity – like the artists I was listening to and as I'd done myself on early Waterboys albums – rather than just a physical space to capture performances in, which was what the studio had become for me since *Fisherman's Blues*. To achieve this I needed a new arsenal of sounds, so for several months I haunted Denmark Street, London's historic Tin Pan Alley where the city's musical instrument shops were clustered in a brightly coloured row, and sought out the effects and gizmos that would enable me to produce the sound in my head. I loved Denmark Street. It was the scuzzy heart of British rock'n'roll and as I tramped its Dickensian pavement I could sense the ghosts of London's musical past; song sellers, bandleaders, sharkskin-suited agents, teddy boys and skifflers, early sixties folkies just off the bus from Glasgow or Newcastle, the spectral figure of Jimi Hendrix strutting past in his brocaded guardsman's jacket, Elton John and David Bowie hustling for breaks at the dawn of the seventies, the Sex Pistols loitering with intent five years later, fighting, fornicating and writing 'I'm A Lazy Sod' in a dingy basement eighteen months before the revolution they unleashed caught fire.

I was walking in all their footsteps, jostling for my own corner once more in the landscape of rock, mining for the means of expression that would help me stake my claim. And I found what I needed. My sonic plunder included a metal device called a Micro Synthesizer, which turned guitars into snakes and made *suckk!* and *ffooopp!* noises; vintage phase and tremolo pedals that wired in tandem resulted in fizzling psychedelic paint-wheels of sound; a royal selection of fuzz, muff, crunch and distortion machines; a splendid scarlet-painted Theremin (a hollow box with an aerial that emitted rubbery-sounding electronic wails when I carved shapes in the air around it with my hands) and a blues harp microphone, which made my voice jagged and grotesque.

In search of additional cultural ballast I went back to vintage gospel music, a passion from the *Fisherman's Blues* days. I bought forty or fifty CDs of recordings from the twenties and scoured them for samples, lyric ideas and song titles, one of which I paraphrased for my album's title *A Rock In The Weary Land*. Next I stashed up on all the BBC and movie sound effects I could find on CD or vinyl and even recorded my own, an absorbing pursuit that found me trudging the streets of Kew holding a microphone under an umbrella to capture the crackling sound of rain on fabric, or sitting on a tube train recording its rattling rhythm and fragments of people's conversation. Finally I went to an Indian music shop in Southall where I picked up a Hindu beat-box, several weird-shaped tambourines that made bright *shrashy* sounds and, mightiest of all, two sweet-sounding harmoniums with inscrutable eastern drones and a button the turbaned dude in the shop called 'the trembler', which triggered a fast *drrrrrrrr* sound like a musical pneumatic drill. Thus was I armed, equipped, suited and booted with the tools I needed to transfer the roaring music in the cave of my skull onto the miracle of magnetic tape, but before I could begin, destiny interrupted with some long-unfinished personal business. Tracking down my dad.

I hadn't seen my father since Christmas 1970. I remembered him from my childhood as a handsome moustached fellow who worked in an Edinburgh music shop and spent his spare time sculpting and painting in his study. His name was Allan and though he wasn't a musician several of my clearest memories of him were musical: leading me and my mum in sing-songs in the family car, giving me my first guitar, telling me how exciting he thought the Stones' 'Jumpin' Jack Flash' was.

When he left he did so gradually: after he moved out of the house, he came round ever more rarely before finally disappearing altogether. He didn't take me aside and explain what was happening, nor did he stay in touch once he'd left Edinburgh. And because children don't know how to process such things, like most abandoned kids I felt I was to blame and that I must be wrong or unlovable in some way. But these feelings got buried over time and my father's disappearance from my life became my normal. As I grew older I pictured him as a wanderer, a free spirit moving from scene to scene from whom I inherited the same tendency. I often wondered where he was and what would happen if I bumped into him; surely he was aware of my life as a musician and must have seen me on TV or read about me in the press.

I'd never tried to find him but as I approached forty something shifted. I'd always imagined our meeting would trigger an awkward process of reconciliation or some form of rejection, and the fact of my lost father had grown in my mind until he occupied a large shadowy corner of my psyche, a domain better left undisturbed. But as I discussed him one day with Janette in the kitchen at Kew I realised I no longer cared about these forebodings. I didn't, as the Glaswegians say, *gie a shite*. What I suddenly understood was that not knowing him was holding me back, stunting me. I needed to find the old man, discover who the hell he was, and most important of all reclaim authority over my own destiny. I needed to say to him: you may have walked out of my life but you can't *stay* out of my life.

The only information I had was that he'd moved to the South of England in 1971. So Janette and I went to the Family Records Office in Islington and spent several afternoons looking for any record of his having remarried. And finally, in one of the huge, medieval-sized volumes of records, we found his name on a marriage certificate for 1972. Bingo! Then, cross-referencing Allan's name and that of his wife, we found details of the births of two children, a half-brother and sister I didn't even know I had! There was an address too, near Birmingham, but it was for 1984 and I figured that after fourteen years they'd surely have moved elsewhere. But when we checked the voters' rolls for the district, to my amazement there he was, the old fucker, still at the same address.

Rather than tip him off in advance and risk denial or some other form of brush-off, I decided to go and knock on his door. So on a sharp, windy December day, a week before my fortieth birthday, Janette and I took a train to a town on the outskirts of Birmingham and walked the mile to my dad's house, the longest mile of my life.

I had the address on a piece of paper and counted down the houses. The Scotts' was the last but one house on a suburban terrace, next to a bare little park. I knocked on the door and a teenage boy answered it – my half-brother, with a question-mark face and blond hair. To my surprise he didn't show any recognition when he saw me. I asked if his father was there and the lad replied warily that his dad would be back in half an hour. I asked if we could come in and wait. But this was Middle England and bohemian outlanders in colourful clothes who come asking questions don't get asked in to wait. Junior held his ground, like the good lad he was, and said no. The boy closed the door but he must have been alarmed because a neighbour woman, roused by telephone, quickly materialised from the opposite house. She bustled up to us and with concern and suspicion in her voice asked us what we wanted. I told her my business and she was immediately mollified but all she said was, 'Oh, well, he'll be here soon' and hurried back indoors.

And so we stood like tinkers on the pavement, feeling extremely out of place. My heart beat like a sledgehammer in my chest and Janette held my arm, a steadying rock until, somewhat earlier than the mooted half-hour, a car approached.

I saw his face through the windscreen but couldn't recognise him. It had been too long. But I knew it was him. He pulled up at the house and stepped out, reaching in his pockets for his key. As we walked towards him I tried to match the man in front of me with the memory traces in my mind. He turned and looked quizzically at us. I searched for the right words but after all these years, having arrived at the moment so long awaited, so often imagined, I couldn't speak. Janette, seeing my difficulty, did it for me.

'Allan,' she said, 'this is your son.' My father's eyes and mine met, and a cocktail of confusion and recognition passed across his still-handsome face.

'I wouldn't have known you,' he spluttered then added, dramatically, 'but I always knew this day would come.' Lost for what to say next he asked us into the house. We walked behind him and I noticed two things: my little half-brother watching us through the window, and the way my father's hair curled round his collar at the back of his neck, exactly like I remembered it from when I was a child. He sent the lad upstairs and sat with Janette and me in the lounge, a room like a million others, with family photos on the mantelpiece, an electric fire in the hearth and a copy of the *Radio Times* under the TV. In this domesticated theatre the long-withheld questions were finally asked: Why did I never hear from you again? Where did you go? Do you understand what your disappearance meant to me?

Allan answered my questions, or tried to. He explained he'd never got in touch because he'd felt it was kinder that way. And clearly he'd done what he'd thought was best according to his wisdom, or lack of it, at the time. But though he tried to sum up what he imagined my experience must have been, it was clear Allan didn't understand how his leaving had impacted on me. I didn't need him to understand my reality, but I needed him to acknowledge that he didn't, and to stop theorising about what it must be like to be the abandoned child. Though I couldn't inch him towards such an acknowledgment now, I was determined I would in future.

It was a weird afternoon; four or five hours that expanded and compressed as the conversation swung from deep waters to commonplace banalities. Much was discovered: Allan hadn't known I'd become a musician and had never heard of The Waterboys, and his kids hadn't known they had an older half-brother. When Allan's wife and daughter arrived home from shopping, the lad was retrieved from upstairs and we were all introduced, sitting together in the living room, a strange uneasy sixsome. The tough conversation continued into evening.

In the process I realised my dad and I were less similar than I'd expected. He was a real character, a cross between a straight Dirk Bogarde and an old-time stage tragedian. I liked him. And second time around he was clearly a loving, solid family man, but he wasn't at all the figure of my imagination. All those years I'd believed I was cast in the image of my father, I'd actually been casting him in the image of *me*. The free spirit shifting from scene to scene was myself: a tendency I now understood came more from my mother, with her penchant for moving house every few years, than my old estranged dad. By learning who he was I'd learned a lot about who I was too, and when Allan drove us back to the railway station that night I'd got what I came for: a headful of answers and the right to have my father in my life.

Next day I was overwhelmed by a tidal wave of feelings. Deep shit was working itself out inside me. At some subterranean level of consciousness I was reporting back to the young Mike whose dad had walked out on him, and the new information was rearranging the framework of my emotional DNA. And there was a new feeling too, an inner buzz of wellbeing and self-honouring that told me I'd done the right thing. I'd faced down my oldest fear and jettisoned a motherlode of obsolete psychological architecture.

For the next year Allan and I corresponded by letter, an exchange that enabled us to express things still unsaid, and to establish the crucial point about his not understanding how his disappearance had impacted on me. These letters didn't flow fast. Replies both ways took a month or more each time, a measure of the emotional depths we were plumbing, and step by step we cleared the debris of the past and emerged into the sunlight of a new and cordial relationship with each other.

The reunion with my dad didn't lead to a stream of new songs; in fact I didn't write anything about it, without actually intending not to. But having confronted my old shadow, when I finally began recording *A Rock In The Weary Land* in early 1999 there was a difference in the way I felt and carried myself, and I worked with a new self-confidence. I needed it, too: I was coming back from career rock bottom without a record label, with only a headful of songs and the skin I stood up in. And because this was the first album I'd ever made without record company money and I'd lost my shirt on the *Still Burning* tour, I hadn't anything to spend. But the gods of rock'n'roll sent me two benefactors. My ex-lawyer John Kennedy lent me money and I found myself a new manager who got me cheap recording time in a decent studio.

His name was Philip Tennant and ten years earlier he'd worked as a recording engineer on *Fisherman's Blues*. I can still picture him turning up on his first morning at Rockfield Studios, bright as a pin, to find me red-eyed and stubble-chinned, deep in late album burnout, having been up all night doing a very bad mix of 'The Stolen Child'. Mercifully he took over and we finished *Fisherman's Blues* together, becoming friends in the process. By the time our paths re-crossed a decade later, courtesy of a chance meeting on the ever-fateful Portobello Road, Philip had become a manager and promptly offered to represent me. As the Svengalis of rock weren't exactly queuing up to have me on their books, and I remembered Philip as a good guy, I said yes. It would turn out to be my best managerial relationship since good old Z.

The studio Philip found for me was called Maison Rouge, a faded old joint on the Fulham Road where I'd done a couple of sessions in the early eighties. Soon I was set up with my gear and gizmos, having a serious creative experience and a whole lot of first-rate fun at the same time, just as it should be. And as the project progressed I called in some fellow explorers.

First was Thighpaulsandra, a Welsh keyboard warlock with a penchant for Mohawk haircuts and bloodcurdling prog-rock riffs. I'd seen a photo of him loitering by stone circles like a fur-clad gnome in Julian Cope's 'Earth mysteries' book *The Modern Antiquarian*. Expecting a lunatic genius, possibly speaking in Elvish, I was surprised to be greeted at the studio by a soft-spoken, casually dressed chap of about forty, smiling placidly behind a bank of keyboards, a cup of tea in one hand and his Mohawk grown out into a sensible crop. It was like meeting an assistant scientist or a technical boffin at the BBC. I couldn't equate the gentle fellow before me with either his outrageous sexually charged name or his reputation as a sonic terrorist. But when the music began, someone else appeared.

Thighpaulsandra's first contribution was on 'Crown', a blues-hewn fuzz-Mellotron battle charge, and as the track blasted out of the speakers, I found myself watching a wild moonstruck elf, a brilliant Gollum locked in the frame of a man, and it was the elf that was making the music! The keyboard spoke in tongues, a ferocious but disciplined torrent of sound filled with brainstorms, shards of metal, lightning-struck towers and vengeful Druid horsemen, all of which seemed to materialise in the air of the room, passing before my imagination, conjured and manifested by the exultant elf-wizard.

I'd seen such things before, trad players who morphed from shy farmers into flame-eyed centaurs the moment they stuck a tin whistle between their lips or a fiddle under their jaw, and I knew how to deal with it. I directed the music in terms of what the elf was capable of (which appeared to be anything) but I addressed myself only to the man, who stepped seamlessly back into control every time the playing stopped. Thighpaulsandra had mastered the art of allowing his inner wizard, his genius, full expression while he played, without it hijacking or overwhelming his persona. Man and daemon co-existed in dynamic harmony.

My next playmate was a teenage drum programmer called Rowan who lived in a top-floor bedsit on Ladbroke Grove, where I spent three days listening while he prepared rhythm tracks for me. Rowan's sampling gear was state of the art, all shiny effects racks and wall-sized speakers meticulously assembled, and clearly meant more to him than life itself. But everything else in the bedsit was squalid and scum-encrusted, especially a vast pile of dirty dishes, not unlike the one in the opening scene of *Withnail And I*, that teetered round the filthy sink, abuzz with flies, and had been there long enough to become a culture. This tower of grime emitted a thin, curdled, somehow *satisfied* smell that haunted the room, though Rowan, like any teenager in his own mess, was oblivious and quite immune to it. I sat amidst the sordid scene till I could stand it no more, whereupon I fled to a local supermarket and bought rubber gloves, scourers and a bottle of yellow washing up liquid. I heroically cleaned Rowan's abominable crockery mountain while he sat unperturbed on the far side of the room, sampling the drummers on ancient jazz records and turning fragments of their playing into slick, cunning grooves as pristine as his flat was vile.

I had my own history in the teenage mess department. When I was seventeen my mother went off to teach at summer school for a fortnight, leaving me a set of keys, a list of instructions and a huge fresh chicken on the sideboard, which I absently picked at for a week. One morning I heard a strange sound of distant munching as if an army was gobbling food several miles away. To my horror I saw the chicken had metamorphosed into a vibrating mass of maggots the size of a rugby ball. I sprang into action and did what any sensible teenager left on his own in a house would do: ran and got the woman next door. Neighbour Maggie took one look and whisked my unplanned nature project into a dustbin outside the back door, plate and all, then poured a kettleful of boiling water after it.

Fortunately there was nothing alive in Rowan's pile of dishes; I'd got to it in time. And his work was brilliant, well worth the price of three days' purgatory. Using a young creative spirit added a hip freshness to the music, but I needed older heads too. Anthony Thistlethwaite played fuzz mandolin on several sessions; Kevin Wilkinson, veteran of the first Waterboys shows, Dave Ruffian from the 1986 band and Jeremy 'Swipe' Stacey all drummed. Palestinian jazz sax-man Gilad Atzmon, The London Community Gospel Choir and a procession of backing singers, including 'Bjorn' from the Abba tribute band Bjorn Again, all added their notes. By the summer of 1999 the album's style was established and my songs nestled in a glittering beautiful-cum-grotesque psychedelic soundscape.

Then midway through the assemblage of this sonic architecture Kew imparted its next revelation. Whenever I'd moved in the previous two decades I'd put my stuff in storage, and by the late nineties I had container-loads of tea chests and boxes stashed in several different cities. In the summer of 1999 Janette and I moved to a house with a large attic, and for the first time I had space to store them all myself – and to go through them.

There were boxes from teenage Ayr, punk-wars Edinburgh, eighties London, Dublin and Spiddal, nineties New York and Findhorn, each a memory capsule with a power to immediately transport me back in time and place, and put me in touch with how I'd felt at all the stages of my long strange road. I found over a thousand books dating from as early as childhood; stacks of music weeklies from 1969 onwards; colourful piles of superhero and underground comics; reams of ancient fan mail and press cuttings documenting the rise of The Waterboys; over a hundred lyric notebooks; my teenage record collection; photo albums of my first bands; cassettes of early Waterboys music I hadn't listened to in ten years; old clothes; shoeboxes full of personal letters, maps, tour itineraries, promo pictures, menus from restaurants in Jerusalem and Skibbereen, notebooks, scrawled addresses and sets of playing cards.

Lots of things made me cringe – early lyrics, lists of grandiose plans for records and tours that had come to naught, reminders of friends lost or neglected when I'd moved on. And some curious mysteries were explained; for example, why Simon Le Bon of Duran Duran had been weird and standoffish every time I'd passed him in Maison Rouge Studios that spring. An old press cutting I found revealed the answer: in an early eighties interview I'd gratuitously slagged off Duran Duran, and it would appear that Simon remembered. I made a mental note to apologise to him next time our paths crossed.

But the process was inspiring too: my old lyric books enabled me to re-inhabit the Mike Scott of my twenties, a bracing experience like standing on a cliff top in a fierce wind. That young guy had been so wildly on fire, so drunk on wonder, that it was a wonder all over again just to make his acquaintance. Similar glimpses allowed me to re-engage with my teenage dreamer, my west of Ireland trad explorer, my Findhorn seeker, and so on, and to discover that all these characters were still inside me like a set of wavelengths, and that if I chose to I could re-think myself into each one of them.

I'd always wanted to be the kind of artist who could draw on every strand of his music and personality at will, but I hadn't known how. If I played a rock'n'roll tour I wasn't able to weave acoustic or Celtic music into it, and vice versa. Now, for the first time, all my past selves and the inspirations they'd worked with were accessible. The discovery reminded me of the concert I'd attended once in New York by The Native American Dance Theatre, the highlight of which was the Hoop Dancer. I'd wanted then what the Hoop Dancer had, the ability to balance my worlds within me and move between them with ease. Seven years later in an attic in Kew, with the contents of two-dozen tea chests strewn around the floor, I'd found the key.

At a one-off solo show that summer I flung songs from all my eras into the set and tried on their different personas like stage costumes. It worked. I could move between them like a shape-shifter, maintaining contact with the original streams of inspiration that had driven each stage of the music. I was the sum of my parts at last. Getting my fire burning again with Steve Wickham, for our two-man Sligo concert occurred shortly after, dovetailed with this process. My partnership with The Fellow Who Fiddles was another wavelength I could tune into, and now it had a future, not just history. But for now the music said 'wait' and so I finished *A Rock In The Weary Land* without Steve.

Philip Tennant, meanwhile, had hustled me a deal with BMG, one of the few record companies I'd never been with (all I needed was Warner Bros and I'd have the set). The guys who signed me were a Swedish A&R man called Per and a wily old label boss called Harry McGee, no relation to Alan, known in the business as 'the silver fox'. Per and Harry thought they were getting Mike Scott and were gobsmacked when halfway through negotiations I told them *A Rock In The Weary Land* was going to be a Waterboys album.

This was no light decision; I'd thought about it for three years. I'd come to detest the idea that there was some difference between Waterboys music and Mike Scott music, and I recognised that only by using the better-known name could I gather it all under one banner. Then there was the size of The Waterboys' audience, several times larger than I commanded as a solo singer. And thirdly, most of all, I missed the alchemy of the name, the sense of being part of something bigger than myself, with band members who had the status of fellow Waterboys, not just backing musicians. So in the summer of 2000, as the release of *Weary Land* approached, I assembled a new Waterboys. And in the same way that I'd created the original band by selecting musicians who'd played on that era's album, *A Pagan Place*, so this line-up comprised three players who'd worked on *A Rock In The Weary Land*: Jeremy Stacey, Livingston Brown and a new keyboard player, Richard Naiff.

Richard was one of those rare musicians who'd come to my attention, like Steve and Anto, through my hearing them by chance and wondering, who the hell is *that*? I was working in Maison Rouge late one night when the liquid tones of David Bowie's 'Lady Grinning Soul', a favourite song from my teens, floated from a room down the studio corridor. The original had been played by the great Mike Garson, an avant-garde jazzer shoehorned into Bowie's Spiders From Mars in 1972 in an inspired piece of cross-cultural casting by David and his bandleader Mick Ronson. Surely it couldn't be! I walked down the corridor, stuck my head round the door and caught a glimpse of a bearded young guy, not Garson, hunched at the piano, a river of sound spilling from his blurred hands.

I didn't want to interrupt so I asked my assistant engineer to run in when the music stopped and get the guy's details. At the end of the evening I was handed a scrap of paper bearing the scrawled name Richard Naiff and a north London phone number. Next day I called Richard and invited him to come and record with me. On the appointed day he turned up at the studio, not looking much like anyone's idea of a rock'n'roller. Thickly bearded, walking with a Monsieur Hulot bounce, clad in a patterned woolly jumper and with an extremely shy, self-deprecating manner – no eye contact whatsoever – Richard was more like a librarian than a rocker. I asked him what bands he played with and he replied, looking at the wall behind me, that he only did a few part-time gigs. 'What do you do the rest of the time then?' I said. 'Oh,' he told the wall in hesitant, embarrassed tones, 'I'm working in a library.'

I'd found myself a real live talent in the raw: librarian or not, when Richard played he could turn his hand to anything. High melodic beauty? No problem, mate. Thundering storms of chordal passion? All in a day's work, guv. Classical intros played on an outrageously distorted Hammond organ? House speciality, sir.

Most of the keyboards on *Weary Land* had been played by me or Thighpaulsandra, whose day job with the druggy British band Spiritualized precluded him from touring with The Waterboys. But as Richard's version of 'Lady Grinning Soul' suggested, my new discovery was able to master whatever musical parts were put in front of him; he just needed the sounds that had been used on the album and his fingers would do the rest. So Richard's first task as a neophyte Waterboy, a week before our tour commenced, was to make a pilgrimage to Thighpaulsandra's remote Welsh farmhouse, commune with the prog-rock elf, and transfer the crucial sound samples into a travelling keyboard module.

Richard and a mate set out in an old banger. They journeyed through the West Country, over the Severn Bridge and deep into Wales until they reached Thighpaulsandra's lonely farmhouse, high on the side of a hill. Like me, Richard was expecting to meet an Elvish wizard and he too was surprised to be greeted by a softly spoken Welsh gentleman. But once in the house, things turned strange. The lights were dim, the curtains were drawn and the temperature was dramatically high. Richard assumed this was because Thighpaulsandra lived with his mother, who was unwell, but as his eyes got used to the gloom he realised that slithering freely round the floor and walls, or poised unnervingly still on the arms of chairs, were numerous geckos and lizards.

Thighpaulsandra acted as if it was absolutely normal to live in perpetual twilight with a crowd of reptiles and made Richard a cup of tea. Then they went through to the music room, Thighpaulsandra leading the way while Richard loped behind, followed by several scurrying lizards, to find himself in a dark chamber filled wall-to-wall with vintage keyboards and art-rock paraphernalia. He squeezed himself into a smidgen of space, plugged in and proceeded to download Thighpaulsandra's Mellotron samples under the baleful eye of a gecko, motionless on a nearby shelf.

Keyboard sounds assembled, the new four-piece Waterboys gathered for a crash course of London rehearsals and a six-gig romp around Norway to warm up. This was the debut live outing for the *Weary Land* sonic rock music, and it took until the final couple of nights for us to fully gel as a band. Unfortunately our second show, a scrappy affair in a Bergen aircraft hangar, was reviewed nationally and the Nordic journalists were aghast at the difference in sound and personnel from the old band. 'This isn't The Waterboys!' fumed *Aftenposten* and *Bergens Tidende*, two newspapers which a helpful native translated for us on a ferry midway across a fjord as we travelled to the next gig. But the scathing headlines only motivated the band and our last two Norwegian concerts, in a packed theatre in Oslo, were shot through with defiance as we began to hit our groove and catch fire.

A few days later we played to five thousand punters at the Glastonbury Festival, in a rammed Acoustic Tent with a set that was anything but: a maelstrom of electric guitar, fuzz keyboards and Mellotron powered by the funk-blown Stacey/Brown rhythm section. We hurled out half a dozen songs from *Weary Land* – 'Let It Happen' and 'The Charlatan's Lament' our opening salvo – and recast totemic old numbers like 'Savage Earth Heart'. Standing on stage with a multi-coloured whirlwind of noise wailing around me, I felt the power of playing under the Waterboys banner for the first time in a decade and sensed the sum of all my changes. I was the hoop dancer at last, moving between my worlds connected to everything The Waterboys had ever meant to me or the audience: adventure, passion, The Mysteries, musical brotherhood. And it was *right*.

Backstage I was surrounded by happy well-wishers. The Silver Fox slapped me on the back while Philip Tennant shook my hand, thrilled to have played a part in the return of The Waterboys. Paul Charles, the agent who booked the Acoustic Stage, told me 'this one will run and run'. Fans appeared at the fence outside the tent shouting their congratulations, and I recognised one of them, a wild-faced chap with straggly hair, from another festival in another age, fourteen years before, reappearing like the spirit of Glastonbury past.

After gathering our stuff, the band clambered into a minibus to go back to our hotel. Slowly we drove through the mad midnight of Glastonbury, amid biblical crowds, past crackling bonfires and huge dance tents from which thundering bass grooves boomed apocalyptically across the blackness. I leaned back in my seat, Janette's head on my shoulder, my ears ringing from the show, and wondered into the future. The Waterboys were back but I still had everything to prove. How would *A Rock In The Weary Land* be received? Would radio still play us? There were lost highways to recover, a Fiddler yet to return, and who knew what challenges and adventures ahead.

We passed the main gates of the Festival and reached the open road. I leaned over to kiss Janette's head and smelt the womanful scent of her hair. Down the hill behind us the last bass notes were booming through the air, and as we sped through the night they faded until I could hear them no more, and the music in my head took over.

APPENDIX 1
NOTES

CHAPTER 1: MUSIC IN THE HEAD

24 "A mysterious language I didn't understand, full of esoteric words like cans and foldback." Headphones and the sound played through them.

24 *The Sooty Show*. A British children's TV programme featuring glove puppets, popular in the fifties and sixties. Sooty was a glove puppet bear operated by Yorkshire entertainer Harry Corbett.

CHAPTER 2: THE REALM OF THE TEENAGE BAND

27 *There wasn't a whole lot of anything going on in Ayr*. Other combos struggling to get something going in the musical backwater of Ayrshire included accomplished older bands like Garbo and Southbound, who played bluesy rock covers; local stars The Dead End Kids, who supported the Bay City Rollers on tour and had a hit in 1977 with a remake of the sixties oldie, 'Have I The Right?'; Corpus, featuring Davy Flynn, lead guitarist in my first band Karma; Paradox, the best band in town, led by the charismatic Mij; teenagers Fragile Sky, whose guitarist Gordon Goudie went on to play with Echo & The Bunnymen, Simple Minds and others in the nineties and noughties; and the luckless Groper, who played semi-punk originals, were reviewed (badly) by the music weekly *Sounds*, and had what must be the worst-ever band name in rock history.

31 *My mother's waiting car*. My mother, Anne, regularly drove our gear to and from gigs.

33 *Orange Lodge*. A Protestant-only fraternal club, deeply tied to Northern Irish (and Scottish) sectarianism, and named after William of Orange, who defeated the Catholic King James The Second at the Battle of the Boyne in Ireland in 1690.

CHAPTER 3: WHERE'S THAT SCOTTISH BOY?

36 *A pen pal in Wales*. His name was David Thomas.

36 *Unlikely song titles*. Very unlikely indeed: several, presumably guessed at by whoever issued the bootleg album, were wrong. 'Strained On Strange' was a mishearing of 'Ain't It Strange' and 'The Smooth Stone Beyond' was a mistitling of 'Pumpin' (My Heart)'.

CHAPTER 4: A FRIEND CALLED Z

48 *Tull-head*. A follower of the band Jethro Tull.

49 *We hitchhiked to concerts in Glasgow and St Andrews.* Z and I hitched to see The Jam at St Andrews University and spotted Paul Weller drinking in the bar of his hotel. We talked to him and I asked him to autograph a cigarette for my mod drummer mate, Crigg, a devoted Jam fan. Weller kindly obliged, etching his name ultra-carefully along the side of the cigarette. Crigg received this artefact with great solemnity and Blu-Tacked it to his bedroom wall, where it remained for some months until one night, desperate for a fag, he smoked it. In the late nineties I was working in a London rehearsal studio at the same time as Weller. We co-existed in daily proximity but hadn't bumped into each other till one day I was standing behind him in the queue at the studio's café. He turned round and said, 'Scuse me, Mike, did I sign a fag for your mate in St Andrews twenty years ago?'

50 *Richard Hell.* Inventor of spiked hair, ripped t-shirt and clothes held together with safety pins, founder member of Television, short-term colleague of Johnny Thunders in The Heartbreakers, and leader of Richard Hell & The Voidoids. Richard was also the writer of 'The Blank Generation', a song I loved so much that I proclaimed 'Hell is a Genius' on the cover of my fanzine *Jungleland*. Richard, spotting the fanzine on the counter of Hot Licks record shop in Edinburgh during his 1977 tour, was so gratified with this accolade he bought every copy.

53 *'All The Boys Love Carrie'*. Produced by Ali Donaldson, better known around Edinburgh in those days as William Mysterious, bassist with The Rezillos.

54 *A&R* stands for 'artiste & repertoire'. The duties of A&R men vary, depending on the individual and the record company they work for, but their principal role is twofold: 1) to act as talent scouts who discover artists and 2) to steward artists' recording careers, suggesting producers, consulting as to song selection, musical direction etc. A&R staff range from deeply intuitive music men like John Hammond who signed and worked with Billie Holiday, Bob Dylan and Leonard Cohen, to cloth-eared clowns who get the job because they're a record company boss's drug dealer or son-in-law.

55 *I went to New York, for the first time, to record some of my new songs with Lenny Kaye.* The band was Lenny on bass, me on guitar, and David Donen, from

Lenny's band The Lenny Kaye Connection, on drums. We worked in a studio called Songshop and cut four songs, all remakes of stuff I'd already demoed in London. The New York recordings were good but the demos had more freshness and magic so they went on The Waterboys' self-titled first album. The Lenny material remains unreleased.

55 *The Waterboys*. I found the word 'waterboy' in the lyrics of 'The Kids', on Lou Reed's album *Berlin*. I loved the sound and mystery of it. What on earth was a waterboy?

56 *A retro glam/punk scene that festered round some of the city's music pubs, and for a while I was so lonesome I even took comfort there.* I was sometimes accompanied by Nikki Sudden, with whom I'd go to The Golden Lion in Fulham or the Moonlight in West Hampstead to watch long-forgotten Faces-type artful dodger bands like Dogs D'Amour. Nikki was an English songwriter and bohemian spirit, real name Adrian Godfrey, and as 'Nikki Mattress' he'd been a member of late seventies DIY punk band Swell Maps. He was devoted to The Rolling Stones, Marc Bolan and Biggles the fighter pilot, had impeccable taste in clothes and song titles, and wrote good tunes. He couldn't sing remotely in key, but this never stopped him living the life of a troubadour or making albums. I contributed piano and guitar to several tracks of Nikki's 1982 record *Bible Belt*, including one called 'The Road Of Broken Dreams', which I also produced, and I was lead guitarist in his band for one gig. I came home once from a recording trip to find Nikki had moved into my flat with a girlfriend and a French drug dealer. We were never such good friends after that, but he left his mark on The Waterboys by turning me onto Anthony Thistlethwaite, whose sax I first heard on Nikki's album *Waiting On Egypt*. My rendering of one of Nikki's songs, 'Cathy' (my vocal over his original backing track), is on the remastered version of *A Pagan Place* (EMI, 2002). Nikki died in 2006.

58 *Mike's Cafe on Blenheim Crescent*. I always ate the same thing in this semi-legendary greasy spoon caff: breast of chicken, chips and baked beans. For some curious reason there was always one green pea among the beans.

58 *The gay punk rocker Gene October*. I'd met Gene once before. His band Chelsea was signed to a company called IRS, and in 1979 Z and I turned up at their offices to see if they'd distribute the first Another Pretty Face single. Chelsea were hanging around the reception area like a gang and Gene, acting the big man, asked if he could listen to our record. We handed him a copy and he disappeared into another room. Five minutes

later he stuck his head round the door long enough to say, 'It'll do well,' and then, after a deliberate pause, added, 'They ain't goin' for the real stuff anymore' (ie *his* stuff), and disappeared before we could reply. It was very satisfying to say no when he asked me to join his band years later.

59   *My musician-seeking ad in the NME.* The ad was for 'lead guitarist, into Iggy Pop.' Karl was the only person to reply. He phoned me up and said he wasn't a guitarist but he played keyboards and liked Iggy. I still have a cassette recording of him walking into his audition, and our lives, with the words, 'Uh … hello … it's Karl.' The first song he played was 'The Three Day Man', and within ten seconds of it he'd got the gig.

61   *A look halfway between Billy The Whiz and a Mohawk.* Billy The Whiz, the fastest boy in the world, was a cartoon character in the weekly British comic *The Beano.* His hairstyle was an aerodynamically efficient shaved head with two lone hairs standing rigidly on end.

61   *We had to change money every few days.* Like most touring British bands, rather than keep track of the names of local currencies, we referred to all foreign money as 'shitters', as in, 'can you lend me any shitters, mate?'

64   *His global wanderings would take him to Madagascar, Brazil and the Far East.* Z still sends me emails, about one a year, always from somewhere exotic. And in a cheesy but reassuring way that immediately recalls the days of our early friendship he usually puts one of my old Another Pretty Face song titles in the subject box.

CHAPTER 5: THE BLACK BOOK AND THE MOON

65   *A witches' store.* Magickal Childe, West Nineteenth Street. The shop closed in 1999.

66   *The man behind the counter, a lantern-jawed character with an air of brusque authority.* Herman Slater, author and owner of Magickal Childe.

67   *Steve Reich's album of sacred music, Tehillim.* I bought this by mistake while recording with Lenny Kaye in New York in 1982. I was browsing in a record store on Times Square when I found an album in a dark blue patterned cover with the strange title *Tehillim.* The artist's name was Steve Reich, which I mistook for Peter Reich, whose memoir *A Book Of Dreams* had been the inspiration for a Patti Smith song. Thinking I was buying an album with some esoteric Patti connection, I shelled out my bucks. When I got back to London and read the sleeve notes, I discovered my error. Steve Reich was a New York 'minimalist' composer, whatever that

was, with no connection to Patti Smith. I stuck the record on and heard a teeming rhythmic flow of bells, hand drums and fiddles overlaid with exquisite female voices chanting Hebraic words in complex yet organic patterns. It was like listening to blood vessels coursing through the body, or the ministrations of angels transformed into music. I was spellbound and quickly tracked down Reich's other records. From these, particularly *Variations For Winds, Strings And Keyboards* and *Music For 18 Musicians*, I learned arrangement techniques and tricks which I deployed in Waterboys music. They included sudden offbeat chordal bursts or 'pops' (on 'Don't Bang The Drum' and 'This Is The Sea'); long brass harmonies sustaining across chord changes ('This Is The Sea'); instrumental motifs played without emotion but having emotional impact because of their placing and context ('The Whole Of The Moon', 'Trumpets', 'Beverly Penn', 'The Pan Within'); recurring melodies played in different time signature to the main rhythm therefore constantly changing in relation to it ('The Return Of Jimi Hendrix'); and groups of tambourines emphasising multiple beats in the bar ('This Is The Sea'). The overall sound and atmosphere of Reich's work loosely influenced other Waterboys tracks such as 'A Pagan Place', 'The Stolen Child', 'High Far Soon', 'Spirit' and 'We Will Not Be Lovers'.

68 *Anthony Thistlethwaite, who'd turn up in his car and whisk me off.* Anthony had a Keith Richards bootleg perpetually on his car stereo. Wherever we drove we were accompanied by Keith's doleful tones croaking out 'Let's Go Steady' and 'Somewhere Over The Rainbow'. When I walk down certain streets in West London today I immediately hear Keith's cracked dulcets in my head, crooning, 'Birds fly over the rainbow ... why oh why can't I?'

68 *Many of the sounds that would define This Is The Sea had their sonic dress rehearsal at Seaview.* These sketches can be heard on CD2 of the remastered edition of *This Is The Sea* (EMI Records, 2004).

69 *I had a shimmering wall of music.* Variations of this sound can be heard on the following: 'December', 'The Three Day Man', 'Savage Earth Heart' (*The Waterboys*, released 1983, recorded 1981–82), 'Where Are You Now When I Need You' (*The Waterboys*, remastered version 2002, recorded 1982), 'Church Not Made With Hands', 'Rags', 'The Big Music', 'A Pagan Place' (*A Pagan Place*, 1984, recorded 1983), 'Don't Bang The Drum', 'The Pan Within', 'This Is The Sea' (*This Is The Sea*, 1985), 'The New Life' (*Dream Harder*, 1993), 'The Hosting Of The Shee', 'News For The Delphic Oracle' and 'White Birds' (*An Appointment With Mr Yeats*, 2011).

69 *When Kevin Wilkinson's epic drums and Anthony Thistlethwaite's sax were subsequently added, the musical picture became huge.* Best heard on 'Red Army Blues' (*A Pagan Place*, 1984, recorded 1982).

69 *John Brand*. John later discovered and managed the band Stereophonics.

70 *Chris Whitten*. A doleful skin-basher with bog-brush haircut who later played with Dire Straits and Paul McCartney. Chris's finest moment with The Waterboys is his drum performance on 'The Whole Of The Moon', overdubbed in place of the original drum loop after everything else was recorded. But my defining memory of him is of us recording a fast Stax-style R&B version of 'This Is The Sea'. We were closing in on the perfect performance, every musical element coming into focus and victory in sight, when Whitten broke the spell to say, 'This is my two-take warning', meaning he'd had enough and would play the song only two times more, and if we hadn't got it right by then, tough luck!

71 *A carnival of trumpets*. Played by Roddy Lorimer, the Glaswegian trumpeter whose solos and horn work were a hallmark of the early Waterboys sound. Roddy was introduced to me by Anthony Thistlethwaite in 1983 and he features on the first five Waterboys albums, as well as *Still Burning* (1997) and *Book Of Lightning* (2007). For the solo on 'The Whole Of The Moon' I asked him to do for the song what the piccolo trumpet did for The Beatles' 'Penny Lane', though without copying its melody, and to enter 'like a bolt of sunlight streaming through a gap in the clouds'. Roddy began drafting a score and within an hour had recorded a four-part solo, in a cleverly structured series of heraldic fanfares, which did the job beautifully.

71 *Candy-flavoured 'la-la' backing vocals*. Sung by Liz Wilcox, an Australian friend of Anthony Thistlethwaite's. At the time of 'The Whole Of The Moon' she was calling herself Max Edie.

CHAPTER 6: DON'T FORGET TO GET ON THE BUS

74 *My record company bosses, Nigel and Chris*. As well as partnering Nigel Grainge at Ensign Records, Chris Hill was and still is a top British soul and funk DJ. The third member of the Ensign team was Doreen Loader, who ran the company business. Doreen was the background hero of The Waterboys' first incarnation and handled our day-to-day affairs for many years. She remained a good friend after I left Ensign.

75 *The Fellow Who Fiddles*. Steve's pre-Waterboys activities, other than playing with In Tua Nua and Sinead O'Connor, included playing fiddle on

U2's 'Sunday Bloody Sunday' and guesting with them on a 1982 Irish tour.

88 *He'd met Steve when In Tua Nua had played support to him in Ireland a year earlier*. Slane Castle, July 1984. Steve guested on Bob's encore, playing fiddle on 'Leopard Skin Pillbox Hat'.

89 *Top Of The Pops*. A weekly BBC show that ran from 1964 until 2006. It's often said that I refused to appear on *Top Of The Pops* with 'The Whole Of The Moon'. I'd loved watching *Top Of The Pops* in the sixties and early seventies, but by the eighties the show had degenerated into a garish celebration of everything I liked least about pop, and was a filter through which I felt it was impossible to convey authentic energies of rock'n'roll, power, inspiration, or even an attitude. An appearance on *Top Of The Pops* could increase a band's audience but at the cost of being tamed, and I agreed with The Clash, who throughout their lifespan refused to appear on the show. I even discussed it with Joe Strummer after a Clash show in Edinburgh in 1980, during my Another Pretty Face days. We exchanged baleful views on the programme, and though my band hadn't yet had a sniff of a hit I zealously told Joe, 'We won't do *Top Of The Pops* either!' 'That makes two of us,' he replied, sealing the deal. Five years later, when 'The Whole Of The Moon' reached the charts, the offer came for The Waterboys to do *Top Of The Pops*, thus testing both my conviction and my fealty to Chairman Joe. But we were playing Boston on the night of the TV filming, midway through an American tour, and I chose not to cancel the gig and fly back and forth across the Atlantic. If we'd been in the UK I might have conquered my resistance and done it; no one will ever know. When 'The Whole Of The Moon' was a hit in 1991, *Top Of The Pops* broadcast the promo video. My attitude had softened by 1993 when The Waterboys finally appeared on the show with 'Glastonbury Song'.

89 *A young piano player, Guy Chambers*. Now a successful songwriter, best known for his work as writer/producer with Robbie Williams.

91 *I wrote to Gary Kurfirst and split with him*. I'd signed a three-year contract with Gary and after our split the spectre of some form of legal action hung over me for several years, adding an extra frisson of stress to the making of *Fisherman's Blues*: what would happen if the album came out while the contract was still in force? An injunction, lawsuit or other drawn-out battle seemed likely, and perhaps it was fortuitous that the music slowed me down. When the album appeared some months after the contract expired, Gary took no action. In fact, he never charged me

for the nine months in 1985 when he actively managed me, for which I'm grateful. In 1991 we bumped into each other at Los Angeles airport, a cordial reunion. Gary died in 2009.

CHAPTER 7: YOU GUYS ARE THE WHIZZ!

94 *B.P. Fallon ... seems to have been present, Zelig-like, at every significant moment in rock since 1965.* Including both of John Lennon's 1970 *Top Of The Pops* performances of 'Instant Karma', and The Rolling Stones 1969 Hyde Park concert, which he watched from a lighting scaffold above the stage. Showing me a picture of the gig twenty years later, B.P. pointed to a pair of legs at the top of the frame, the rest of their owner cut out of the shot, and said, 'Those are my legs, man.'

97 *A bustling dining hall with a vaulted ceiling and fantastical stained glass windows.* The windows in Bewleys Cafe, Dublin, were created by Harry Clarke (1889–1931).

105 *I'd got to know Paul McGuinness when The Waterboys had supported U2 on some shows.* Twenty dates in the UK and North America in November and December 1984.

114 *Nothing we could put on a record.* Three Keltner/Patitucci tracks have since been released. I returned to the tapes in 2001 and 2005, edited three extended workouts to song length and filled in the missing lead vocals. They are: 'Blues For Your Baby' and 'Lonesome Old Wind' (*Too Close To Heaven*, BMG 2001/*Fisherman's Blues Part Two*, *Razor & Tie*, 2002) and 'Soon As I Get Home' (CD2 of *Fisherman's Blues* remaster, EMI 2006).

CHAPTER 8: THE POWER OF THE MUSIC GIVES EVERYBODY WINGS

116 *We Free Kings.* Named after a 1961 Roland Kirk album, and also the 'Wee Frees', the nickname of the Scottish Free Church. Joe Kingman's band played round Britain and Ireland from 1985 to 1991. They released one album, *Hell On Earth And Rosy-Cross* (1988).

121 *A crowd of several hundred had converged on the docks, including every busker in Dublin.* Among their number was a teenage Glen Hansard, later of The Frames and The Swell Season.

121 *A Yosser Hughes moustache.* A character in the early-eighties British TV series *Boys From The Blackstuff*, Yosser was a doomed Liverpudlian hard-man who entered national folklore.

122 *Letham Village Hall was a lonesome-looking redbrick building on a hill overlooking a tiny hamlet.* Five months before The Waterboys' appearance at The Pictish Festival, Letham Village Hall hosted Scottish accordionist Jimmy Shand's televised 1986 *Christmas Eve Party.*

124 *The Cibeal.* Pronounced 'Ki-bal'. Loosely translated it means 'hubbub'.

CHAPTER 9: GO SLOWLY AND YOU MIGHT SEE SOMETHING

133 *Many of the tunes I'd been hearing in Dublin, I realised, were Scottish.* The majority of the trad melodies that pepper the *Fisherman's Blues* and *Room To Roam* albums are Scottish. To compound the cultural cross-fertilisation, most of these were introduced to the proceedings by our *Irish* members, Steve Wickham and Sharon Shannon. We didn't care where the tunes came from; we played what we liked, and anyone who says The Waterboys somehow appropriated 'Irish' music is talking through their hat.

133 *In the bloom of their youth on the Isle of Mull.* Mull is one of the Scottish Hebridean Islands.

134 *The Joshua Tree, on which I heard the spiritual seeker vision and big music of the last two Waterboys album re-calibrated.* Orthodox rock history doesn't acknowledge any Waterboys influence on either U2 or their album *The Joshua Tree.* Even broaching the subject of a Waterboys influence on U2 is to risk appearing churlish because convention considers it unseemly for one artist to claim influence over another, and not without reason. But the evidence of my ears tells me Bono and The Edge were paying rapt attention when we supported them on tour and when they listened to *A Pagan Place* and *This Is The Sea.*

136 *Boreens.* Irish country back roads.

136 *Bodhrán.* Irish goatskin hand drum, pronounced 'bow-rawn'.

136 *The Crock Of Gold.* A novel by the Irish author James Stephens (1882–1950), published in 1912.

136 *The locals conversed in Irish.* Also referred to in the text as Gaelic, this Celtic language is still spoken in regions of Ireland and on some of the Hebridean isles of Scotland.

136 *I'd … work … late into the night, often till dawn.* Often, in fact, late enough to see the top of the Spiddal postman's green minivan bobbing over the stone walls as it chugged along the country lanes delivering the morning mail. This vision had resonance for me because often, after staying up all night recording at Windmill Lane the previous year, I

would wind down in the studio lounge watching early morning kids' TV, which in those days featured *Postman Pat*, the top of whose green minivan bobbed over the stone walls as he chugged along the country lanes delivering the morning mail.

137 *Galway was a convivial city then as now, but in 1988 it had a slow, magical character*. And a lawless streak typified by the Harbour Bar, a festering Fellini-esque dockside den with peeling flock wallpaper and sticky carpets where, due to some arcane by-law, the coastguard had jurisdiction instead of the police. This resulted in it being 'legal' to smoke reefers in the bar. It was demolished in the nineties.

138 *The Islandman*. Irish title *An t-Oileánach*, first issued in 1929, currently published by Oxford Paperbacks. This is an Irish classic, a wonderful book describing the now-extinct life of the Blasket Islanders off the Kerry coast.

139 *Irish was the same language as the Scottish Gaelic my grandmother spoke, and I was separated from it by only two generations*. The passage of the language down generations was broken when my grandmother's family moved from Gaelic-speaking Mull to Glasgow in the early twentieth century. Her children, my mother and uncle, grew up speaking only English.

140 *Inishmore, largest of the Aran Islands*. The three Aran Islands – Inisheer ('eastern island'), Inishmaan ('middle island') and Inishmore ('big island') – can be reached by plane or ferry from Connemara or by boat from Doolin on the Clare coast. They are every bit as strange and rewardingly unique to visit as I've indicated in the text. Among the best books on Aran are Tim Robinson's two volumes *Stones Of Aran: Pilgrimage* (Lilliput Press/Faber 1986) and *Stones Of Aran: Labyrinth* (Lilliput Press/Penguin 1995, both published in the USA by New York Review Books Classics). Also recommended: *The Aran Islands* by J.M. Synge (1907).

141 *Kilronan, a cluster of white buildings hunched on a hill round a little harbour*. Kilronan has grown a lot since my first visit, with many new buildings, a new pier and much tourist development. When I returned in 2009 after a break of eighteen years such were the changes that I felt like a character in a movie who's been catapulted a hundred years into the future.

141 *Vinnie was staying in a house a few yards away*. Vinnie Kilduff was on Inishmore to record local Gaelic singers. Some of the recordings he made appeared twenty years later on a 2CD set called *The Aran Lifeboat Collection* (Aran Recordings, 2008).

141 *Sean Watty*. His real surname was Flaherty, but Sean was known to

everyone on the island as 'Sean Watty' because he played in Joe Watty's Pub. Like most Irish box players, Sean played button accordion, not piano accordion. He died in Galway in the nineties.

142 *Sean Watty and another local musician called Máirtín were waiting with accordion and banjo at the ready.* Pronounced 'Mawr-cheen'. Twenty years later, Máirtín told me that on that first night at the American Bar he and Sean decided to play as fast and wild as they could, in order to show up the pop musicians, but that Anto and I 'kept up with everything we threw at ye'.

143 *We'd become part of the local colour.* But not quite acclimatised. On the day we were due to catch the plane back to Galway, Anto and I were having such a good time we decided to stay longer. From the one phone box in Kilronan I called the island's airfield to cancel our tickets and book some new ones. But the chap on the other end of the line, an older man with a slow island voice, wasn't best pleased. 'If you bought a ticket you have to take the flight,' he said, 'you can't be goin' changin' it.' Maybe this was how they did things in Aran, but I was used to the mainstream world where if plans change you cancel or postpone a journey, and it's nobody's business but your own. I argued with the fellow and stuck fast to my position despite the waves of disapproval coming at me down the phone line. The conversation ended with me, royally cheesed off, telling him to forget it, that we'd take a boat instead. In a Kilronan pub that afternoon I told Anto about the phone call. When I'd finished the story, he said, 'The guy who runs the airline is Colie Hernon. Is that who you spoke to?' I wasn't sure if it was, but I'd heard of Colie Hernon all right. He was the island's equivalent to a mayor, the man who brought the airline to Aran, who'd organised the island's first supply of electricity in the seventies, and who ran the lifeboat. The local Big Man. Still, I thought, that didn't give him the right to give me a row for cancelling our flight tickets like I was a naughty schoolboy. With indignation I thumped my fist on the bar and said, 'Well, I don't care who he is, he doesn't have the right to speak to me like that!' A few moments later we got up to leave. As we stepped down from the bar, sitting a few feet behind us quietly reading a newspaper was Colie Hernon. He looked up at us with a hint of mirth in his eyes, said, 'Hello there, lads,' in a jaunty but unmistakably matter-closed way that was impossible to reply to, and returned to his paper.

CHAPTER 10: MANSION OF MUSIC

147 *Our young recording engineer Pat McCarthy.* Now a successful record producer. Pat produced R.E.M. for ten years.

151 *Even this didn't work for poor old 'Rose', and the song was filed away.* 'In Search Of A Rose' was re-recorded for *Room To Roam*.

152 *Dunford nipped down to Hughes's bar to enlist some dancers.* He could only find five but by happy coincidence a young chap turned up at Spiddal House who'd met us when we played a benefit for the Irish Green Party six months before. His name was Trevor Sargent and he made up the third waltzing couple. Years later he became leader of the Irish Greens and a member of the Irish Parliament.

152 *For one song I wanted the sound of a distant faery band.* This can be heard on 'The Stolen Child' from 2:35 to 2:52.

154 *Galway drummer Padraig Stevens.* Pronounced 'Paw-rig'.

154 *Stig Of The Dump.* A British children's book, written by Clive King, about a strange caveman boy called Stig (Puffin Books, 1965).

154 *Tomás Mac Eoin.* Pronounced Taw-mosse (emphasis like *finesse*) M'Kyo-in.

155 *Sean-nós.* Prounced 'shan-noas'. Translates literally as 'old style' and refers to an unaccompanied, ornamented style of traditional Gaelic singing.

158 *Rockfield Studios on the Welsh/English border.* I'd recorded at Rockfield before. In 1983 The Waterboys made half of *A Pagan Place* there, but my first visit was two years earlier with the last line-up of Another Pretty Face. We drove from London and arrived at the Rockfield farm at night. We couldn't find the reception but saw some lights in a long barn-like building. We knocked on the door, someone shouted 'Come in!' and we pushed it open to find ourselves in a studio control room face to face with Robert Plant and his entourage. Robert looked us up and down and said, 'Where are you guys from?' Our sax player, a punk rocker called Gordon with a deep dislike of Led Zeppelin, stepped forward, put his hands on his hips, tilted his head slightly in a well-practised defiant pose and replied, 'We're fae Edinburgh.' Robert said 'Edinburgh? Oh, you must know Ray Thomas,' whoever that was, as if Edinburgh were a village in which everyone knew everyone else. Gordon, motionless, said, 'Whit gang was he in?' Discomfited by this unexpected line of questioning, and trying to be the coolest person in the room, Robert sputtered, 'Er ... the Led Zeppelin gang, mate,' with a little aggressive edge on the word

'mate'. To which Gordon, nonchalantly delivering the coup de grace, replied, 'Oh? That wis before our time.' It wasn't the last blow in the punk wars, but it was a good one.

CHAPTER 11: SHARON HAS A TUNE FOR EVERY BEAT OF HER HEART

162 *Winkles Hotel*. A legendary haunt of trad musicians in the West of Ireland, owned by Tony and Phil Moylan. Tony's grandfather Bartholomew 'Ballo' Winkle bought the premises in 1913, and after his death in 1938 his daughter Tiffy ran Winkles for over forty years. Her husband Ciarán Moylan was a musician, and his friends, who included trad heavyweights of the day like box player Joe Cooley and fiddler Joe Leary, played sessions in Winkles, establishing its reputation as a music hotspot. From the fifties to the seventies, Irish broadcaster Ciarán Mac Mathuna recorded trad singers and players in Winkles, and during the sixties the bar was a playground of John Huston, Peter O'Toole and Richard Harris. Winkles experienced a late heyday in the eighties and ninenties when Sharon Shannon, Jackie Daly and Seamus Begley were regular performers. Decreasing business and ill health forced the Moylans to sell Winkles in 2003, and the building was demolished in 2007.

166 *The empty shop in Temple Bar where we rehearsed*. 7 Crow Street, now the Crow Street Bazaar. This was only one of many places we rehearsed in Dublin. Others included the Top Hat Ballroom in Dun Laoghaire, the Revenue Club, the Royal Hotel in Howth, and professional studios the Warehouse and the Factory.

166 *By the second night, in Mallow, she was a veteran*. The venue in Mallow was the Majestic Ballroom, a country dance hall with a legend that the devil had once appeared there. A well-dressed stranger, the tale went, turned up at a ceilidh and proceeded to dance with every unattached woman. During the last dance his partner dropped an earring, bent to pick it up and saw his cloven hooves. She screamed and he ran out, never to be seen again.

167 *A trad duo called Cooney & Begley*. The same 'Cooney' Steve Wickham had told me about the day we first met.

167 *Cooney … played a battered old nylon string guitar like he was driving a tank*. Steve Cooney revolutionised Irish music. Before Cooney, string accompanists (guitarists and bouzouki players) strummed along with jigs

310

and reels providing depth and chordal colour but rarely any driving or eruptive power. Cooney changed that forever. He introduced backbeat and an entire vernacular of triplets, skirls, rallies, stop-starts and dizzying runs of impossible chords, which no one else has yet figured out how to do. His influence on Irish trad guitar is akin to Hendrix's on rock: he raised the bar and the rest of the world is still catching up. Since Cooney, and in his image, guitar accompanists have driven Irish music with momentum and visceral energy, though none has yet matched Cooney's genius.

169 *Handfaster*. Person who performs a pagan or traditional non-church wedding.

171 *Mattie Mullen had a bottle of potcheen*. Irish spelling: *poitín*, pronounced 'poh-cheen'. A violently strong form of moonshine whiskey distilled from potatoes or barley. It's now legal in Ireland and some companies manufacture a tame version somewhat less combustible than the 'field' variety. Once, during the prohibition days, Tomás Mac Eoin took me out in the middle of the night to buy a bottle from a rustic smallholder in Connemara. We knocked on the man's door, Tomás and he exchanged a look, and the man promptly disappeared into the fields behind his house. Five minutes later he returned, in an advanced state of excitement and agitation, with a lemonade bottle filled with a coarse alcoholic brew so strong it almost had hair.

171 *A guest slot with The Saw Doctors*. I befriended this band of Galway ragamuffins after their guitarist Leo Moran blagged a slot with Wickham and me at an impromptu gig one summer. We gave them their early break as support on the *Fisherman's Blues* tour, and I produced their first single, 'N17'. Years later I realised my song 'And A Bang On The Ear' was subconsciously influenced by their number 'I Used To Love Her', with its comedic mentions of an old girlfriend, which I remember them playing in local pubs around the time The Waterboys were working in Spiddal. The Waterboys team photograph on the inner sleeve of *Room To Roam* is from the day we played The Saw Doctors at football in the grounds of the Gaelic college at Spiddal. The score was 2–2.

173 *The name Dingle sounds cutesy*. Dingle isn't even the original Irish name of the place at all, but a clumsy medieval (probably Norman) phonetic translation of the local town An Daingean (pronounced An Dan-gan), which means 'the fort'. The town is also known as An Daingean Uí Chúis (the fort of O'Cuis). The correct Irish name for the peninsula on which

Dingle stands and Seamus Begley lives is Corca Dhuibhe (Corka-gwinney).
175 *The music he and Begley recorded that September … remains unheard.*
Cooney & Begley finally released an album titled *Meitheal* (Irish for 'working together') in 1993, credited to 'Begley & Cooney', though no one in Irish music ever refers to them with the names that way round. The album includes one live track from the pub session detailed in Chapter 11. Unfortunately Cooney & Begley weren't 'meitheal' for much longer and fell out in the mid nineties. Begley now works with a variety of guitar players and has made two albums with Jim Murray (*Ragairne*, 2001 and *Eirí Go Lá*, 2009), and one (*Disgrace Notes*, 2011) with Tim Edey. Cooney is a perpetually in-demand accompanist in the Irish trad world and was married to Sinead O'Connor from 2010 to 2011.

CHAPTER 12: LIKE A HOUSE OF CARDS COLLAPSING
178 *In L.A. where we were joined by The Scottish Fiddlers Of Los Angeles.* And also by several members of The Tannahill Weavers.
183 *In my zeal to blend the worlds, I'd neglected the needs of the songs.* And overlooked the unique power of my two closest bandmates. After the split of the *Room To Roam* band I realised how the large ensemble had crowded Steve and Anto, denying them the space they needed to continue making their remarkable two-man-orchestra sound of 1985–88.
184 *Even his trademark holey hat was gone, taken by the ex-wife.* A friend returned the holey hat to Steve in 2000, in time for him to wear it when he guested with The Waterboys at Dublin's Olympia Theatre that December. After his first song the audience went mental and started chanting his name. Inspired by this reception Steve whipped the hat off and flung it, Frisbee-like, into the crowd, never to be seen again.
188 *But if I wasn't ready to let go, Sharon was.* A successful solo career awaited Sharon Shannon. She's now recognised as one of the finest acoustic musicians in the world and is, as far as I know, the only accordion player to have achieved several number one albums and a number one single ('The Galway Girl') in Ireland. John Dunford has managed her since 1991.

CHAPTER 13: A WALK IN THE LAKE SHRINE
190 *Seven shows in a circus tent round the Highlands and Islands of Scotland.* Our then-agent Denis Desmond presented band and crew with Waterboys denim jackets to commemorate this tour. At my request each had a row of

coloured medal ribbons sewn above the left chest pocket, one for each tent show. We'd earned them.

194 *'Moon' had become a hit at Balearic clubs and English raves.* 'The Whole Of The Moon' was made popular on Ibiza by DJ Alfredo (Alfredo Fiorillo), Andrew Weatherall, Tony Wilson and Terry Farley.

194 *I received the phone call telling me 'The Whole Of The Moon' was in the charts.* 'The Whole Of The Moon' also won the Ivor Novello award for Best Song, Musically And Lyrically, 1991.

196 *Did you hear what happened to Charlie Minor?* He was shot dead by former girlfriend Suzette McClure. In 1998 Charlie's dramatic demise was turned into a TV film with the tongue-twisting title *Death In Malibu: The Murder Of Music Mogul Charlie Minor*.

201 *A friend in Chicago called Jim Powers who offered to show me round the city's blues clubs.* On some of our explorations we were accompanied by Chicago resident and former Supertramp member Dougie Thomson.

CHAPTER 14: SHUTDOWN IN THE BIG APPLE

209 *A young L.A. producer called Brendan O'Brien.* Later to work successfully with Bruce Springsteen, among many others.

209 *The closest I got was a trio of guys I played with on a musician-seeking trip to Texas: Bukka, Joey and Brad.* Bukka Allen, Joey Shuffield and Brad Fordham.

CHAPTER 15: THE PHILOSOPHY ROOM

218 *I ask another assistant where the Philosophy Room is and she points to a small archway in the far corner.* The room is on the top floor of Foyles overlooking the corner of Charing Cross Road and Manette St, and is now a private staff area.

219 *Elgin Books.* Sadly, this shop closed in 1999. Its owner, the lady who directed me to Foyle's, was Mary Mackintosh. She died in 2003.

219 *I came upon a scarlet-covered volume of A Season In Hell and The Illuminations.* Arthur Rimbaud: *A Season In Hell / The Illuminations*, translated by Enid Rhodes Peschel (Oxford University Press, 1973)

220 *'Lettre Du Voyant'.* The 'Lettre Du Voyant' can be found in *Rimbaud: Complete Works, Selected Letters*, translated and with notes by Wallace Fowlie (University of Chicago Press, 1966), pages 305–11.

220 *A biography of him written by an Irish scholar. Arthur Rimbaud* by Enid Starkie (Faber, 1961).

220 *A contemporary Frenchman called Eliphas Levi, author of something called The History Of Magic.* Histoire De La Magie par Eliphas Levi (1860). English version: *The History Of Magic*, translated by A.E. Waite (Rider & Co, 1913). Levi's real name was Alphonse Louis Constant.

221 *The dozen books I purchased at Foyles that day.* I no longer remember what they all were, but they included *The History Of Magic* (Eliphas Levi, Rider & Co); *The Esoteric Orders And Their Work, The Training & Work of An Initiate, Practical Occultism In Daily Life* (all Dion Fortune, Aquarian Press); *A Book Of Pagan Rituals* (Herman Slater, Weiser Books); *The Opening Of The Third Eye* (Dr Douglas Baker, Thorsons) and *The Secret Tradition In Arthurian Legend* (Gareth Knight, Aquarian Press).

221 *More things in heaven and earth, Horatio, than are dreamt of in your philosophy. Hamlet*, Shakespeare, Act 1, Scene 5.

221 *A transcendent, attainable reality to which all the world's religions pointed: that all is one.* A profound exploration of this, with references to countless spiritual texts, is Aldous Huxley's *The Perennial Philosophy* (Harper & Brothers, 1945). A shorter but excellent exposition can be found in Peter Russell's *The Awakening Earth* (Routledge & Kegan Paul, 1982), Chapter 8, 'The Quest For Unity'.

221 *My favourite book was Peter Russell's The Awakening Earth.* See entry above.

222 *Dion Fortune.* Born Violet Mary Firth in Wales, 1890, Dion Fortune was author of many spiritual books including several novels, and founder of The Society Of The Inner Light. She died in 1946.

227 *I read everything on the Findhorn community I could find.* Two of the best books about the community are *The Findhorn Garden* (Harper & Row, 1975, republished by Findhorn Press as *The Findhorn Garden Story*, 2008) and Eileen Caddy's autobiography *Flight Into Freedom* (Element, 1988, republished by Findhorn Press as *Flight Into Freedom And Beyond*, 2002).

227 *The community was in Northeast Scotland.* The Findhorn community – comprising the settlement at the caravan park, Cluny Hill College and a network of associated people living in the local area – is a separate entity from the Scottish village of Findhorn, built on the shores of Findhorn Bay, with its own traditions and character.

230 *I went to a lunchtime meditation at one of the community's sanctuaries.* This experience is also described in the song 'Long Way To The Light' (on *Bring 'Em All In*, Chrysalis/EMI 1995)

CHAPTER 16: SOME KIND OF POP STAR LIVING UP AT CLUNY

233 *The Findhorn community is celebrating Burns Night.* Also known as a Burns Supper. This ceremony is held around the world wherever Scots are gathered on 25th January, the birthday of our national poet Robert Burns.

233 *Ceilidh.* Pronounced 'kay-lay'. Gaelic word for a social gathering featuring energetic country dances.

238 *I wasn't the first interloper from the world of show business to descend on Findhorn.* Nor the first rock star to have a connection with a mystery school. By their nature such connections are often discreet, but musicians with esoteric interests have included Richard Thompson (a practising Sufi for several years, still a Muslim), Van Morrison (numerous references to spiritual teachings in his songs circa 1979–83 and a palpable spiritual atmosphere in his records of the time, especially the album *Common One*) and Kate Bush (many clues in her songs suggest that Kate is an explorer of The Mysteries).

242 *I found myself called on to sing at holidays, funerals, weddings and, most of all, charity shows.* I was also cajoled to join The Findhorn Jazz Band, though my then-miniscule knowledge of jazz meant our repertoire comprised only four songs: 'Accentuate The Positive', 'It Ain't What You Do (It's The Way That You Do It)', a clarinet-led instrumental of 'Rudolf The Red-Nosed Reindeer' and a comedic number of mine titled 'Universal Hall' (not the title track of the 2003 Waterboys album).

242 *News Of The World.* A British tabloid Sunday newspaper, which folded in 2011.

244 *Niko Bolas ... whose name I'd seen on a couple of Neil Young album covers.* Niko co-produced *This Note's For You* (1988) and *Freedom* (1989). He worked again with Neil on several albums in the noughties, sharing production credits with Neil as The Volume Dealers.

244 *I'd hired Niko to record B-sides for the singles off the Dream Harder album and it turned out to be a momentous session ... ten cracking tracks, which had all the power and passion Dream Harder itself lacked.* I wanted to use several of these on *Dream Harder* but Dick Lackaday and Geffen's Tom Zutaut disagreed on the grounds they had too different a sound from the tracks already recorded. Only two Bolas-recorded numbers were cherry-picked by Zutaut, 'Corn Circles' and 'Wonders Of Lewis', and added to the

album. Seven other songs from the session were released as B-sides and bonus tracks over the next few years.

246 *Five Rhythms on a Monday*. The Five Rhythms is a movement meditation practice developed by Gabrielle Roth.

CHAPTER 17: MY WANDERINGS IN THE WEARY LAND

257 *The spectre of the blonde-bobbed geezer preening away*. Actually I liked Dave Jaymes a lot. Of all the people I've jousted with in the music business, Dave was one of the most honourable and honest.

258 *A gregarious Scottish skinhead invariably dressed in a checked shirt*. Alan McGee had hundreds of checked shirts on clothes rails, and a dedicated room at his flat to store them in.

260 *When we played, Keltner was as great as I remembered*. And he almost got a Beatle to play on my record. Jim Keltner offered to ask his friend George Harrison to do a guitar solo on the *Still Burning* album. As a long term George fan, and a believer that *All Things Must Pass* is one of the greatest albums ever made, I was thrilled and suggested a poppy number called 'Big Lover', which I thought would suit George's style. 'Uh, no Michael,' replied Jim, 'George loves songs with fat snare sounds. The one to give him would be "Questions".' Questions was a brass-driven soul stomper with a very fat snare sound indeed, but it already had a guitar solo worked out note-for-note by my favourite Scottish rocker – myself, and Beatle or no Beatle, George or no George, I didn't want to scrap it. So I insisted 'Big Lover' was the track. 'Well, all right Michael,' said Jim dubiously, and a DAT of the song was couriered down to George's house at Henley-on-Thames. Two days later Jim announced he'd had a call from George who couldn't think of anything to play on 'Big Lover' but sent this enigmatic message: 'Tell Mike I'll meet him somewhere down the road and Bob's your uncle.' George died before we got to have that meeting and I now wish I'd sacrificed my solo.

265 *The charts had become so manipulated, so gamed by the music industry, that they were stretched out of all shape and logic*. Some of this shape and logic has been restored, though in constantly changing and unpredictable ways, by the democratic influence of the internet.

267 *He used wonderfully meaningless Father Dougal-esque phrases*. Father Dougal McGuire is a character played by Ardal O'Hanlon in the nineties Irish/English comedy TV series *Father Ted*.

267 *My commercial standing was at an all-time low*. On the way to my 1997 tour of Japan, I spotted a photo booth in Heathrow Airport and went to get my picture taken for a laugh. Inside I discovered it was actually a video booth; if I put a five-pound note in the slot it would film a three-minute VHS video. I had a quick brainwave and dug into my bag for a cassette player. I slotted in a tape of my next single 'Rare Precious And Gone', pressed play, clicked the 'film' button on the booth's control panel, then mimed the vocal to camera. Instant promo video. All the band members stuck their heads in to see what was happening and they got on the film too. When the video popped out of the machine ten minutes later I packaged it up, addressed it to our promo man and popped it in a mailbox in the airport departures hall. Within a week it had been shown on several TV shows, exceeding the combined broadcast tally of the last three £50,000 videos I'd done for Chrysalis and Geffen. But even this exposure, and the dubious distinction of having made a video for a fiver, couldn't propel a Mike Scott song into the charts in 1997.

CHAPTER 18: A MAN WITH A FIDDLE AND A DOG AT NUMBER 12A

273 *As I greeted him I felt like Dean Moriarty in On the Road*. Jack Kerouac's classic book, published in 1957.

274 *The Connacht Ramblers*. Connacht is the northwestern of Ireland's four provinces. The name of Steve's band came from a well-known Irish jig called 'The Connachtman's Rambles'.

CHAPTER 19: HOOP DANCING

281 *That May I returned to Spiddal to film a performance for Irish television*. A one-song performance on an Irish language soap opera, set in Spiddal, called *Ros Na Rún*. I appeared under my own name with a six-piece band playing the Waterboys song 'Killing My Heart' in a fictional local pub. The band included Anthony Thistlethwaite, Trevor Hutchinson and 'Fingers' from my Still Burning band.

283 *'I'm A Lazy Sod'*. Officially titled 'Seventeen', but always referred to by its more colourful chorus line in early press reviews of Sex Pistols shows.

283 *My sonic plunder*. The Micro Synthesizer can be heard on 'Let it Happen', 'It's All Gone', the outro of 'Crown', the background of 'Is She Conscious?' and almost every sound on 'Dumbing Down The World'. The

'psychedelic paint-wheels' are on 'His Word Is Not His Bond'. The blues harp microphone was used on 'Crown' and the outro of 'The Charlatan's Lament'. The Indian harmonium with 'the trembler' is at the end of 'My Love Is My Rock In The Weary Land'. The Hindu beat-box lay unused for several years till Steve Wickham unlocked its secrets.

283 *The Theremin.* An electronic musical instrument created in the twenties by Russian inventor Leon Theremin and most notably played by Clara Rockmore. Film clips of Rockmore's uncanny performances are included in the documentary film *Theremin: An Electronic Odyssey* (1993). The most famous example of a Theremin in pop music is The Beach Boys' 'Good Vibrations' (the instrument enters at 0:25 with a distinctive high-pitched 'whee' sound). In 2000 Richard Naiff played Theremin on The Waterboys' *Rock In The Weary Land* tour.

287 *Allan hadn't known I'd become a musician, and had never heard of The Waterboys.* My father finally saw me performing at a Waterboys show in Warwick, England, in 2001.

289 *Maison Rouge.* The studio was knocked down in the early noughties and turned into a car park.

292 *Reams of ancient fan mail.* Among the letters was one sent to me in 1985 by a sixteen-year-old James Dean Bradfield, later of Manic Street Preachers. His enthusiastic communication ended with the postscript 'Look out for my name, preferably in lights', and the paper had been carefully singed round the edges for dramatic effect. Twenty-five years later I bumped into James on an aeroplane and greeted him with the words, 'I got your letter.'

294 *A new keyboard player, Richard Naiff.* Richard went on to play with The Waterboys for nine years. He features on the albums *A Rock In The Weary Land* (BMG, 2000), *Universal Hall* (Puck, 2003), *Karma To Burn* (Puck, 2005) and *Book Of Lightning* (Universal, 2007).

295 *Walking with a Monsieur Hulot bounce.* Jacques Tati's classic comic character, immortalised in the films *Monsieur Hulot's Holiday* and *Mon Oncle*.

VISIONS OF STRAWBERRY FIELDS

"I assumed the images I 'saw' when I listened to any piece of music were somehow encoded in the record. Surely everybody knew the outro of 'Strawberry Fields' represented a procession of brightly clothed Beatles jigging in and out of traffic during rush hour in an Asian city, pursued by water buffaloes and snake charmers? But when I asked my friends, they either imagined nothing at all or saw totally different images."

Soon after writing the above (from Chapter 1), I asked some friends and colleagues what they imagine or feel when they hear this piece of Beatle music, either now or when they first heard it. I requested they listen from 3:34 to the end of the record, and here are some of the responses I received.

Alan Berry (musician): Scores of anthropomorphised lemmings whistling happily as they march off the end of a half-finished version of the Forth Road Bridge.

Norrie Bissell (poet): Some kind of industrial complex in another world, slightly menacing, almost nightmarish after the dream-like-floating-in-clouds quality of the main song.

Patrice Brennan (Waterboys fan): A colourful, noisy Indian market, high walls (the market in the courtyard of a castle perhaps). Definite image of snake charmer with turban and straw basket.

Rosanne Cash (musician and author): I felt the outro was spoken directly to me. I felt it was the first drug I ever took, that I understood something not everyone could understand. I thought if I understood that music, I could enter a world of art just beyond my reach. It also made me feel angry at 'the people who were trying to box me in': my mother, my teachers. Not my father. I knew he understood this wildly expansive, dark, wake-up call of a song, but he didn't know he could talk about it to such a young girl. Shortly after I first heard the record I wrote a letter to my dad, who was on the road, saying I knew there was something bigger out there for me, and that I wanted to do creative things, important things, and that I had IDEAS and passion. He saved that letter his whole life, and I found it after he died. I'm not saying the outro to 'Strawberry Fields' caused the inspiration, the awakening, the rebellion, but it came at exactly the right moment to help me begin my life.

Paul Charles (booking agent and author): Two bands coming, one from left to right, one from right to left. They meet in the middle and pass on. I also used to have an image of Lennon jumping in and out of the tree (from the video) when I heard this section.

Richard Curtis (screenwriter and film director): Well, it's a strange thing. I can't remember what my original feelings were about the last 45 seconds – though I can remember where I was when I heard them, sitting with two other boys in a master's room at boarding school. We sat on the couch and listened to both sides of the single with Mr Foster-Watson, and we knew that they were good. But now, when I listen to the end of 'Strawberry Fields', all I see is that wonderful image of the five of them – The Beatles and George Martin in his tie – clustered round a machine, listening back and delighting in what they'd made. The joy of the creative freedom, the delight in everything new, the intimacy of the five of them in a room, in the knowledge that millions of people all over the world would listen to it – but it didn't matter, because they were liking it, and pushing boundaries, and laughing and arguing and free.

Dave Depper (singer and musician): As I was raised in a fanatically pro-Beatles household, 'Strawberry Fields Forever' was one of the first songs I ever heard. Even at such an early age, I was able to identify Ringo's frenetic martial pounding as the product of drums, conjuring up images of disembodied sticks clattering hard against a mass of floating drumheads. And my interpretation of the piercing electric guitar notes was similar then to how it is now – an infinitely long, thick guitar string, stretching out of sight down a dark tunnel and glowing as if charged with electricity. But the elephant in the room is the crazy Mellotron flute line that dominates the coda and sounds like nothing else on earth. I didn't know what a

Mellotron was until I was twelve, and even given a Mellotron now, I would have no idea how to recreate whatever John is playing on it. And having no real-world associations to make, my visual representation of this sound was forced to get deeply psychedelic. As best I can describe, the Mellotron looks like two butterflies made of audio tape fighting in mid-air, as viewed through a kaleidoscope. It's a big bundle of shimmering ribbon that pulsates along with the vibrations of the sound, growing and collapsing with the volume. And, for the record, 'cranberry sauce' is yawned out by a comically giant John Lennon lying prostrate on the floor.

Chris Difford (singer and songwriter): With a wobble I saunter off towards the garden with my water wings on both arms. I dive into the green of the garden and embrace the blue of the sky above, and life seems strange from upside down. In the potting shed a magazine with hand-drawn pictures folds into my hands. There I journey prancing like a horse going over fences and through bushes in slow motion. There is danger in the arc of a clown. He smiles, she cries. I melt like butter into a dish. Back in the house and the sun throws light suddenly into my eyes. I wake for one last time and see nothing but colour, nothing but green, nothing but blue, nothing like lemon. It's over and I wake by the side of the bed, next to me the pillow I chewed in the night, this now, me now, we now and one. Strawberry Fields Forever.

Ger Eaton (musician): A marching band winding its way backwards through a fairground.

Dave Eggers (author and publisher): Growing up, I was a bit of an Anglophile and was fascinated by London. Everything I knew about the city I learned from Paddington Bear, and later, Monty Python. So when I would hear that section of 'Strawberry Fields', I pictured Paddington trying to get on a bus somewhere in the city, and just as he was doing so, a constable would walk by, harrumphing – maybe disapproving of a small bear riding the bus? – and after Paddington gets on the bus it heads into a tunnel of some sort (do they have tunnels in London? I don't know), while another vehicle is going the other way, honking. That was always what I pictured when I heard the end of the song.

Gillian Ferguson (poet): Blue birds like huge kingfishers are playing pear-shaped stringed instruments on a small stone stage in the space bar where Luke Skywalker and Obi-Wan met Han Solo. Amid the hazy purple smoke, everyone is from different species but just getting with the groove, even although the music is alien; phraseology, notation, key, structure, all different to Earth music. Then a golden trumpet call – fanfares, flutes, drumming. Everybody rushes outside to see a vast marching band coming over the turquoise horizon. Enormously oversized strawberries and Magic Roundabout flowers cluster all around. Then I notice childhood toys are among the marchers. Something sinister has darkened the atmosphere. Why are they gathering? Are they hostile? There are Nutcracker dolls like generals. A disturbing voice drags from a tall black-hooded figure, striding at the front like a spindly Pied Piper, saying, 'I marry swans' as he passes. What does it mean? The music and marchers are no longer happy; the trumpets have called them and they must answer. There is fear in the dazzling sunlight. All children are called – and all children, bar one, must leave their dreams and march forwards.

Eamonn Forde (journalist): The outro always spooked me as a kid. It still does. Those low strings and brass stabs during the song were bad enough as they conjured up images of the devil, fat on the bones of the dead, dreaming up something looming and sinister. But the outro was something else entirely, amplifying the disquiet and taking you off guard by making you think this strange, sinister song is finally over. But, no. Here it comes back from the dead, crawling out of the speakers like a determined, demonic electric snake. It still scares me, like *Rosemary's Baby* still scares me, through what's implied rather than what's seen or heard. Whatever is happening, I don't like it. Not one bit.

Nancy Franklin (journalist): I was ten when 'Strawberry Fields' came out, and it was the first Beatles song that felt like it wasn't quite a Beatles song. John's depressed and draggy voice pulled me into a place where I wasn't comfortable. The last 30 seconds struck me in a literal way. The horns were train whistles, the scratchy, rhythmic sounds of who knows what instrument or found object were wheels turning, and the darting flutey sounds and jumble of voices were people trying to get somewhere in a crowd. The horn got louder as the train left the station, perhaps away from the place where "nothing was real". Or were we going towards that place? Though I listened to the song a lot, I was always relieved when it was over. My internal life was already chaotic enough. I was more at home in 'Penny Lane' (the flipside of 'Strawberry Fields'), where everything was reassuringly real.

Irakli Gaprindashvili (musician): I live in New York, but I was born and grew up in Georgia, at the time a Soviet republic, now an independent country. I and all my friends were huge Beatles fans. The way we accessed western records in Georgia was by giving a blank cassette tape to 'recording booths' on the street run by guys who had smuggled in LPs. After a couple of days you'd go back and get your cassette with the music on it. No titles, no artwork, nothing. But because 'Strawberry Fields' was only a single, not on an LP, I hadn't heard it. In 1990, when I was fifteen, I got an invitation to go for two weeks to Saarbrücken, West Germany, in a school exchange program. That was my first time in a western country, and my mind was blown with all the available music in record stores. The family with whom I was staying were Beatles fans and had every release. I spent most of my time listening, reading credits, lyrics and copying the music to cassettes. Finally I got to 'Strawberry Fields Forever'. I can't exactly describe or remember any mental images at the time, but I do remember everything sort of stopping around me. I listened to it over and over again, trying to figure out words (my English was below basic at the time) but it didn't matter that I didn't know what John was singing about. That song, more than any other, had power to take me out of any situation and to take me with it; to space, or some other form of place in time. I returned back to my summerhouse in Georgia and reunited with my friends, proudly holding the cassette with 'Strawberry Fields' and other newly acquired treasures ('I Am The Walrus' was another mind-blowing discovery). We spent every evening until we had to go back to school sitting on my porch listening to that tape, rewinding and rewinding, really FEELING 'Strawberry Fields'. Now, whenever and wherever I listen to Strawberry Fields, I see the balcony of my house, moonlight peeking through the apple trees in my garden, peace and quiet of a summer evening, and three of my friends sitting around the table dealing another hand of cards. I'm there.

Clive Goodwin (live sound mixer): A surreal shambolic merry march of toy soldiers, teddies, and rag dolls.

Steve Gullick (photographer): Spinning treetops, dirty hands, an evil circus master; general unpleasant woodland chaos.

Hugh Gunderson (schoolboy): A band in uniform marching off a cliff overlooking the sea but instead of plunging into the sea they plunge into a melting candle.

James Hallawell (musician): I'm at John Lennon's place out in Weybridge or Ascot or somewhere. It's 5am and the sun's coming up, me and him in the kitchen drinking tea, talking about everything and nothing. I'm looking at myself in the reflection of his round blue shades. Then I'm in a room at Paul's listening to a track. The speakers are clad in purple silk and Paul's wearing a suit of the same material. We listen to the playback. It feels strange to be making music with a Beatle. The track ends, then I hear a toy box melody and wonder what song this is the intro to. Flying backwards, with shapes and colours streaking past me, I awake in a London bedroom to the toy box alarm tone of a Nokia phone.

Martin Harrison (live sound mixer): Like having the just faded-out main song spurted back, but with all the sweetness taken out of it and its dark, malignant side exposed, and the flutey Mellotron phrase, which I associated as a child with the music of Space Patrol, a UK puppet series, being particularly pernicious. The most prevailing image is a train or some other monstrous machine, emerging from the pitch dark, but like a circus procession inhabited by mischievously malevolent beings.

Leonard Hawker (musician): Summer wheat fields, fire engines, tractors, swaying dancers in Bollywood garb, and a guy with a megaphone driving a crane, which veers madly from side to side.

Martin Herbert (guitar technician): An infinite dark background with diagrams in the left-hand side representing all the percussive elements of the music and sheets of colour coming from the right, which represent the textures laid on top by the other sounds and instruments. The repeated dirty guitar note is an impostor, which looks like a zigzag.

Jools Holland (musician and broadcaster): I was nine in 1967 when this was released. On hearing the song I visualised The Beatles in the recording studio and me hanging out with them as a precocious nine-year old playing piano on the track. I would be making musical suggestions that they agreed would be brilliant. It is often these sort of fantasies that can lead to a career in music.

Mary Hopkin (singer): On first listening (1967), I watched in awe as amorphous, swirling figures danced on a path ahead of me. Later that year, when *The Prisoner* enraptured the nation, the song and the series became inextricably linked in my mind. Bizarre, colourful, brainwashed characters from Portmeirion joined us on the path, while Rover (the huge white balloon that was sent to capture escaping prisoners) hovered menacingly alongside.

Stephen Jobes (theatrical director & playwright): A fife-and-drum band in tight trousers and loud jackets, ragged and unknown, turning the corner at the bottom of a street. I wasn't happy to hear the outro when young; my longing to be free was large, my longing to be wooed by some muse, some gamine lovely gal to take me away. 'Strawberry Fields' is where, I imagined, she might take me and free me into exactly what, I didn't know. I longed for it; I feared it too, the chaos as well as the sweetness and lift. Didn't know if I went, if I'd come back. It wasn't a band I could follow.

Daniel Levitin (neuroscientist, musician, and author): Just when you think it's over, they're back with their Mellotron (like a flute with the hiccups) and those oddly military drumbeats. As an eight-year-old I envisioned a fairground with sawdust and wood chips on the ground, a warped and broken-down calliope, live horses bobbing up and down on its rotating platform, big toothy grins and floppy ears taking in the scene of chaos unfolding around them: Beatles dressed in *Sgt Pepper* costumes running around like keystone cops, a marching band dispersing in all directions with drummers beating bass drums the size of small cars, kids with balloons and stuffed animals scrambling every which way, and a clown ambulance whizzing past in time with the siren-like electric guitar at 3:44. All was in fun, as though watching a movie rather than a newsreel, amusing non-threatening chaos.

James Maddock (songwriter and singer): I picture myself as a four-year-old, sat on the floor in front of one of those suitcase record players in the living room at our house on Lanesborough Road in Leicester. My mum in the kitchen making some tea and me just sat there alone, totally immersed in a fantasy made by this band called The Beatles, the only band I had ever heard of. Playing the songs over and over and over, hours at a time, feeling the music so deeply but never understanding any of it.

Nicola Meighan (journalist): From my vantage point as a four-year-old the exotic chaos of 'Strawberry Fields'' final, fitful flashes of brilliance merged the anarchy and tradition around me. The outro evoked the lawless pop and free jazz of The Muppets' band, Dr Teeth & The Electric Mayhem; and processions of bagpipe players marching up the Abbey Craig to the Wallace Monument, their uneven, reedy chanter echoes billowing into my tiny back garden. I still see Muppets and pipers whenever I hear 'Strawberry Fields'. And I see a child outside a bungalow, embracing the end of a much-loved song, populating its notes and beats with bricks and history and puppets.

Colin Meloy (singer, The Decemberists): Marching, a grand procession of some sort. Vibrant colours: magentas and deep blues. There's an urgency to the procession. It's loping and maybe a little drunken, but deliberate in its movement. And there's a darkness behind it all, a little dangerous like it's inviting you to come along but with a strong caveat that you will be taken beyond the pale of your comfort and experience. And there are definitely elephants involved.

Andrew Merry (singer): A military band in a busy city watching a spinning coil collide with oncoming traffic.

Kieron Moyles (record plugger): A groundswell of dwarves grumbles to the left and a giant army of weighted plastic birds bobbing into water troop past as a questing eye moves through the undergrowth and then everything fades away to vibrations.

Caoimhín Ó Raghallaigh (musician and composer): A long-forgotten chaotic carnival world, spinning on a dismal little record player in the corner of a junk shop. In one of the grooves is a curious chap wearing wellies and squelching in the mud, running against the grain and staying ecstatically stationary. There is a wind-up carnival organ, the workings of which have gone wonky, doomed to dementia. There's that fire brigade going past, of course, and disappearing – not to a fire though. And a train rattling down the tracks. Under the glass between the sleepers stands a strange old man with an ungainly moustache, reasonably well dressed but wearing runners, smoking a cigar and slurring his mutterings, quite drunk. He's obnoxious, yet somehow magnetic. All these people are engaged in these activities for an eternity. There is no way out. They are doomed.

Peter Paphides (music journalist): As far as I'm concerned it is – and always has been – the sound of what the woodland animals get up to when the last humans have left.

Nick Pegg (author and playwright): Some sort of motley Bohemian raggle-taggle procession of figures, walking, dancing, and marching across a field away into a golden sunset with horses and gypsy caravans in tow; a circus leaving town.

Ali Pike (concert lighting designer): White flying birds, possibly Liver Birds, with a trail of white sparks behind them swooping overhead, and a marching band in bright red jackets and busbies; an almost cartoon-like quality to the scene.

Ian Rankin (author): All a big carnival funfair, with the Beatles as ringmasters. Floaty, too. Summery. But summer with an edge. The smiling balloon-seller holds a knife behind his back. His thick black moustache is fake. Hints of Indian mysticism (I didn't know what a sitar was). Yes: dreamy, floaty, but a bit scary. This at a time when a hall of mirrors could freak me out, and ghost trains were a definite no-no.

Comrie Saville-Ferguson (schoolboy): A zooming carousel with horses bolting backwards, wheeling so fast it takes off and flies into the ether. Birds playing the xylophone. A rocket-powered train, with a black hole in tow, sucks everything in before imploding and spitting out a new universe. Munchkins breakdancing. John Lennon fighting elves. Panpipes in a blender. Hyper Fireman Sam on drugs. Time-travelling string and pipe band flung through the vortex, landing at an Indian rave.

Mark Smith (musician and producer): A huge space (warehouse? cave?)

full of strange people and things, chaos and activity. The trumpet a call to arms (not fighting, necessarily, but something exciting and a bit scary but brilliant).

Wesley Stace (novelist and musician): I think of it like the soundtrack for one of those weird old sci-fi films like *The Incredible Melting Man*, where some bizarre transformation occurs, though the victims are completely unaware. The strange, perhaps inebriated, pipe and drum band, dressed possibly à la *Sgt Pepper*, are marching down a country road, going about their merrily un-tuneful business. We see their progress through the warped blurry eye of the lava-like extra-terrestrial. The insistent guitar represents the moment when this invisible alien force possesses them (in the movie this would be represented by some throbbing psychedelic effects) but they don't know! They just carry on regardless. Even their own families won't be able to tell the difference, but bizarre behavioural changes will give the game away. They are no longer human. They are now a Pipe Band of Zombies.

Thighpaulsandra (musician): For some reason the end section always reminded me of the sound of empty trucks being shunted on lonely railway sidings; the grass and weeds creeping up through the gravel and around the oily sleepers. This had a melancholic feel with a slight edge of menace. I must have been about nine when 'Strawberry Fields' was released and often took the train with my grandmother from Pontypridd to Cardiff. We passed lots of empty coal trucks and box wagons, which always seemed abandoned. Why they scared me I don't know. Such are the miseries of childhood. I'm sure what I saw in the music was totally different from other people but then I had a rather strange childhood.

Graeme Thompson (journalist and author): A small army, by which I mean an army of very small people, marching – speeded up – over some kind of moor, until they disappear entirely.

Kondo Tomohiro (singer): A scene where a mysterious band takes me to a strange and foreign town, like the ending of the Grimms' fairy tale, 'The Pied Piper'. Very colourful landscapes and darkest black at the same time.

Annie West (illustrator): A merry-go-round going backwards, as if I'm standing right up close to it (too close maybe) with all the colours and lights going by me then shifting and going in the opposite direction. And I'm very small.

Steve Wickham (musician): I'm on a train with George Harrison playing sitar then we pass through to a tunnel of silence/darkness to the magical place of strawberry fields where some Technicolor strawberry people are going about their business (making lovely roundy sounds as they waddle through their strawberry town). The train steams right on through.

Heidi Wickham (painter): A thousand white-faced harlequin clowns on a loud protest march through the streets of New York.

Damon Wilson (musician): Landed gentry on a foxhunt with horses, red coats, dogs, and bugles in an idyllic English setting.

INDEX

Words in *italics* indicate album titles unless otherwise stated. Words in quotes indicate song titles. Page numbers in **bold** refer to illustrations.

ACKNOWLEDGEMENTS

My love and gratitude always to Janette Campbell Scott, who read every draft of this book and edited it with me.

Thank you for help with facts, advice, etc: Stuart Bailie, Willem Beekman, Edward 'Z' Bell, Norrie Bissell, Colin Blakey, William Bloom, Paul Charles, Peter Chegwyn, Crigg, John Dunford, Cait & Mairtin Flaherty, Lyndsay Guttridge, Gerry Hanberry, Hanna at The Portobello Hotel, Sharon Hickey, Seb Holbrook, Stephen Hunt, Theresa Kereakes, Vinnie Kilduff, Philip King, Joe Kingman, Roddy Lorimer, Maureen Martin, Chris Merry, Tony Moylan, Andrew Mueller, Richard Naiff, Carol Napier, Jim Powers, Mary Quinn, Mike Rogers, Simon Reynolds, Robbie The Pict, Anne Scott, Sharon Shannon, Annie Siggins, David Spangler, Mark 'Stan' Stanton, Wesley Stace, Frank Surgener, Anto Thistlethwaite, Crispin Thomas, Graeme Thomson, Alex Walker, Andy White, Steve Wickham, Ali Wilson. Special thanks to these 'angels' in my musical life: Doreen Loader, John Kennedy, Mark Astaire, Philip Tennant, Nigel Grainge.

PICTURE CREDITS
The pictures used in this book came from the following sources, and we are grateful for their help. Please contact the publisher if you feel there has been a mistaken attribution. **Jacket front** Sean Brady; **spine** Colm Henry; **jacket rear** Frank Miller; **2–3** Stefano Giovannini; **6** Anne Scott (top two images), Mike Scott; **7** Virginia Turbett (APF), Ally Palmer (Caldwell); **8** Jill Furmanovsky, rockarchive.com (1982), Patrick Durand (USA); **9** Mike Scott; **10** Philippe Herriau (Werchter), Pete Vernon (Keltner), Mike Scott; **11** Sean Brady (Kenmare), Frank Miller (Sirius); **12** Steve Meany (both images); **13** Colm Henry; **14** Shona MacMillan (Shannon), unknown; **15** unknown; **16** Mike Scott (Universal Hall), Jeff Alexander (Findhorn).

ALSO AVAILABLE IN PRINT AND EBOOK EDITIONS FROM JAWBONE PRESS

Strange Brew: Eric Clapton & The British Blues Boom Christopher Hjort

Metal: The Definitive Guide Garry Sharpe-Young

Lennon & McCartney: Together Alone John Blaney

Bowie In Berlin: A New Career In A New Town Thomas Jerome Seabrook

Beatles For Sale: How Everything They Touched Turned To Gold John Blaney

So You Want To Be A Rock'n'roll Star: The Byrds Day-By-Day Christopher Hjort

Hot Burritos: The True Story Of The Flying Burrito Brothers John Einarson with Chris Hillman

Million Dollar Les Paul: In Search Of The Most Valuable Guitar In The World Tony Bacon

To Live Is To Die: The Life And Death Of Metallica's Cliff Burton Joel McIver

Jack Bruce Composing Himself: The Authorised Biography Harry Shapiro

Return Of The King: Elvis Presley's Great Comeback Gillian G. Gaar

White Light/White Heat: The Velvet Underground Day-By-Day Richie Unterberger

The Impossible Dream: The Story Of Scott Walker And The Walker Brothers Anthony Reynolds

Forever Changes: Arthur Lee & The Book Of Love John Einarson

Shelter From The Storm: Bob Dylan's Rolling Thunder Years Sid Griffin

Becoming Elektra: The True Story Of Jac Holzman's Visionary Record Label Mick Houghton

Seasons They Change: The Story Of Acid And Psychedelic Folk Jeanette Leech

Won't Get Fooled Again: The Who From Lifehouse To Quadrophenia Richie Unterberger

The Resurrection Of Johnny Cash: Hurt, Redemption, And American Recordings Graeme Thomson

Crazy Train: The High Life And Tragic Death Of Randy Rhoads Joel McIver

The 10 Rules Of Rock And Roll: Collected Music Writings 2005–11 Robert Forster